Moving with Research

Evidence-Based Practice in Sherborne Developmental Movement

Edited by

Elizabeth Marsden
and Jo Egerton

The right of the authors to be identified as authors of this work has been asserted by them in accordance with the Copyright, Designs and Patents Act 1988.

In this selection of chapters, copyright © Sunfield Publications 2007
In the individual chapters, copyright © the individual authors 2007

First published in Great Britain
by Sunfield Publications 2007.

Published by
Sunfield Publications
Sunfield, Woodman Lane, Clent, Stourbridge DY9 9PB.
www.sunfield.org.uk

ISBN: 0-9550568-3-7

All rights reserved. No part of this publication may be reproduced in any material form (including photocopying or storing it in any medium by electronic means and whether or not transiently or incidentally to some other use of this publication) without the written permission of the copyright owner except in accordance with the provisions of the Copyright, Designs and Patents Act 1988. Applications for the copyright owner's written permission to reproduce any part of this publication should be addressed to the publisher.

Warning: The doing of an unauthorised act in relation to a copyright work may result in both a civil claim for damages and criminal prosecution.

Printed and bound in Great Britain

To the memory of Veronica Sherborne and all those who, like her, create beautiful movement

Contents

Acknowledgements

Firstly, thanks must go to Professor Barry Carpenter, chief executive and director of the research institute at Sunfield, for his vision and willingness to take the risk of allowing me to bring together so many diverse pieces of research into compiling *Moving with Research*. Without Barry's support, we would never have even begun this project. Jotham Konaka was to have shared the editing of this book, but unfortunately, due to illness, was not able to do so – my thanks to Jo Egerton for taking over part of his role. Her tremendous skill and commitment must be recognised and applauded. There are few editors who would be willing to eat egg curry at 1.30 a.m. in order to keep going until the job is completed!

The contributing authors have been remarkable in keeping to publishing deadlines, and I have great respect and admiration for their work presented here. Each one has responded to requests immediately, and this has made editing a pleasure. Thank you all for your wonderful work. Jotham Konaka has been the leader of the project, 'Sherborne @ Sunfield'. Cyndi and George Hill have not only been consultants on this project, but have been my personal supporters and very good friends in the Sherborne Association for the last 16 years. The continuation of Sherborne Developmental Movement (SDM) since the untimely death of Veronica Sherborne owes a great deal to these two stalwarts.

It has been so encouraging to receive research reports from European colleagues. The Polish and Swedish reports would have remained inaccessible if we had not discovered our amazing translators: Maggie Malgorzata (Poland), Marie Janson and Anne Sparrow (Sweden). These women are not professional translators, and have been willing to give up many hours to struggle with two languages. They have done a truly superb job. The research paper from Lapland was translated in Finland by Tove Ruuskanen and Kaisu Laasonen. Kaisu organised both the accessing of the paper and the translation, and I am indebted to her for her efficiency.

Searching for the background material for Chapter 2 led me to several of Veronica's early colleagues who were delightful and so willing to add their thoughts about how she developed her philosophy over the years; so I would like to thank Geraldine

Stephenson for a lovely telephone conversation, and Valerie Preston-Dunlop and Walli Meir for returning my questionnaires. Sincere thanks also go to Sarah Sherborne for giving me a rich insight into her early childhood and for providing the photograph of her mother. Your contributions continue to be invaluable, Sarah.

The Sherborne Association (UK) and the International Sherborne Co-operation Group (ISCO) have, for many years, given me encouragement, enthusiasm, assistance, friendship and humour. They have worked together tirelessly, and as volunteers, because they know the value of SDM. They are looking forward to the publication of *Moving with Research* and have been supportive since its conception.

The Sherborne Association (UK) and the research committee of the School of Education and Media, University of Paisley, Scotland provided funding to secure the implementation of the research carried out in Herne Infants School, Kent (described in Chapter 5). I would like to thank: the head teacher of the school; the Sherborne practitioner, Fiona Ong; the movement observer, Carolyn Childs; the social development observer, Carrie Weston; and all the children in Year 1 for their hard work and commitment during this project.

Finally, I must thank my friends and especially my family – Scott, Jamie, Lucy and Rose – for their continued interest in my work and for their attempts to keep me sane. Too bad it didn't work!

Elizabeth Marsden

Contributing Authors

Birgitta Althoff is a registered physiotherapist and educator in Sweden. During 30 years working in the field, she has lectured at different conferences concerning research in movement and communication. She is the author of articles on movement, pain, body awareness and Sherborne Developmental Movement (SDM). She has wide experience of children with both physical and mental disorders. She has worked with people with autistic spectrum disorder (ASD) and profound and multiple learning difficulties for 10 years.

Berit Astrand works as director of the Kristina School in Sweden, which she founded 10 years ago for children from pre-school to the ninth year with ASD and functional disabilities related to autism. The school uses the Kristina model of communication, which was developed according to structured educational principles. Beginning as a specialist teacher, Berit has worked for many years in different capacities and contexts with and for children who are in need of special support and suffer from various difficulties, including neuropsychiatric functional disorder, functional disabilities and communication difficulties. Her work has also entailed supervision and consultancy for teachers and others, teaching and lecturing on various teachers' training courses, and taking responsibility for development, projects and leadership. She also writes educational books, and carries out research in the area of science.

Marta Bogdanowicz (Professor dr. hab.) is a clinical psychologist, specialising in children. She works as director in the Institute of Psychology, University of Gdansk, and also continues her professional psychology practice. She is an author of over 300 publications, including 26 books related to work with children, and 6 films. Her professional interests are: child clinical psychology; developmental dyslexia; left-handedness; prevention of school failure; and remedial teaching. (She developed the 'Good Start' method, which uses a multisensory approach.) Marta Bogdanowicz has worked with SDM since 1980, and is one of five international course leaders in Poland. Since 1991, she has been leading research on the effectiveness of SDM, and has published four books on SDM (including the Scale for Assessment of Children and Parents' Behaviour). She is a vice-president of the European Dyslexia Association and the Polish Dyslexia Association, which she founded in 1990.

Barry Carpenter joined Sunfield as chief executive/principal in 1997. He has over 30 years' experience in special education, having held the leadership roles of head teacher, inspector of schools, and principal lecturer. In 1992, he established the Centre for the Study of Special Education at Westminster College, Oxford, which became a national teaching and research centre. As part of his role at Sunfield, he now directs the recently established Sunfield Research Institute. He has been awarded honorary professorships by the Universities of Northumbria and Worcester. Barry has written extensively in the field of special educational needs. His book, *Enabling Access*, won the National Association of Special Educational Needs' Academic Book Award. He has recently edited, with Jo Egerton, *Early Childhood Intervention: International perspectives, national initiatives and regional practice*. He lectures nationally and internationally. He represents the UK on the European Union Working Group on Early Intervention, and Europe at the International Society for Early Intervention. He has been appointed by the Disability Rights Commission as their representative on the General Teaching Council for England. Barry is the father of three children, one of whom has Down syndrome. He was awarded the OBE by the Queen in 2001 for services to children with special educational needs.

John Dibbo, Ph.D., was senior lecturer in primary physical education (PE) and head of PE at the Faculty of Education, University of Plymouth, until retirement in 2006. During the early part of his career (1972–1988), he taught extensively in primary and secondary schools in the UK, holding a variety of posts of responsibility up to assistant principal, and was also an advisory teacher for primary PE. He taught mainstream PE to all ages from reception children (aged 4 years) to adults in a variety of educational contexts. His involvement in SDM initially came through work with Bill Richards (University of Plymouth) from 1988 onwards, where the elements of trust and confidence (essential qualities of SDM) for the self and others, and the underlying philosopohy of SDM teaching, became an important part of his teaching with primary-aged children and trainee teachers. His research, teaching and writing centred around a holistic approach to PE in which the learners are central to the experience and where performing and understanding (doing and talking) are linked to understanding of movement.

Jo Egerton is research fellow/publications manager at Sunfield School for young people with severe and complex intellectual disabilities in Clent, Worcestershire. She has worked in the field of special education for 10 years, and during that time has held posts in teaching, research, residential care, leisure and development. She holds a Postgraduate Certificate in Education and has a master's degree in learning disability studies. She has co-edited two books with Barry Carpenter, and has authored and co-authored several journal articles. While working in Oxfordshire, she developed *On Track*, a Mencap-funded accessible newspaper for young people with intellectual disabilities in the county. She has presented at a number of conferences.

Janice Filer, Ph.D., formerly a teacher of PE and Dance, has used SDM as the foundation for her work with children and their families since the early 1980s. In 1989, she developed an innovative early intervention programme to address the needs of two generations by providing a service for the child and parent. The intervention, Developmental Movement Play, is based on knowledge and skills of early childhood education and development alongside a lifelong interest in dance and movement. The programme uses movement as a means of communication, and incorporates SDM to address issues concerning communication, relationships, emotional, behavioural and mental health difficulties for parents and children in mainstream education. Since 1999, as part of a multidisciplinary project for vulnerable families, she has used Developmental Movement Play alongside parenting methodologies to provide a means to address the issues of poor parent–child attachment relationships.

Mario Hair is a lecturer and a member of the Statistics Consultancy Unit at the University of Paisley. His special interests are in survey design, sampling methods and the analysis of survey datasets. He has had over 25 years' experience of analysing survey data. He is a fellow of the Royal Statistical Society and a member of Assess, the SPSS European users group. As a teacher, he has taught and presented academic papers on statistics and survey methodology. As a consultant, he is routinely involved in providing statistical consultancy to health service staff. He has also completed projects involving large-scale surveys for a wide range of commercial clients.

Jotham Konaka is a teacher/researcher with over 25 years' teaching experience in the area of special educational needs. He is currently working at Sunfield School for young people with severe and complex intellectual disabilities, including ASD. As a founder member of the Special Schools Sports Association of Kenya, he contributed immensely towards the development of a physical education curriculum for children with physical and neurological disabilities in the country. Jotham holds an MA degree in special education as well as being a level 3 SDM practitioner. He has recently completed a two-year research project exploring the use of the SDM programme to support social engagement with young people with severe ASD. Jotham is currently exploring ways of extending this work as part of his doctorate studies. He has presented at conferences nationally and internationally, and run training courses based upon the 'Sherborne @ Sunfield' programme. He has contributed chapters about the programme to several publications.

Kirsti Lassila took her degree in physiotherapy at Oulu Health Care Institute in 1981, and specialised in internal diseases and child neurology in 1990. She took her M.Sc. in education and special education in 2000, and a degree in multiprofessional work counselling in 2004, both of them at the University of Lapland. Kirsti Lassila has worked as a health centre physiotherapist in Finland and Sweden, and has taught adapted physical education for young people with special needs. Since 1991, she has been working in her own physiotherapy enterprise. Most of her clients are children and adults with neurological disorders. She participates in a multiprofessional team in a kindergarten, and she operates in close contact with parents. From 1998–2002, she also acted as a counsellor and lecturer in a project aiming to develop special education in northern Finland. Kirsti has used SDM for about 12 years, both in group sessions and individual therapy.

Elizabeth Marsden, Ph.D., is Physical Education course leader at the University of Paisley. She trained at Bedford College of Physical Education where she first met

Veronica Sherborne, who was a guest lecturer for just one day. Two years later, while teaching children with severe disabilities in Canada, Elizabeth contacted Veronica for advice, and their communication lasted for the next 30 years. While raising three children, Elizabeth continued to seek ways of using movement to bring out the best in very young children, adolescents with behaviour problems, populations with special health problems and special needs, and the elderly. This led her into doctoral study at Glasgow University and, after teaching in a variety of schools for over 20 years, she now works in the university sector. Elizabeth has seen for herself, time after time, how SDM can change lives. This way of working with movement crosses cultural, age, gender and disability barriers in leading people to become at home in their own bodies and to learn to form relationships. She has been delighted to gather research projects from all over Europe into this book.

Melanie Peter, Ph.D., is senior lecturer in education and early childhood at Anglia Ruskin University. She has worked in special education for over 20 years, and is widely published. She has contributed to professional and academic journals and edited books, and has published a number of books on drama and the arts with David Fulton Publishers, including *Developing Play and Drama in Children with Autistic Spectrum Disorders,* written with Dave Sherratt. She lecturers nationally and internationally. She has three children, one of whom has profound autistic spectrum disorder.

Janet Sparkes has recently retired as principle lecturer at the University of Winchester, where she worked in the area of movement studies, special education and education for 30 years, preparing students for the teaching profession. Her particular interest lies in the area of movement and special needs, which became her main teaching and research area. She has applied her knowledge in this area to working with the young and old with a wide range of learning and physical disabilities. Since 1980, she has worked at different times in Romania, initially as part of a mixed arts team, using the creative processes with disadvantaged and disabled children and adults, and more recently training Romanian workers in using movement work with different population groups. All the movement work draws on SDM practices and principles, which have been part of Janet's teaching since her first meeting with Veronica Sherborne in 1972.

Maarit Uusitalo took her degree in nursing in 1983, and specialised in public health nursing in 1991, obtaining both qualifications at Lapland Health Care Institute. She took her master's degree in education and special education in 200 at the University of Lapland. Maarit has worked as a teacher of health care subjects in Ylitornio Christian Institute since 1991. SDM is a part of her courses in special education. Her students study to be children's instructors and practical nurses.

Carrie Weston is currently a Ph.D. research student at the University of Paisley. Prior to that, she lectured in early childhood education and special needs at two universities. Carrie's area of research is PE in the early years, which has brought her into contact with SDM as an inclusive and holistic example of PE for young children. Carrie has worked with Elizabeth Marsden and other colleagues on a study of the physical and social benefits of SDM and written collaborative papers on this research. She has also published a number of children's fiction books.

Foreword

Melanie Peter

This is a milestone text in several ways. Over 20 years ago, I had the privilege to train with Veronica Sherborne, and was introduced to her unique approach using creative movement experiences based on relationship play. At the time, I was an enthusiastic student on a one-year Postgraduate Certificate in Education course at Bristol Polytechnic (as it then was), specialising to teach children with severe learning difficulties. Veronica was a much loved, inspirational tutor, who set me on track for my own lifetime's professional quest to access arts education for children with special needs. Regrettably, the course was axed in the mid-1980s, along with other initial teacher training in special needs. This was under the guise of a more 'integrated' approach to special needs, and marked the onset of massive education curricular reform which lasted through the 1990s. It has taken a long time for the pendulum to swing back, and for systems to revalue Veronica Sherborne's legacy.

Why now? Legislation in Great Britain, especially since 1997, has pushed special needs to the fore – there is a real transformational opportunity out there to be grasped! The 'Every Child Matters' (Department for Education and Skills (DfES), 2003a, 2004a) agenda has prompted awareness of children's holistic needs, and strengthening of a more nurturing philosophy and partnership working. This is being rolled out into contexts where structural reforms require an inclusive approach to children of all abilities fulfilling their potential (Special Educational Needs and Disability Act, 2001; Disability Discrimination Act, 2004). Learning for everyone now is expected to be personalised and fun (DfES, 2003b, 2004b). As pressures grow globally for social cohesion and ability to respond to the rapid pace of change, prompted by technological advances, so the need is being recognised for future generations to be creative, confident, adaptable individuals, able to get along with others. Daniels (2006) calls for a Russian form of flexible, imaginative instruction known as 'obuchenie', whereby the practitioner 'rummages around' to meet the individual on a psychological level.

This always used to be the hallmark of special education practice, but became subsumed for many years by the quest to access an entitlement curriculum that prioritised academic attainment. 'Sherborne Developmental Movement' (SDM) became a victim, and disappeared as a regular feature from many special school timetables, resulting in a whole generation of educators being ignorant of its significance. Fortunately, Veronica had managed to publish her work (Sherborne, 1990), just ahead of her tragically untimely death, and a core group, steered by the Sherborne Association, battled to keep her body of work alive for many years. For example, I endeavoured to embed SDM within the National Curriculum for dance, as the movement experiences to underpin creative expression and communication (Peter, 1997). For me, this was logical, and a way of bringing her work into a developing curricular context. (I think she would have been pleased with what I did!)

SDM needs to be recognised for its continuing relevance both in the special education arena and in mainstream education – a rationale shared by this book. A physical educator and physiotherapist by training, Veronica Sherborne had originally developed her approach from the work of Rudolf Laban, the founder of Modern Educational Dance. Initially working with children in mainstream secondary schools and student teachers primarily as a dance teacher, she was later asked by Laban to help him offer movement therapy to adults with severe psychological difficulties in long-stay provision. She gradually came to apply her developmental creative movement programme across the educational spectrum, including with actors in training at the Bristol Old Vic Theatre. However, those who were hardest to reach were always at the heart of her work – and it is appropriate, therefore, that this cohort has a significant presence in this text. The past decade has seen considerable advances in understanding disabilities such as autism, and the research team at Sunfield have drawn upon findings in their skilful, sensitive refinement of SDM in the 'Sherborne @ Sunfield' programme, a contemporary approach to meeting complex needs. Research has extended globally, embracing practice overseas and a broad range of learning needs and contexts, developing Sherborne's work in a way that is compatible with current and future trends.

The contributors to this book have helped to ensure the survival of SDM, which is so much more than just an approach to support children's physical development: it is a holistic, integrated and creative pedagogy – an exemplification of 'obuchenie'! SDM was always an important counter-balance to pressures within both special and mainstream education that favoured dry, detached, heavily directive, adult-led practices that focused on clearly observable skills as outcomes. It continues to offer a child-led, interactive approach that values relationship-building and shared experience as the foundation for all learning within a social world.

…And I should know! It is one of life's ironies that several years after I had been teaching in special schools, my middle son was born to me. Coincidentally, he turned out to have severe and complex learning needs. Many parents of children with autism describe how their child began to slip away from them around the age of 18 months – to disappear into a world of their own. It can be heart-breaking: the struggle to reach them as your guts sear with the pain of rejection by your own flesh and blood. Luckily, I had my teaching experiences to fall back on, and could switch into professional mode. Having had success forging relationships with some very remote children, I used SDM with my own son: we persisted in being playful …and held on to him.

While his autism is by no means 'cured', my son realised many years ago that there is something in it for him to bother with other people, and he can enjoy even rowdy occasions – Christmas shopping, Norwich City football matches, theatres and pop concerts. I am enormously proud of him: despite his level of intellectual functioning, people often comment how surprisingly sociable he is, how he expects others to be a source of pleasure and, all else considered, how well he can cope with change. His gait too, is integrated – he carries himself well – indicative of a true sense of self. He has a truly joyous attitude to life – and I don't think it is a total coincidence that he has always been played with, not just by family members, but by those practitioners too, over the years, who have sustained him via Sherborne's legacy.

Elizabeth Marsden is a Physical Education teacher who worked alongside Veronica Sherborne for many years. Now, as a university lecturer training student teachers, she has begun to test, through the rigours of academic research, some of Sherborne's hypotheses, and has been instrumental in gathering together the work of others engaged in a similar quest throughout Europe. Jo Egerton is research fellow/publications manager at Sunfield. In addition to the 'Sherborne @ Sunfield' research project carried out by Jotham Konaka, Sunfield, through their Professional Development Centre, have supported the Sherborne Association in its continued promotion of Veronica's work through holding regular training and qualificatory courses, and do so now with the publication of this book.

Moving with Research, and the projects that led to it, offer an enhanced way to apply SDM for the whole spectrum of children's learning and needs. Via this book, practitioners may enable the families too of the children they work with to find in the approach a key to sustaining the bond with their child, to sharing joys and having fun.

I wish them all every success, and commend this book to you whole-heartedly.

Dr Melanie Peter
Senior Lecturer in Education, Anglia Ruskin University
October 2006

References
Daniels, H. (2006) 'The dangers of corruption in special needs education', *British Journal of Special Needs Education*, 33 (1), 4–9.

Department for Education and Skills (2003a) *Every Child Matters*. Norwich: The Stationery Office. [Online at: http://www.everychildmatters.gov.uk/]

Department for Education and Skills (2003b) *Excellence and Enjoyment*. [Online at: www.standards.dfes.gov.uk]

Department for Education and Skills (2004a) *Every Child Matters: Change for Children*. Annesley: DfES Publications. [Online at: http://www.everychildmatters.gov.uk/]

Department for Education and Skills (2004b) *Removing Barriers to Achievement: The government's strategy for SEN*. Annesley: DfES Publications. [Online at: http://www.teachernet.gov.uk/]

Peter, M. (1997) *Making Dance Special*. London: David Fulton.

PART 1
Introduction

CHAPTER 1

Introduction

Jotham Konaka

Sherborne Developmental Movement (SDM) presents exciting opportunities for exploring, enquiring and undertaking projects that can improve knowledge and interrogate understanding of practice focusing on movement education, communication and interpersonal relationships. There is an on-going need to examine the theoretical frameworks and their contribution to our understanding of movement as a fundamental construct in every child's development. This understanding can derive only from our accumulated body of knowledge, reasoning and research.

Developed by Veronica Sherborne between 1950 and 1990 (Sherborne, 2001), SDM came to be recognised as a unique and distinctive programme with the potential to contribute towards the development of body awareness, social interaction, communication and relationship-building with all individuals whatever their level of ability (Hill, 2006; Peter, 1997; Sherborne, 2001). The work was developed from Sherborne's Physical Education (PE) and physiotherapy training backgrounds, and her later knowledge of the work of Rudolf Laban (Kirby, 1984). Sherborne's brief, three-day encounter with Laban during her initial teacher training at Bedford College of Physical Education was an experience that had a profound effect on the rest of her professional life (Hill, 2006).

Following her graduation as a teacher, Sherborne taught at Cheltenham Ladies' College in Gloucestershire for three years. It was during her first year of this appointment that she had a second encounter with Laban and Lisa Ullman during summer courses organised by the pair in Sheffield. On her return to Cheltenham Ladies' College, she started implementing what she had learnt (Kirby, 1984). She later enrolled for a one-year course at Lisa Ullman's Art of Movement Studio in Manchester where Laban was a lecturer. During her time at the studio, she contributed towards the writing of Laban's first dance book, *Modern Educational Dance* (1948). Kirby (1984, p. 35) highlights Laban's acknowledgement, thus: 'Mrs Sherborne, then Miss Veronica Tyndale-Biscoe, helped me to make the text as readable as possible.' On completion of the course, her exemplary performance resulted in an invitation for her to stay on at the studio, which she declined, feeling that she would be restricted in this setting.

After the short period at the studio, Sherborne embarked on a long teaching career as a lecturer in dance, starting at Bedford College of Physical Education and then moving to Bath Academy of Art. However, in 1950, Rudolf Laban once more called upon her to join him at the Withymead Centre in Exeter as a visiting movement thera-pist, which was to crystallise the development of her movement ideas. As Hill (2006) asserts:

> *...an awareness of the basic principles of both Laban's movement analysis and SDM reveals how much Sherborne used Laban's work as the foundation of her own.* (p. 4).

Given that her work at Exeter over a period of 15 years up to 1965 was on a part-time basis, she used her spare time to work in the field of education as a dance, movement and drama tutor in several teacher training institutions around the Bristol area. It was during the mid-1950s that she tested out her ideas with student teachers, who started applying the techniques with children in schools. She later recognised the potential of her ideas, and started developing her techniques with children with special education needs.

Sherborne's practical approach to movement teaching was recognised by, and gave inspiration to, many practitioners who had the privilege of watching her at work. However, it has been argued that she spent so much time in the development of prac-tice that she did not articulate in detail the theoretical perspective underpinning her methods, which could have allowed an informed evaluation of her work and facili-tated its subsequent development (Kirby, 1984). Although Sherborne's work acquired an international recognition and acknowledgement in the 1980s, this omission to doc-ument her way of working led some professionals to question the future of the pro-gramme when she ceased to practice. During this period, the programme gained immense popularity in the UK, Scandinavia and other parts of Western Europe, Canada and Australia. The popularity arose from Sherborne's conviction and resolve to pass on her ideas to student teachers at Bristol Polytechnic, as well as through the many workshops she conducted in different parts of the world.

At later stages of her life, she not only embarked on producing videos exemplifying good practice, but also, in 1990, published *Developmental Movement for Children*. She encouraged many practitioners to begin leading courses and workshops, locally and internationally, on her behalf (Hill, 2006). After her sudden death in 1990, several colleagues who realised the uniqueness of SDM continued to develop her work, and inaugurated the Sherborne Association. Hill (2006) writes:

> *In recognition of her work and also as a way of preventing it becoming frag-mented in the future, the Sherborne Association has been set up in the UK, Belgium and Sweden, and there are many other countries – amongst which are Australia, Brazil, Canada, Finland, Germany, Italy, Japan, the Nether-lands, Norway and Poland – where there is an ongoing interest in her work.* (p. 5)

The International Sherborne Association continues to perpetuate Sherborne's work in the belief that her ideas and ways of working can make a positive contribution towards maximising the abilities and qualities of life for children, young people and adults through shared movement experiences. Sherborne's way of working is based on two main assumptions: that relating to one's own body and feeling at home in it, and relating to other people through movement, are essential for the satisfactory development of every human being. SDM places equal importance on the development of body awareness, a good self-esteem and the ability to form positive relationships with others through shared movement experiences. The movement experiences used take many forms, but all are designed to encourage specific developments in the child (Sherborne, 2001).

While Sherborne's unique approach was rooted in facilitating the development of communication and social relationships with children whose formative years have been deprived of the above basic human needs, there has always been the knowledge that children in mainstream schools, students in higher education, and individuals of all ages and backgrounds, have the need to experience good movement education. However, the difficulties posed by the ever-changing population of children and adults with challenging needs (Carpenter, 2005) demand that practitioners question the best methods of delivering the SDM programme in different contexts. In his foreword to *Communication through Movement* (Hill, 2006), Barry Carpenter cites the dynamic, evolving and child-centred approach of SDM as an 'effective and meaningful way of meeting the children at their point of need' (p. xi). Sherborne's open-ended teaching approach encouraged practitioners to develop their own approaches to meet the needs of the individuals they worked with. She stated:

> *Each teacher or caregiver can make use of the materials described in this book [Developmental Movement for Children] in his or her own way. Teachers develop their own variations and ideas as do the children they teach.* (Sherborne, 2001, p.111)

In my own research, this led to an exploration of more structured teaching approaches to enable children with autistic spectrum disorders (ASD) to access SDM at their point of learning.

In *Developmental Movement for Children,* Sherborne (2001) highlighted the significance of practical participation in her movement experiences in order to develop a sound understanding of its underlying philosophy. The social constructivist, participative nature of Sherborne's approach is particularly consistent with the current trends of encouraging effective intervention techniques and approaches that can enhance social engagement with vulnerable individuals, regardless of their physical or mental conditions. As evidence provided by various contributors to this book suggests, practitioners have endeavoured to apply Sherborne's techniques to develop the foundation of good movement education, good social engagement and good psychological wellbeing. They have also subsequently explored, examined and evaluated the effectiveness of the philosophy underlying the programme in relation to the groups they work with. This philosophy has remained elusive as Sherborne was essentially a practitioner, not an academic.

The impetus for producing this book has arisen from the current high demands for evidence-based practice (Rose, 2002; Carpenter, 2007) and repeated questioning by head teachers, therapists, funding bodies and local educational authorities regarding evidence demonstrating the efficacy of the SDM programme and its beneficial and worthwhile effects on various populations. Under these prevailing circumstances, some practitioners who know the value of SDM, but lack the research evidence to back their claims, have been denied financial support or time allocation to apply SDM as an educational or therapeutic strategy to ameliorate some of the difficulties encountered by individuals in their care.

There seems to be an emergent interest among SDM practitioners in conducting enquiries to resolve this deficit; and, indeed, research has been carried out both in the UK and Europe. Some of these pieces of work have been published in educational and therapy journals, but remain within academia and are not easily accessible to practitioners. However, while the recent publication of Cyndi Hill's book, *Communication through Movement* by Sunfield Publications (Hill, 2006), has changed this trend by explaining and making much of Sherborne's work accessible to students and new practitioners, it has equally provoked a quest for further exploration into the potential benefits of SDM as an interactive approach. *Moving with Research* will therefore, confirm, encourage and, hopefully, inspire both new and experienced practitioners to take a proactive role in testing out Sherborne's claims (Sherborne, 2001).

The following chapter of this book interrogates in depth the main influences on Sherborne's life and makes a brave attempt at suggesting the essence of her evolving philosophy. The third and fourth chapters describe a major project undertaken by Sunfield School and its partners in placing SDM within a framework which can enhance the learning and lives of children with ASD. Chapters 5, 6 and 7 show the versatility of the movement programme with differing UK populations, and Chapter 8 reveals the affects of SDM training on the attitudes, confidence and practice of teachers. Chapters 9 to 12 of the book describe a valuable collection of research studies carried out in Poland, Finland and Sweden. Although educational practices differ throughout Europe, Sherborne's influence has been applauded and welcomed in these and many other countries of the Union. The concluding chapters identify the common threads discovered in the findings of the research carried out with such diverse populations and in very different cultures, and propose future directions for SDM, with reference to contemporary research and the aims of Every Child Matters (DfES, 2003, 2004) in the UK.

It is imperative that practitioners play a proactive role in advancing knowledge and skills which are based on valid research evidence, and in ensuring these are shared with other service providers and professionals interested in applying Sherborne's techniques (Carpenter, 2005). The pieces of work in this book will be a great resource to a wide range of people, including students, new and experienced practitioners in education, care and therapy, head teachers, directors of therapy units, physical educators and university departments.

References

Carpenter, B. (2005) 'Early childhood intervention: possibilities and prospects for professionals, families and children', *British Journal of Special Education,* 32 (4), 176–183.

Carpenter, B. (2006) 'Foreword'. In: C. Hill (2006) *Communicating through Movement: Sherborne Developmental Movement – towards a broadening perspective.* Clent: Sunfield Publications.

Carpenter, B. (2007) 'Schools as research organisations'. In: B. Carpenter and J. Egerton (eds) *New Horizons in Special Education: Evidence-based practice in action.* Clent: Sunfield Publications.

Department for Education and Skills (2003) *Every Child Matters.* Norwich: The Stationery Office. [Online at: http://www.everychildmatters.gov.uk/]

Department for Education and Skills (2004) *Every Child Matters: Change for children.* London: DfES. [Online at: http://www.everychildmatters.gov.uk/]

Hill, C. (2006) *Communicating through Movement: Sherborne Developmental Movement – towards a broadening perspective.* Clent: Sunfield Publications.

Kirby, M. (1984) *Sherborne and Movement (unpublished thesis).* Bristol: Bristol Polytechnic.

Laban, R. (1948) *Modern Educational Dance.* London: Macdonald and Evans Ltd.

Peter, M. (1997) *Making Dance Special.* London: David Fulton.

Rose, R. (2002) 'Teaching as a "research-based profession": encouraging practitioner research in special education', *British Journal of Special Education,* 29 (1), 44–48.

Sherborne, V. (1990) *Developmental Movement for Children: Mainstream, special needs and pre-school.* Cambridge: Cambridge University Press.

Sherborne, V. (2001) *Developmental Movement for Children: Mainstream, special needs and pre-school (2nd edn).* London: Worth Publishing.

CHAPTER 2

Understanding the Philosophical Basis of Veronica Sherborne's Approach to Movement

Elizabeth Marsden and Janet Sparkes

Veronica Sherborne worked at a time (1943–1990) when the teaching style in evidence in both the classroom and the physical education space was changing from almost strict 'military style' and didactic teaching methods, in which rows of children stood in lines on the football field or in a hall carrying out the orders of the teacher, into a child-centred, creative and free-thinking approach, in which the teacher's role was that of educator rather than commander. Sherborne never explicitly explained her philosophy of education, but she wrote in 1990 in her book, *Developmental Movement for Children*, that her movement education was firmly based upon the work of Rudolph Laban (1879–1958), and part of this chapter will scrutinise this remarkable man's influence on her. It is possible also to glean some ideas about Sherborne's broad educational philosophy through the papers that she wrote for conferences, and also by considering her spoken words delivered during workshops. Conversations with her friends, ex-students and colleagues, and her daughter, Sarah, have further enlightened the authors' understanding and experience of who Sherborne really was. Like any good educator, she continued to learn over a teaching career spanning nearly five decades, by trial and error, by reflection and by careful observation of the ways in which children learn and develop, so that her philosophy was one that evolved throughout her life (Sparkes, 2001). This chapter will examine the main influences on Sherborne's approach to movement, especially that of Rudolph Laban, and it seeks to explore Sherborne's perceived views about children's learning.

The influence of her initial teacher training
Sherborne trained at Bedford College of Physical Education in the early 1940s. The training at Bedford during this time resulted in students being granted recognition both as physiotherapists as well as Physical Education (PE) teachers. Her training as a PE teacher at Bedford would have thoroughly equipped her with formal teaching skills in games, gymnastics and dance, but the emphasis was definitely on *formal* training. In an interview with

Margaret Kirby in 1984, she described the strict regime which was prevalent at that time:

> *Our teaching practice preparation was learning how to give commands and we spent the whole of the autumn term in the evening learning to say, 'Forward,' 'Sideways,' 'Bend,' 'Forwards and downwards,' 'Drop,' and we learned how to command each others from long distances away...and you had to prepare your apparatus lesson, your free standing exercises and so on. Everything was in four lines and the apparatus was very carefully organised and structured... I had to unlearn so much at the Studio [where she later trained with Laban] that had been ingrained in me at Bedford. (p. 31)*

There was, however, one bright light in her training. Bedford College of Physical Education was particularly forward-looking in dance, and had been a focus for visiting lecturers from abroad since the 1920s (Thornton, 1971). Joan Goodrich, the dance lecturer in 1940, had trained under Leslie Burrows and Mary Wigman who were the first to bring Laban's style of dance and movement to Britain. Sherborne, as an 18-year-old student, had entered her PE training with the ambition of being a dance teacher, and so she was drawn to the 'modern educational' style of Goodrich. Then Laban himself, along with Lisa Ullman, came to the college for three days to teach the students. This first encounter with Laban had a stunning effect upon her (Kirby, 1984), and after several years of teaching in mainstrean secondary school, she sought him out in Manchester for further training.

The influence of Rudolph Laban

Conversations with Geraldine Stephenson, who had also undergone training at Bedford Physical Education College and who joined the Art of Movement Studio in Manchester at the same time as Sherborne, revealed that Laban's approach to movement was unorthodox and completely different from anything they had encountered at Bedford. Laban sought out the expression of a person's feelings and inner attitudes. He applauded controversial interpretations of the world, and allowed his students the space to discover movement qualities for themselves. He gave students the confidence to find their own way. For some, like Geraldine Stephenson, it would be into the world of theatre and dramatic movement; for others, it would result in a lifetime of dance (Preston-Dunlop, 1963); for Sherborne, it would eventually result in Developmental Movement (Sherborne, 2001).

Laban was a truly charismatic personality, and his impact and influence on his students was profound. In order to understand the nature of his influence on others, it is useful to explore those factors which had shaped his personality and approach to movement many years earlier and many miles away in a troubled and unstable Europe. Rudolph Jean-Baptiste Attila Laban was born in 1879 in Bratislava to a well-to-do military family. At the turn of the century, aged 21, he realised he did not want to follow in his father's military footsteps, and left the army to pursue his burning interest in art forms. Moving to Paris with his young wife, he found the capital to be blossoming with new experiences, as this was the period when names such as Picasso, Monet, Matisse and Rodin were becoming part of the scene. Preston-Dunlop (1998) suggested that it was at this time that Laban encountered Rosicrucian thinking and practice upon which he built his philosophy. He learned about the suppression of the energy-sapping ego and promotion of the belief that all are equal but different. We see Sherborne's teaching style reflecting this thinking, as she always accepted her pupils' 'differences' gladly and created an environment where all felt accepted and equal in status (Hill, 2006). Laban also learned to focus on the energy of the centre of the body, and many of his compositions show gathering and scattering movements. Similarly, Sherborne also stressed the importance of the centre of the body, particularly with her work with disabled children and adults. Douglas (1995) refers to both Laban's and Sherborne's attention to this:

> *Consider the focus on body awareness; perhaps because of his origins as a dancer and choreographer, Laban was much concerned with the centred body in the context of the space but Sherborne's focus is on the centre of the body as critical in knowing the self and giving confidence in the body.* (p. 15)

Laban used painting, drawing, architecture, music, drama and dance in his search for rhythm and harmony, expression of inner attitudes and the creativity of the soul. He encountered many difficulties and hardships after the death of his wife and father, yet he continued on his quest. He began to see the problem that music and a set pattern of steps somehow constrained dance, keeping the natural rhythm of the body fettered. He began to experiment without these traditional tethers, and used only the voice and tambour, and the body's natural rhythm. The experience was tremendously freeing for him and his dancers. He called the resulting form 'movement'.

Preston-Dunlop (1998) describes Laban's growing confidence in his movement/dance discoveries:

> *For the dancer, the body took on a new significance through Laban's lived assurance of the power of the unified human being. He implicitly denied Cartesian dualism. Body–mind oneness was found in its essence in the dancing dancer, the lived body, the dynamic person.* (p. 32)

With these discoveries, he realised that such experiences were hard to describe in words and so his long battle with notation began.

Laban's life took many twists and turns through two world wars, and eventually he took up residence in Britain where he influenced many British educators including Sherborne. By the time he was in his 60s, he had developed certain principles of movement (Laban, 1948) and, during the 1960s and 1970s, the teaching of PE in British schools was often based on these principles (Slater, 1974). Russell (1958) described 'movement' as an activity that involves the whole person and as a far wider concept than that then accepted within the physical training community, and prevalent in both primary and secondary schools of the day. Jordan (1966) wrote of the huge effect the adoption of movement education was having in schools in the 1960s:

> *To many teachers even today, it is so different from the physical education <u>they</u> experienced at school that they think it is a different subject...for others it is, as it should be, a better approach to physical education which gives*

greater scope to children, whatever their physical and mental endowment: one which brings the whole child into play – bodily, mentally and expressively at the tempo and in the manner which is personal to the individual at each successive stage of growth and development. (p. xiv)

The *Expressive Arts 5–14: Guidelines for Physical Education* (Scottish Office Education Department, 1992), which are still in force today, show a clear foundation on Laban's principles (p.57). These movement principles provided a framework for teachers both to successfully observe movement and also to teach movement holistically, creatively and inclusively (Davies, 2001) It was upon these principles of movement that Sherborne developed her movement work which she used with mainstream children, student teachers, and children and adults with moderate and profound physical, emotional or cognitive disabilities. The main principles are centred around *Body*, *Space*, *Dynamics* and *Relationships*. Table 2.1 shows these in a form that the authors find useful for explanation and clarity. Those movement elements included are only

Table 2.1. Laban's Movement Principles

BODY	SPACE
Actions: Stepping, jumping, rolling, sliding, vaulting, twisting, turning, swinging, balancing, gesture, stillness	**Levels:** High Medium Low
Parts of body: Can lead, can support, can relate, can move symmetrically, can move asymmetrically	**Directions:** Left – right High – deep Back – forwards
Body shape: Arrow, ball, pin, Wall, screw	**Extensions:** Near – far
	Air and floor patterns: Straight, curved, twisted, angular
DYNAMICS/ EFFORT	**RELATIONSHIPS**
Time: Sudden/quick. . . . . .sustained/slow	**With others:** Alone Partner Small group Large group
Weight: Strong/heavy. . . . . .light/fine touch	
Space: Direct/straight. . . . . .flexible/circuitous	**With apparatus:** The floor Small (mats, benches) Large (climbing materials, ropes, boxes)
Flow: Bound. . . . . free	**With equipment:** Small (balls, hoops, cones, etc.) Large (tunnels, goals, weights, etc.)

examples. They are not meant to represent all the possibilities of human movement. Laban maintained that any human movement, whether a single movement or a sequence of movements, could be analysed into these four categories (Laban, 1998). Humans tend to favour certain movement qualities, and ignore others; for example, some tend to move in strong, flexible, slow and free-flowing strides, favouring the use of large amounts of space, and using both arms and legs as they move. They might find the use of light, quick movements particularly difficult, and so their movement vocabulary would be restricted to their favoured types. Laban encouraged his students to experience a wide movement vocabulary by encouraging them to try out those movements which did not come naturally to them so that, in turn, they would gain body mastery and movement confidence.

As well as analysing, Laban used his movement principles to build up his students' understanding and experience of movement. By working upon a movement idea from each of the four categories, his students' movement vocabulary would gradually be built up so that they would have a solid movement bank from which to draw for experimenting, creating and gradually increasing their body confidence and ability to express their inner attitudes. As they developed physically and were given room to practise, so their movement confidence and fluency would increase.

Once her time at Laban's School was completed, Sherborne would have left with a deep understanding of, experience in and training for, human movement. Her attitude towards the fundamental importance of movement for adults and children, with or without disabilities, was now assured. Initially, she returned to teaching dance to student teachers, and then, with Laban's recommendation, she used movement in therapeutic work with emotionally distressed adults at the Withymead Centre in Devon. Both Sherborne and Laban had realised the psychological effect of movement many years before research in Sport and Exercise Psychology had been considered.

The influence of other contemporary educational thinkers
During Sherborne's early years as a teacher, educational theories were changing slowly. Her own attitude to movement had changed as a result of working with Laban, and then her experiences changed as she used movement with different populations, including her own three young children (Hill, 2006). The physical bonding encountered during motherhood and subsequent physical play with her developing children gave her a new and profound insight into the importance of movement, play and relationships in child development. Her children were born between 1956 and 1962, and her daughter Sarah recalls how her mother built a large climbing frame in the garden which was copied by the local school because of its innovation. The dressing-up box was always filled and well-used, and, while motherhood would have been demanding enough for most women of the time, Sherborne continued to work part-time. Occasionally, her busyness meant that the boundaries became blurred, and her students one day were stunned to see her appearing for a dance lecture in her apron!

In educational thinking, the notion that the education of young children should be child-centred, both active and interactive, and reflect the social world of the child became more acceptable during the 1950s and 1960s as educational theorists and pioneers of early childhood education became more established and more numerous (Dewey, 1938; Erikson, 1950; Fröbel, 1826; McMillan, 1930; Montessori, 1965; Piaget, 1953). Although educational theories tended to focus on the cognitive aspects of child development and the way that thought processes were organised and developed, Sherborne realised that the ability to think, reason, understand and learn also involved perceptual and sensory skills and that these cannot be separated from the physical development of young children. She could clearly see that physical and intellectual development were closely intertwined during the early years as her children moved to explore, play and make sense of the world and people around them.

The educational value of movement for young children had been recognised in some circles as long ago as 1914 when the Christian Socialist sisters, Margaret and Rachel McMillan, having worked with children in inner-city environments, noted the relationship between poor physical development and poor intellectual development of young children. We do not have explicit writing from Sherborne to suggest that these pioneer women had influenced her thinking, but we do know how much she stressed space and environment and opportunity. In setting up their first 'open air' nursery, the McMillan sisters recognised the need for children to have space and opportunity for physical movement in order to enhance both their learning and well-being. Likewise, Maria Montessori organised education for young children based on the notion that children learn best by interacting positively with a safe, familiar, stimulating environment. Montessori (1965) stressed that the role of the educator was to provide the best possible environment and physical learning experiences for the child in order to help them explore and learn purposefully. She also believed that reflective observation of children learning was a key tool for effective planning. Similarly, Piaget (1968) stressed the central importance of the familiar environment in which children are safe and stimulated to explore and learn. He placed an emphasis on the role of *social interaction* in learning

The influence of Sherborne's own reflections and personality

Sherborne was living and working in an innovative time with exciting new philosophies of education as well as the controversial worldview of Laban. We can only infer that she was indeed influenced by these new forces. Politically, there were also changes which affected her work. During the early 1970s, children with special needs were transferred from the authority of the Department of Health to that of the Department of Education, and Sherborne, with her vast experience of movement education, became more involved with the challenge of providing movement experience and opportunities for moderate and profoundly disabled youngsters. She wrote:

> *Over the years I have noticed that children make progress in certain fundamental areas as a result of movement experiences of different kinds. It is possible to help developmentally retarded children to relate to their bodies, to become more self aware and more confident. It is possible to help them form relationships and it is possible to help them focus attention and to concentrate.* (Sherborne, 1975)

The concern of these movement experiences was to engage children sufficiently that they became aware of how they use their bodies; to give them confidence and opportunity to move with control, qualitative awareness and with ease alongside and among others. The concern was to help children to re-experience, rebuild or maybe even experience for the first time those elements upon which a healthy body image and body schema is built. In fact, it is the focus of Sherborne's movement experiences for the whole child and their needs, rather than movement technique itself, that sets it apart from most other movement programmes which either seek to improve motor skills or remediate specific motor defects.

Sherborne noticed that one major factor, which children with special educational needs often lacked, was that of a consistent care-giver to act as their guide through the rocky road of growth, development and socialisation. Realising the significance of early relationships and the impact of these on communication, trust and sociability, Sherborne created movement experiences where these could be consistently addressed. She empowered adults, whether teachers, carers or occasional helpers, to work alongside the youngsters and to participate in the movement experiences too.

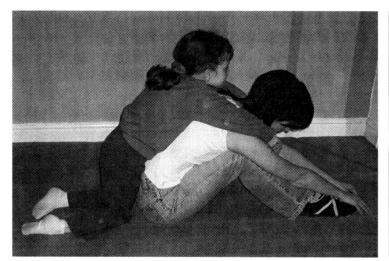 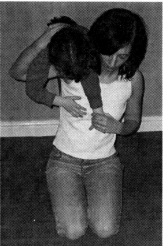

Figure 2.2. Adult and child share together in the movement experience

The nurturing environment that became the hall mark of her movement sessions was created by the *way* she interacted and taught her children as well as by what she chose to present. Her interaction was always one of fun and enjoyment for both the children and the adults so that motivation was stimulated. Sherborne's sensitivity to the quality of the learning environment she created finds support in the writings of Stern (1977) and his analysis of mother–infant, face-to-face play. In this context, he writes of positive interaction being a multifaceted process stemming from the care-giver's ability to engage the interest of the recipient and create a 'fun' environment. Stern (1977) equates fun with the notions of interest and delight:

> *By interest and delight, I mean the mutual providing of stimulus events of such a nature that attention is engaged and maintained enough to allow the build-up and fluctuation of excitement within a tolerable range so that affective, positive experiences are generated.* (p. 82)

Once attention was gained with interest and excitement, then Sherborne would begin a dialogue. Schaffer (1977) refers to dialogue as an essential acquisition in order for the child to realise they are involved in a relationship. This, in turn, involves reciprocity and intentionality. In the early days of building a relationship, Sherborne (1990) outlined the one-sidedness of the care-giver/teacher taking most of the responsibility for the interaction until eventually, the child reciprocates and a real dialogue takes place. As a result of the child being involved in a reciprocal relationship, they will start to realise that personal behaviour communicates, that it might influence the actions and reactions of others, and that others usually respond to their signs and signals. Soon, the child learns to send out signals intentionally expecting others to respond. Eventually the child will show awareness that behaviour can communicate and can be used intentionally to affect the nature of the relationship.

Hill (2006), Loots and Malschaert (1999), Marsden et al. (2004) and Sparkes (2006) have each commented on the way that Sherborne approached her pupils (i.e. her atypical teaching style). Not only did she interact by creating an environment of fun and enjoyment in which a dialogue could begin, but she also provided a sense of equality and sharing between herself and the children. She made it obvious that she enjoyed being there, and valued all the efforts that the children made. She created a learning environment where children felt emotionally and physically safe; where they could experiment with positive encouragement, and where she would be sensitive and responsive in her reactions. She was never negatively critical of anyone's work.

The focus in Sherborne's movement sessions was one where the emphasis was on each child's *process* of learning. Her emphasis was not on the outcome, but she sought to praise achievement also. As mentioned above, her aim was twofold: that children would feel at home in their own bodies; that they would trust and feel emotionally and physically confident to form relationships (Sherborne, 2001). For children with some disabilities, such as autistic spectrum disorder, or those who have suffered abuse, these have always been very difficult challenges. Sherborne's model was one where the environment created was safe and secure so that children could always experience success and happiness. The way of working was characterised by a concern for how the child could learn, interact, communicate, experience movement and feel. The model intentionally created an environment where children could find a way of communication and where their efforts were valued. Within this model, opportunities for working with others and achieving with others naturally developed. Children were encouraged to 'grow' at their own pace. They were not forced to make developmental steps until their inner selves had the strength and confidence to move forwards (Sparkes, 2001).

A lasting legacy
Many years after his death, Sherborne (1982) wrote of her debt to Laban:

> *Everything I teach is based on Laban's theory; I couldn't work at all as an educator or as a therapist without that background knowledge and I was very fortunate in being able to work with Laban himself over quite a long time.*
> (p. 14)

Yet she never became his puppet. She was aware of the treasure of knowledge she had discovered with him, and was aware of his great charisma. Preston-Dunlop (1998), also aware of his charisma, wrote how important it was for his students to see through this and to recognise that empowerment came, not through following him, but through finding one's own way.

In a similar way, Sherborne was a very charismatic teacher. Kirby's (1984) study showed a tendency among many of those taught by Sherborne to 'relate movement education directly to the teaching they had experienced from Mrs Sherborne'. They did not seek an understanding of the theoretical principles underlying the practice, and she was concerned that the temptation would be to 'merely repeat a set of activities which they had learned...without relating them to the movement qualities involved' (p. 223). Douglas (1995) challenges colleagues to take Sherborne's work forward:

> *We need to look at her programme and her activities – to use them, to search for the principles underlying her work and to be creative within those principles. It is important to be dynamic in exploring the potential of the work and to prevent it becoming dead. Veronica's work is worthy of analysis and scrutiny, but I suggest it will only survive if practitioners take the principles and develop within them, mindful that the power is in the <u>movement experience</u> not the system.* (p. 15)

Sherborne was indeed fiercely independent and encouraged her students to stand on their own feet. She did not write down her philosophy nor her theoretical principles. She just knew, in the last decade of her life, that what she did worked. But this was after a lifetime of experience and reflection, and she never lost the joy of discovery:

> *...it's been trial and error all the time but I have learned an awful lot and I'm discovering something new almost every week and that gives you a feeling of achievement...it's exciting.* (Sherborne, 1983, p. 52)

The lasting legacy of Sherborne's philosophy is not only the principles of movement, the acceptance of all persons as being valued, the importance of being at home in one's own body and the ability to form relationships through movement, but it is one of pure joy in discovery and the excitement of achievement.

References

Davies, E. (2001) *Beyond Dance*. London: Brechin Books Ltd.

Dewey, J. (1938) *Experience and Education*. New York, NY: Macmillan.

Douglas, M. (1995) 'The essence of Sherborne's work: the way forward'. In: J. Dibbo and S. Gerry (eds) *Caring and Sharing: Physical education, therapy and Sherborne Developmental Movement*. Exmouth: University of Plymouth Press.

Dunlop-Preston, V. (1998) *Rudolph Laban: An extraordinary life*. London: Dance Books Ltd.

Erikson, E.H. (1950) *Childhood and Society*. New York, NY: W.W. Norton & Co.

Fröbel, F. (1826) *On the Education of Man (die Menschenerziehurg)*. Keilhau/Leipzig, Germany: Wienbrach.

Hill, C. (2006) *Communicating through Movement: Sherborne Developmental Movement – towards a broadening perspective*. Clent: Sunfield Publications.

Jordan, D. (1966) *Childhood and Movement*. Oxford: Basil Blackwell.

Kirby, M. (1984) *Sherborne and Movement (unpublished thesis)*. Bristol: Bristol Polytechnic.

Laban, R. (1948) *Modern Educational Dance*. London: Macdonald and Evans Ltd.

Laban, R. (1998) *The Mastery of Movement (5th edition)*. London: Northcote House.

Loots, G. and Malschaert, E. (1999) 'The use in Belgium of developmental movement according to the work of Veronica Sherborne: a developmental psychology view,' *European Journal of Special Needs Education,* 14 (3), 221–230.

Marsden, E., Weston, C. and Hair, M. (2004) 'Innovative and inclusive physical education'. Paper presented at the British Educational Research Association Conference, UMIST, 16–18 September. [Online at: www.leeds.ac.uk/educol/documents/00003898.htm]

McMillan, M. (1930) *The Nursery School*. London: Dent.

Montessori, M. (1965) *Dr Montessori's Own Handbook: A short guide to her ideas and materials*. New York, NY: Schocken Books.

Piaget, J. (1953) *The Origin of Intelligence in the Child*. London: Routledge and Kegan Paul.

Piaget, J. (1968) *Genetic Epistomology*. New York, NY: Columbia University Press.

Preston-Dunlop, V. (1963) *A Handbook for Modern Educational Dance*. London: MacDonald and Evans Ltd.

Preston-Dunlop, V. (1998) *Rudolf Laban: An extraordinary life*. London: Dance Books.

Russell, J. (1958) *Modern Dance in Education*. London: Macdonald and Evans.

Schaffer, D.R. (1977) *Developmental Psychology: Childhood and adolescence*. Pacific Grove, CA: Brooks/Cole.

Scottish Office Education Department (1992) *Expressive Arts 5–14 Guidelines for Physical Education*. Edinburgh: Scottish Office Education Department.

Sherborne, V. (1975). In: K. Holt (ed.) *Movement and Child Development*. London: Heinemann.

Sherborne, V. (1982) 'Relationship play in movement for developmentally retarded children'. Workshop presented in Queensland, Australia.

Sherborne, V. (1983) 'Personal interview'. In: M. Kirby (1984) *Sherborne and Movement (unpublished thesis)*. Bristol: Bristol Polytechnic.

Sherborne, V. (1990) *Developmental Movement for Children: Mainstream, special needs and pre-school*. Cambridge: Cambridge University Press.

Sherborne, V. (2001) *Developmental Movement for Children: Mainstream, special needs and pre-school (2nd edn)*. London: Worth Publishing.

Slater, W. (1974) *Teaching Modern Educational Dance*. London: MacDonald and Evans Ltd.

Sparkes, J. (2001) 'Foreword'. In: V. Sherborne (2001) *Developmental Movement for Children: Mainstream, special needs and pre-school (2nd edn)*. London: Worth Publishing.

Sparkes, J. (2006) 'Sherborne Developmental Movement in education'. In: C. Hill (2006) *Communicating through Movement: Sherborne Developmental Movement – towards a broadening perspective*. Clent: Sunfield Publications.

Stern, D. (1977) *The First Relationship: Infant and mother*. London: Fontana/Open Books.

Thornton, S. (1971) *A Movement Perspective of Rudolph Laban*. London: Macdonald and Evans Ltd.

Whitehead, M. (2001) 'The concept of physical literacy', *British Journal of Teaching Physical Education,* Spring, 32 (1). [Online at: http://www.physical-literacy.org.uk/concept.pdf]

PART 2

Sherborne Developmental Movement
in the UK

CHAPTER 3

Autism, Engagement and Sherborne Developmental Movement

Jotham Konaka

Teaching approaches for individuals with severe and complex learning difficulties, including autistic spectrum disorders (ASD), have changed over the last few decades (Aird, 2001; Collis and Lacey, 1996; Lewis and Norwich, 2005). Many educationalists during the 1950s up to the 1980s applied behavioural approaches, which were characterised by control and structure with the ultimate goal of changing behaviour. This often led to a focus upon pathology and deficiency within the child with special needs (Porter and Lacey, 2005; Tilstone and Layton, 2004).

In the 1970s, when Sherborne initially introduced her work into the field of special education, she encouraged teachers to engage individuals with severe learning needs as active participants rather than passive learners, and promoted sociability through movement experiences, rather than focusing on prescriptive physical exercises (Hill, 2006; Sheppard, 1996; Sherborne, 2001). Her emphasis was upon inclusion. As Sheppard (1996) writes:

> *[Sherborne Developmental Movement] fits into an interactive model of teaching and learning which has at its heart a focus on the process in which individuals are engaged, rather than the end product.* (p. 144)

SDM offers co-operative movement with the participant and supporter moving together in close proximity, which allows the participant to be aware of the supporter, and allows the supporter to notice and respond to small signals from the participant (Murdoch, 1992; Sherborne, 2001). In this person-centred teaching approach, the onus lies with the supporters to facilitate the development of positive concepts among the participants, and to ensure that the quality of interaction has a profound effect on them (Hill, 2006; Peter, 1997).

The current educational trend encourages engagement-orientated, interpretative approaches in which the emphasis is on inclusion (Carpenter and Shevlin, 2004; Guralnick, 2004; Hewett and Nind, 1998; Jones, 2002; Jordan, 2002; Porter and Lacey, 2005; Powell, 2000; Tilstone and Layton, 2004; Tilstone and Rose, 2003). This stance, which is concerned with the understanding and interpretation of the world in terms of its actors (Kellett and Nind, 2003; Sherratt and Peter, 2002), is particularly important in promoting access and an educational entitlement for all children, in accordance with the statutory inclusion statement (Department for Education and Employment (DfEE)/Qualifications and Curriculum Authority (QCA), 1999) and *Removing Barriers to Achievement* (Department for Education and Skills (DfES), 2004). In the last two decades, the amount of literature focusing on interpretative, engagement-orientated interventions for children with autistic spectrum disorders (ASD) has steadily risen; for example, Intensive Interaction (Nind and Hewitt, 2001), the Options approach (Williams and Wishart, 2003), interactive play for children with ASD (Seach, 2006; Stern, 2002; Thornton and Cox, 2005) and dance (Hills, 2003; Peter, 1997).

The present research

Sunfield provides education and 52-week residential care for 70 children between the ages of 6 and 19 years who have severe and complex learning needs. The organisation also offers specialist provision for children whose needs fall within the autistic spectrum, and for those with challenging behaviour. It is the organisation's aim to develop each individual child's abilities so that they may come to experience life as a worthwhile activity and live as independently as possible.

As one of the main training bases for Sherborne Developmental Movement (SDM) in the UK, Sunfield was interested in investigating the resonance of SDM with the concept of engagement for children with ASD. This formed the focus of a two-year study (September 2004 – August 2006) – a collaborative piece of work between Sunfield and Cyndi and George Hill, two experienced Sherborne consultants/trainers from the Sherborne Association UK. The project was supported financially by the Three Guineas Trust.

While SDM has been used extensively and produced positive results in the context of special education (Peter, 1997; Sugden and Wright, 2001), only exploratory work has been done regarding its implementation with children with ASD (Sheppard, 1996). As Jordan and Powell (2002) assert:

> *A range of phenomena in autistic thinking and behaving suggest that the relationship between self and experience is unique in autism.* (p. 7)

The present research aimed to explore whether this uniqueness affected the engagement of individuals with ASD in SDM sessions, and how their engagement could be enhanced so they would derive maximum benefit from their participation. In this way, it was hoped to begin to address the difficulties children with autism experience in social interaction and communication (Jordan and Powell, 2002).

This chapter provides the literary context for developing an adapted teaching approach to promote social engagement for children with ASD through SDM (see Chapter 4). It seeks to discuss the key issues influencing the effective implementation of such an approach, including the nature of ASD, the concept of an engagement approach (Guralnick, 2005), the resonance of SDM with the concept of engagement and interventions which facilitate access for individuals with ASD.

Social development and individuals with autism

In 1979, Wing and Gould identified a cluster of features common to the experience of individuals with autism – difficulties in social interaction, communication and imagination, later referred to as the 'Triad of Impairments' – that provided a diagnostic platform for autism (American Psychiatric Association, 2000; World Health Organisation, 1992). A plethora of literature has since demonstrated the variability in features and phenomena characterising autism (e.g. Jordan, 2002; Koegel et al., 1996; Wing, 2002; Worth, 2005), and it has, therefore, come to be understood as a broad spectrum of developmental disorders (Jordan, 2002; Jordan and Powell, 2002).

Edelson (1999) and Powell and Jordan (2002) recognise dysfunction in social interaction as the key impairment associated with ASD, and it is probably the greatest obstacle for individuals with ASD to engaging with other people (Jordan, 2002; Wing, 2002). It has been argued that impairments of interaction predetermine other features of the triad (Powell and Jordan, 2002).

Research evidence suggests links between this developmental deficit and the hypothesis behind 'Theory of Mind' (Baron-Cohen, 1995; Frith, 1989; Jordan, 2002). As Edelson (1999) postulates, many autistic individuals do not understand that other people have their own plans, thoughts and points of view. Furthermore, the difficulty autistic individuals have in assuming other people's perspectives ultimately limit their anticipation of what others will say or do in various social situations. According to Hobson (1993), 'the development of a sense of self and others are intricately related and bound up with the understanding of minds' (p. 82). Most importantly, he proposes that it is a lack of participation in social experiences, which explains the failure of the child with ASD to recognise other people's perspectives.

Social learning theorists (Bruner, 1985; Vygotsky, 1978) believe that socialisation emerges from awareness of self and then awareness of others within the immediate surroundings. The foundation of communication and language arises from interpersonal situations with parents and care-givers during the first two years of life (Bruner, 1985). An infant learns these skills by a process of continuous, progressive and accumulative interaction with the environment, including parents and care-givers. In normally developing children, the acquisition of social skills depends on the ability to observe, interpret and imitate the behaviours of competent others, and yet this is problematic for children with severe ASD (Tilstone and Layton, 2004).

Movement and development

Movement is considered to be the most fundamental aspect of a young child's life contributing to early social-communicative development (Davis, 1997; Greenspan, 1995; Maurer, 2003). Due to their sensory sensitivities and social difficulties, many children with ASD have been unable to engage fully in the experiences necessary to enable them to develop even the very basics of social interaction and communication as a foundation for exploring relationships, and developing confidence, intentionality and social protocol (Aitken and Trevarthen, 1997; Werner et al., 2000). Under normal circumstances, children assimilate these during infant play (Seach, 2006; Stern, 2002; Thornton and Cox, 2005) and movement experiences (Davis, 1997). Maurer (2003) and Teitelbaum et al. (1998) argue that deficiencies in early motor development in individuals with ASD are predictive of subsequent developmental difficulties in communication and social interaction. Peter (1997) and Filer (2006) suggest that SDM offers an important compensatory opportunity to capture early sensori-motor experiences (Piaget, 1969) for individuals for whom such experiences may have been impossible at an earlier life stage. Greenspan (1995) and Maurer (2003) suggest that shared spatial and temporal scaffolds can encourage incipient social relationships in children with ASD.

The SDM Programme is recognised as being highly effective in promoting communication and sociability in individuals with severe and complex learning difficulties (Department of Education and Science (DES), 1991; Dibbo and Gerry, 1994; Hill, 2006; Peter, 1997; Sheppard, 1996; Sherborne, 2001; Stewart, 1990; Sugden, and Wright, 2001). Sherborne founded her 'Developmental Movement' on the premise that relating to oneself and relating to other people is essential for the satisfactory development of every human being through active learning (Sherborne, 2001). SDM encourages three strands of relationship play – 'with', 'shared' with and 'against' another person (Sherborne, 2001). Sherborne describes her movement experiences as concerned with:

■ Developing self-awareness, which involves an awareness of 'my body', its parts and the whole of it, 'me' in space that surrounds me, and an awareness of the quality of 'my' movement

■ Developing an awareness of others – an awareness of another's body, of another's movement and of the impact of another's movement on myself. (Sherbourne, 2001)

The 'movement experiences' she developed had a dual focus on physical and psychological learning experiences (Sheppard, 1996; Sherborne, 2001). Hill (2006) recognises the development of personality and self-image as major attributes of Sherborne's work.

Those who use SDM maintain that it is a sound basis for the development of body awareness, a positive self-concept and relationship-building (Dibbo and Gerry, 1994; Hill, 2006; Peter, 1997). Any meaningful engagement requires a sense of awareness of others, and it has been argued that SDM has the potential to contribute towards the development of this awareness by enabling individuals to work together in a caring and safe partnership (Dibbo and Gerry, 1994). These are areas of great difficulty for a child with ASD, and yet they are the tenets forming the basis for any meaningful engagement.

SDM is to be understood in the context of early child development (Sparkes, 2001). As Sparkes writes in the Foreword to Sherborne's *Developmental Movement for Children:*

> *By examining the text and the practices of Veronica Sherborne, it is possible to identify those stages of early development that characterise a 'nurturing relationship', that is, a relationship that is seen to facilitate growth and optimum development.* (Sparkes, in Sherborne, 2001, p. x)

Sherborne's main intention was to develop and adapt movement experiences for children with wide-ranging developmental difficulties whose formative years had been deprived of basic relational skills. She states:

> *Movement experiences are fundamental to the development of all children but particularly important to children with special needs who often have difficulty in relating to their own bodies and other people.*

The development of SDM was influenced by her knowledge of the learning processes during Piaget's sensori-motor stage, acquired from her physical education and physiotherapy training backgrounds (Hill, 2006; Peter, 1997), and Vygotsky's (1978) and Dunn's (1992) perceptions of child development as a fundamental social construct, which involves what goes on between the child and others. Sherborne also recognised the importance of the role of the supporting adult and the quality of interaction (Hill, 2006; Sherborne, 2001). Sparkes (2001) expounds:

> *Understanding the significance of early relationships and the impact of such on communication and sociability is fundamental to understanding the key features of Developmental Movement.* (p. x)

Peter (1997) also emphasises the role of movement education in the stimulation of the mind, as well as, the development of social communicative skills. She reiterates Hobson's (1993) notion that 'effective engagement at a psychological level is considered critical for social and intellectual development, particularly for individuals with autism.'

The concept of an engagement approach

In the 21st century, much of what there is to know about the aetiology of disabilities is already known (Guralnick, 2004), and the focus of educators and researchers is upon 'engagement' of children with intellectual disabilities as the foundation for effective learning (Guralnick, 2004; Mesibov and Howley, 2003). The term, 'engagement', has received many interpretations. It has been defined as 'as a mutual and reciprocal relationship based on a desire and willingness to be with the other person to share wants and needs over a sustained period'. The National Research Council (2001) defines it as 'sustained attention to an activity or person'. SDM, focusing on the interactive relationship between child and supporter,[1] has engagement as its central tenet, although at the time Sherborne developed it, the term was not in use.

For this research, the most relevant perspective derives from other interactional interventions (e.g. Kellett and Nind, 2003). Kellet and Nind (2003) recognise engagement as the most crucial element underlying social communicative development in children with ASD. Kellet and Nind (2003) suggest that any social interaction requires a fully focused and absorbed engagement, and that this is the foundation on which interactive and communicative relationships can be built. It is difficult for individuals with ASD to communicate verbally and non-verbally with other people as often they do not attach meaning to the conventional elements of communication (Frith and Frith, 2003; Jordan, 2002; Wing, 2002). However, evidence suggests that some of these features may improve with time and relevant approaches (Wing, 2002).

The need for adapted approaches to Sherborne Developmental Movement
Understanding the nature and extent of children's difficulties and adapting the teaching approaches to accommodate individual needs are vital for learning to take place (Carpenter et al., 2001; Ofsted, 1999; Powell and Jordan, 2002; Sugden and Talbot, 1998). The emphasis has to be on 'enabling access' (Carpenter et al., 2001). As Jordan (1999) points out:

> *The special needs of any individual may not be determined by developmental difficulties but will be the result of interaction between abilities and disabilities and the learning environment.* (p. 26)

The DfES also recognises that access to learning for a small number of children may require alternative or adapted approaches (DfES, 2001). Thus in order for individuals with ASD to take part in a motor-based, interactive experience such as SDM, it is important to understand the abilities and impairments which underlie the experience of ASD (Clement and Zarkowska, 2000; Jordan, 1999).

The importance of movement as an interactive approach contributing to the kinaesthetic learning has been acknowledged (Peter, 1997; Piaget, 1969). The basic philosophy of the SDM is underpinned by the notion that children need to feel at home in their own bodies, thus, developing their kinaesthetic sense (Sparkes, 2001, p. xiii). While SDM, through its kinaesthetic approach to learning, allows participants with ASD to capitalise on this strength in their learning profile (Farnell, 2003), other factors might be thought to mitigate against their access to SDM.

Potter and Whitaker (2002) argue that if a child with ASD has to be engaged in active learning, environmental considerations must take precedence. There are myriad reasons why children with ASD become less engaged in learning experiences, including influences from both within and outside the classroom (Brewster and Fager, 2000). Tilstone and Layton (2004) argue that a holistic view of the learner's profile 'in different learning contexts must be sensitive to both the task-demands and individual pupils' response to them' (p. 61). While teachers may have little control over many factors that contribute to the interest and level of engagement in learning of the student with ASD (Lumsden, 1994), they can influence their motivation through certain practices that increase time spent on task.

Individuals on the autistic spectrum are more likely to experience symptoms of anxiety than the general population (Bellini, 2004; Carpenter, 2004), and research evidence suggests that professionals implementing any social skills intervention programmes for individuals with ASD ought to consider the role social anxiety plays in the interaction difficulties these children experience (Bellini, 2004). In the context of SDM, this literature review therefore looked at ways in which the levels of anxiety could be generally reduced and learning improved for individuals with ASD by designing the sessions around the 'fundamental strengths and deficits of autism that affect daily learning and interaction' (Mesibov et al., 2005).

One way of achieving this was to incorporate visually based approaches into SDM sessions. Children on the autistic spectrum are generally known to have stronger visual, as well as tactile and/or kinaesthetic, learning preferences (Farnell, 2003). Most children with ASD at Sunfield are familiar with two visually based approaches which are used across site. Individuals with ASD often have difficulties in understanding and predicting the sequence of events, and this can lead to heightened anxiety levels. The structured teaching model advocated by the Treatment and Education of Autistic and Related Communication Handicapped Children (TEACCH) team from North Carolina (Mesibov et al., 2005) uses visual cues arranged on a schedule to indicate the order and nature of forthcoming events. The Picture Exchange Communication System (PECS; Bondy and Frost, 2002) is a visually based communication system which allows both the individual with ASD and their partner to use a physical communication platform from which to ask and answer questions and to request using visual prompts.

For individuals with ASD, impairment in each of the three areas of the triad may be accompanied by additional difficulties in motor co-ordination and movement (Powell and Jordan, 2002; Teitelbaum et al., 1998), personal contact and touch (Grandin, 1995; Williams, 1996) and atypical responses to environmental sensory stimuli such as noise, light, visual distraction, etc. (Jordan, 2002). Individuals with ASD may also display repetitious body movements (stereotypies) such as rocking, hand and arm flapping or unusual attachments to objects, and they may resist any changes to their routines and environment (Sheppard, 1996). These can make it difficult for the individual with ASD to relate to other people and the world around them.

Whereas most people have a strong need for human contact, many children with ASD seem to find being held or touched distressing and avoid physical contact wherever possible (Edelson, 1999; Grandin, 1995; Williams, 1996). Referring to the potential benefits of SDM, Powell and Jordan (2002) write:

> *Touch is very important to the nervous system and any part of the body which does not receive normal tactile stimulation may develop a protective, as opposed to a discriminatory, response. The tendency to react negatively is termed 'tactile defensiveness' and a child with this problem may find many sensations uncomfortable.* (p. 80–81)

Temple Grandin (1995) confirms that while tactile input is problematic for many individuals with ASD, as a child she longed to be touched, hugged and rocked, but found these sensations painful and overwhelming. For the present research study, it was therefore initially anticipated that the design of the movement experiences would need to be changed in order to address issues that individuals with ASD might have with:

- The ability and willingness to share body space in a focused and concentrated manner due to touch sensitivity (Kellett and Nind, 2003)

- Strategies for sharing attention with others, due to perceptual and conceptual irregularities associated with ASD which contribute to lack of a concept of self and others (Jordan and Powell, 2002)

■ Sharing experiences which presuppose joint attention – an important aspect of engagement (Kellett and Nind, 2003).

These are fundamental mechanisms that allow social communicative behaviours to develop (Jordan and Powell, 2002). Jordan and Powell highlight the significance of social interchanges between the care-giver and the individual with ASD towards the achievement of mutual reciprocity of responses in a social context. This reciprocity can be achieved only when control and influence flow in both directions (Clement and Zarkowska, 2001). Vygotsky (1978) emphasises the adult's role in providing early interaction opportunities for normally developing children. Initially, the person interacting with child assumes most of the responsibility for guiding the problem-solving, but gradually this responsibility transfers to the child. This is indeed consistent with Sherborne's (2001) idea of developing 'relationship play' in an environment where no one feels threatened in any way. It requires trust, understanding and a constant awareness of the participant's sensitivities during all movement activities (Sherborne Association UK, 2002).

Conclusion

Clement and Zakowska (2001) maintain that:

> ...being part of a social system requires the individual to play an active role in establishing and maintaining relationships and for the social system to reciprocate in a like manner. (p. 94)

They emphasise the devastating effects that can ensue in an individual's well-being (physical and psychological) when experiencing problems with relationships. The findings from a UK nationwide enquiry into the mental health of individuals with learning difficulties, suggested that people with additional communication difficulties, especially individuals with ASD, are 60% more likely to suffer mental health problems (Foundation for People with Learning Disabilities, 2002). This committee found that the best ways to meet these individuals' emotional needs is through interpersonal relationships and physical exercise. Turner-Bisset (2001) concurs with this committee in recognising physical exercise as an attribute to the well-being and development of the individual.

In seeking to engage children with ASD through SDM, this research aimed to enable these children to experience a system of interaction which is responsive to them and motivates them to engage with another person. The aim of this research is that, in the context of adapted approaches to SDM, students with ASD will be able to find:

> ...the motivation and ability to relate to others in a mutually reinforcing and reciprocal fashion – to wish to, and to enjoy being with, another person and have them enjoy being with you. (Howlin, cited in Hewett and Nind, 1994).

References

Aird, R. (2001) *The Education and Care of Children with Severe, Profound and Multiple Learning Difficulties*. London: David Fulton.

Aitken, K.J. and Trevarthen, C. (1997) 'Self/other organisation in human psychological development', *Development and Psychopathology,* 9, 653–677.

American Psychiatric Association (2000) *Diagnostic and Statistical Manual of Mental Disorders – Text revision* (4th edn). Washington, DC: APA.

Baron-Cohen, S. (1995) *Mindblindness.* Cambridge: Massachussetts: MIT Press.

Bellini, S. (2004) 'Social skill deficits and anxiety in high functioning adolescents with autism spectrum disorders', *Focus on Autism and Other Developmental Disabilities,* 19 (2), 78–86.

Bondy, A. and Frost, L. (2002) *A Picture's Worth: PECS and other visual communication strategies in autism.* Bethesda, MD: Woodbine House.

Brewster, C. and Fager, J. (2000) *Increasing Student Engagement from Time-on-Task to Homework.* Oregon: Northern Educational Laboratory.

Bruner, J.S. (1985) 'Vygotsky: a historical and conceptual perspective'. In: J.V. Wertsch (ed.) *Culture, Communication and Cognition: Vygotskian perspectives.* Cambridge: Cambridge University Press.

Carpenter, B. (2004) 'Health improvement for people with learning disabilities: a view from the outside'. Paper presented at the launch of the Scottish Health Assessment Needs Report, Glasgow (February).

Carpenter, B. and Shevlin, M. (2004) 'Creating an inclusive curriculum'. In: P. Noonan Walsh and H. Gash (eds) *Lives and Times: Practice, policy and people with learning difficulties.* Wicklow, Ireland: Rashdown Press.

Carpenter, B., Ashdown, R. and Bovair, K. (2001) *Enabling Access: Effective teaching and learning for pupils with learning difficulties.* London: David Fulton.

Clement, J. and Zarkowska, E. (2000) *Behavioural Concerns and Autistic Spectrum Disorders: Explanations and strategies for change.* London: Jessica Kingsley.

Collis, M. and Lacey, P. (1996) *Interactive Approaches to Teaching: Framework for INSET.* London: David Fulton.

Davis, K. (1997) 'The value of movement activities for young children', *The Reporter,* 2 (3), 1–3. [Online at: www.iidc.indiana.edu/IRCA/SocialLeisure/movementact.html]

Department for Education and Employment/Qualifications and Curriculum Authority (1999) *The National Curriculum for Physical Education in England.* London: HMSO.

Department for Education and Skills (2001) *Special Educational Needs: Code of practice.* Annesley: DfES Publications.

Department for Education and Skills (2004) *Removing Barriers to Achievement: The government strategy for SEN.* London: DfES Publications.

Department of Education and Science (1991) *National Curriculum: Physical education for ages 5 to 16.* London: HMSO.

Dibbo, J. and Gerry, S. (1994) 'Developments in Sherborne Developmental Movement'. Paper presented at the PE International Conference, Plymouth, UK.

Dunn, J. (1992) *The Beginnings of Social Understanding.* Oxford: Blackwell.

Edelson, S.M. (1999) 'Overview of autism'. Salem, Oregon: Centre for the Study of Autism. [Online at www.autism.org/overview.html]

Farnell, B. (2003) 'Kinaesthetic sense and dynamically embodied action', *Journal of Anthropological Study of Human Movement,* 12 (4), 133–144.

Filer, J. (2006) 'SDM and its role in family therapy'. In: C. Hill (2006) *Communicating through Movement: Sherborne Developmental Movement – towards a broadening perspective.* Clent: Sunfield Publications.

Foundation for People with Learning Disabilities (2002) *Count Us In: The report of the inquiry into the mental health needs of young people with learning disabilities.* London: Mental Health Foundation.

Frith, U. (1989) *Autism: Explaining the enigma.* Oxford: Blackwell.

Frith, U. and Frith, C.D. (2003) 'Development and neurophysiology of mentalizing', *Philosophical Transactions of the Royal Society London – Series B: Biological Sciences,* 358, 459–473.

Grandin, T. (1995) *Thinking in Pictures and Other Reports from My Life with Autism.* New York, NY: Doubleday.

Greenspan, S. (1995) *The Challenging Child.* New York: Addison-Wesley Publishing.

Guralnick, M. (ed.) (2004) 'Early intervention for children with intellectual disabilities: current knowledge and future prospects.' Keynote address to the 12th IAS-SID World Congress, Montpellier, France (15 June 2004).

Guralnick, M. (2005) *The Developmental System Approach to Early Intervention.* Baltimore: Paul H. Brookes.

Hewett, D. and Nind, M. (eds) (1998) *Interaction in Action: Reflections on the use of Intensive Interaction.* London: David Fulton.

Hill, C. (2006) *Communicating through Movement: Sherborne Developmental Movement – towards a broadening perspective.* Clent: Sunfield Publications.

Hills, P. (2003) *It's Your Move: An inclusive approach to dance.* Birmingham: The Questions Publishing Company Ltd.

Hobson, R.P. (1993) *Autism and the Development of the Mind.* Hillsdale, NJ: Lawrence Erlbaum Associates.

Jones, G. (2002) *Educational Provision for Children with Autism and Asperger Syndrome: Meeting their needs.* London: David Fulton.

Jordan, R. (1999) *Autism with Severe Learning Difficulties.* London: Souvenir Press.

Jordan, R. (2002) *Autistic Spectrum Disorders: An introductory handbook for practitioners.* London: David Fulton.

Jordan, R. and Powell, S. (2002) *Understanding and Teaching Children with Autism.* Chichester: John Wiley.

Kellet, M. and Nind, M. (2003) *Implementing Intensive Interaction in Schools: Guidance for practitioners, managers and coordinators.* London: David Fulton.

Koegel, L.K., Koegel, R.L. and Dunlap, G. (1996) *Positive Behavioural Support: Including people with difficult behaviour in the community.* Baltimore: Paul H. Brookes.

Lewis, A. and Norwich, B. (2005) *Special Teaching for Special Children: Pedagogies for inclusion.* Milton Keynes: Open University Press.

Lumsden, L.S. (1994) 'Student motivation to learn', *ERIC Digest,* 92 (June). [Online at: http://eric.uoregon.edu]

Maurer, R. (2003) 'Autism and the cerebellum: a neurological basis for intervention'. [Online at: http://www.autcom.org]

Mesibov, G. and Howley, M. (2003) *Accessing the Curriculum for Pupils with Autistic Spectrum Disorders.* London: David Fulton.

Mesibov, G., Shea, V. and Schopler (2005) *The TEACCH Approach to Autism Spectrum Disorders.* New York, NY: Kluwer Academic/Plenum.

Murdoch, H. (1992) 'Multi-sensory impairments'. In: R. Gulliford and G. Upton (1994) *Special Educational Needs*. London: Routledge.

National Research Council (2001) *Understanding Dropouts: Statistics, strategies and high-stakes testing*. Washington, DC: National Academy Press.

Nind, M. and Hewitt, D. (1994) *Access to Communication: Developing the basics of communication with people with severe learning difficulties through Intensive Interaction*. London: David Fulton.

Nind, M. and Hewitt, D. (2001) *A Practical Guide to Intensive Interaction*. Kidderminster: British Institute of Learning Disabilities.

Office for Standards in Education (Ofsted) (1999) *Special Education 1994–1998: A review of special schools, secure units and pupil referral units in England*. London: The Stationary Office.

Peter, M. (1997) *Making Dance Special*. London: David Fulton.

Piaget, J. (1969) *The Psychology of the Child*. New York, NY: Basic Books.

Porter, J. and Lacey, P. (2005) *Researching Learning Difficulties*. London: Paul Chapman.

Potter, C. and Whittaker, C. (2001) *Enabling Communication in Children with Autism*. London: Jessica Kingsley.

Powell, S. (2000) *Helping Children with Autism to Learn*. London: David Fulton.

Powell, S. and Jordan, R. (2002) *Autism and Learning: A guide to practice*. London: David Fulton.

Seach, D. (2006) *Interactive Play for Children with Autism*. London: Routledge.

Sheppard, S. (1996) 'The implementation of Sherborne based development with pupils on the autistic spectrum'. In: *Therapeutic Intervention in Autism: Perspectives from research and practice* (Conference proceedings). Durham: University of Durham.

Sherborne, V. (2001) *Developmental Movement for Children: Mainstream, special needs and pre-school* (2nd edn). London: Worth Publishing.

Sherborne Association UK (2002) *Teaching Notes and Guidelines*. Sherborne Association. [Online at: http://homepage.ntlworld.com/esbester/Sherborne/page2.html]

Sherrat, D. and Peter, M. (2002) *Developing Play and Drama in Children with Autistic Spectrum Disorders*. London: David Fulton.

Sparkes, J. (2001) 'Foreword'. In: V. Sherborne (2001) *Developmental Movement for Children: Mainstream, special needs and pre-school* (2nd edn). London: Worth Publishing.

Stern, D. (2002) *The First Relationship: Infant and mother*. Cambridge, MA: Harvard University Press.

Stewart, D. (1990) *The Right to Movement: Motor development in every school*. London: Falmer Press.

Sugden, D. and Talbot, M. (1998) *Physical Education for Children with Special Needs in Mainstream Education*. Leeds Metropolitan University: Carnegie National Sports Development Centre.

Sugden, D. and Wright, H. (2001) 'Physical education'. In: B. Carpenter, R. Ashdown and K. Bovair (eds) *Enabling Access: Effective teaching and learning for pupils with learning difficulties*. London: David Fulton.

Teitelbaum, P., Teitelbaum, O., Nye, J., Fryman, J. and Maurer, R.G. (1998) 'Movement analysis in infancy may be useful for early diagnosis of autism', *Proceed-*

ings of the National Academy of Sciences of the United States of America, 95 (23),13982–13987. [Online at: http://www.pnas.org]

Thornton, K. and Cox, E. (2005) 'Play and the reduction of challenging behaviour in children with ASD and learning disabilities', *Good Autism Practice,* 6 (2), 75–80.

Tilstone, C. and Layton, L. (2004) *Child Development and Teaching Children with Special Educational Needs.* London: RoutledgeFalmer.

Tilstone, C. and Rose, R. (2003) *Strategies to Promote Inclusive Practice.* London: RoutledgeFalmer.

Turner-Bisset, R. (2001) *Expert Teaching.* London: David Fulton.

Vygotsky, L.S. (1978) *Mind in Society: The development of higher psychological processes.* Cambridge, MA: Harvard University Press.

Werner, E., Dawson, G., Osterling, J. and Dinno, N. (2000) 'Recognition of autism spectrum disorder before one year of age: a retrospective study based on home videotapes', *Journal of Autism and Developmental Disorders,* 30 (2), 157–162.

Williams, D. (1998) *Autism and Sensing: The unlost instinct.* London: Jessica Kingsley.

Williams, K.R. and Wishart, J.G. (2003) 'The Son-Rise Program intervention for autism: an investigation into family experiences', *Journal of Intellectual Disability Research,* 47, 291–299.

Wing, L. (2002) *The Autistic Spectrum: A guide for parents and professionals.* London: Constable and Robinson.

Wing, L. and Gould, J. (1979) 'Severe impairments of social interaction and associated abnormalities in children', *Journal of Autism and Childhood Schizophrenia* 1, 256–266.

World Health Organisation (WHO) (1992) *ICD-10 International Statistical Classification of Diseases and Related Health Problems* (10th edn) Geneva: WHO.

Worth, S. (2005) *Autistic Spectrum Disorders.* London: Continuum.

Endnote

[1] Staff supporting students on a one-to-one basis during SDM sessions are referred to as supporters throughout this summary.

CHAPTER 4

Developing Social Engagement through Movement

An Adapted Teaching Approach for Children with ASD

Jotham Konaka

Introduction

The aim of this study was to adapt the traditional teaching approach to the SDM programme in order to meet the needs of children and young people with ASD, and then to explore staff perceptions of the effectiveness of the adapted approach in supporting the development of social engagement for these young people. A description of Sunfield, where the research was based, together with the relevant definitions and a review of literature to support this research can be found in the previous chapter.

Aims

Through an illustrative, school-based study, the researcher sought to:

■ Develop an adapted teaching approach to the Sherborne Developmental Movement programme which would be designed specifically to address the diverse and unique learning patterns of children with profound ASD and which could become rooted in classroom practice

■ Facilitate the implementation of the adapted teaching approach to the SDM programme to enhance social engagement for children with profound ASD.

■ Explore staff perceptions of the effectiveness of the adapted teaching approach to the SDM programme in terms of supporting the development of social engagement with children with ASD.

Methodology

The project took place within a research management structure which provided the researcher with opportunities for professional development and consultancy from two experienced Sherborne Association UK consultant/trainers to ensure consistency of high quality SDM delivery, and with access to constructive discussion with other experienced professionals in the areas of special educational needs and research through a project management group.

The action research approach (Robson, 2002) was implemented through a cyclical series of teaching episodes across various sites, resulting in the production and refinement of SDM teaching techniques to take account of the learning needs of children with ASD.

The research was organised into four phases:

Phase 1:   (September 2004 – January 2005) Introduction of SDM using a traditional teaching approach, and identification of possible adaptations to delivery. Changes to be made in response to data collected using supporter/leader observation and corroborative video footage.

Phase 2:   (February – October 2005) Trial of a teaching approach to SDM which incorporated Phase 1 adaptations. Further changes to be made during Phase 2 in response to data collected from the Phase 1 participant group, and participant groups from two other schools.

Phase 3:   (November 2005 – February 2006) Verification trial of the final adapted teaching approach to SDM among 10 schools, including those taking part in the earlier phases. Data collected to be analysed with reference to social interaction and communication as indicators of engagement.

Phase 4:   (February – August 2006) Data analysis, research write-up and implementation of adapted SDM approach.

For the successful implementation of the phases, it was important that:

■ Staff involved in the project received training in both Sherborne Developmental Movement, the adapted approach and data collection techniques

■ Data collection instruments were identified or devised.

■ An adapted programme was developed during Phases 1 and 2

Research sample

A purposive sampling strategy involving pupils and staff was adopted (Denscombe, 2003). One hundred pupils between the ages of 7 and 19 years and all with a diagnosis of severe ASD were identified and participated in the project. Staff members from Sunfield and 10 other schools working with these pupils were also surveyed to provide their insights in relation to the effectiveness of the programme in various phases (see Table 4.1). Each pupil required one-to-one support, with the session leaders and non-participant observers being supernumerary.

The selection of participating schools was based on their provision for pupils with complex learning difficulties including ASD and each school's ability to support the proposed research. Once the individual schools had agreed to take part, they were then asked to identify a pupil group with a session leader and supporters from among their staff to fit the following criteria:

■ Pupils were diagnosed as having severe or profound ASD

■ The leader(s) were able to commit to leading every session

■ Maximum possible consistency of support for pupils.

Table 4.1. Sampling framework

Phase	Numbers of pupils		Numbers of staff	
	Sunfield	**Other schools**	**Leaders**	**Supporters**
1	29	–	1 (researcher)	35 (Sunfield)
2	29	14	2 (researchers)	52 (inc. 35 Phase 1 staff)
3	11	56	23	62 (inc. 17 Phase 2 staff)
Total *	40	71	23	145 (inc. leaders)

* taking account of involvement in more than one phase

Ethical considerations

Approval for the research was sought from the Sunfield Research and Ethics Committee prior to the commencement of the study. Following the identification of the schools, an information sheet providing full details (the purpose, modalities and ethical guidelines) of the study (Bell, 1999), together with a letter of invitation to take part in the project, was sent to head teachers of potential schools. Thirteen schools were approached with 10 head teachers accepting the invitation to be involved. Once head teachers had agreed, then full consent was obtained from staff members. Consent forms indicating preservation of confidentiality, anonymity, and participants' rights to withdraw from the research without prejudice at any time for any reason were signed at the introductory session. All participants knew they would have the opportunity to see reports on the research outcomes.

Stalker (1998) highlights the difficulties of gaining the informed consent of people with learning disabilities. In relation to the children in this study, this was particularly difficult due to their level of intellectual ability and communication difficulties. Teachers were, however, empowered to judge any unwillingness of a child to take part in the activities, and allow withdrawal as appropriate.

Fully informed written consent for pupils' participation was obtained from parents/carers. They were told of their rights to withdraw their son/daughter from the research at any time should they feel the study was detrimental to their well-being. Additionally, they were asked to sign a consent form indicating their willingness for video recording of the sessions to monitor pupils' response to the programme.

Given that SDM involves extensive, close interpersonal contact, there were important ethical issues around touch and safeguarding children to be explored in the context of the schools' child protection policies and national guidelines. Hill (2006) argues that there is no place for SDM where the school's policy prohibits touch. Adherence to the research code of practice was assured throughout the study to minimise any risks (British Educational Research Association (BERA), 2004; Sunfield, 2006).

Staff training

Prior to the implementation of Phase 2, all the staff (those from Sunfield and the additional two schools) involved in the project received training on the basic SDM teaching techniques and the use of the adapted materials. At the beginning of Phase 3, two session leaders from each of the 10 participating schools, including staff from Phases 1 and 2 who were scheduled to work with new groups of pupils, were invited for a one-day preparatory training on basic Sherborne techniques and the adapted programme implementation. The training was delivered by the researcher and the Sherborne consultant advising on the project, and then was cascaded down by leaders to supporters in the schools. .

Designing the movement programmes

Unlike the traditional way of delivering SDM, where the lesson development is driven by participants' responses and cues, the researcher prepared four lesson plans in advance of Phase 1. The lesson plans were important in maintaining consistency of sessions across different venues for data collection purposes and later comparison. Each programme/plan incorporated movement experiences based on three distinct relationships (with, against and shared), derived from *Developmental Movement for Children* (Sherborne, 2001). Each of the plans focused on specific social communication skills, class organisation and assessment opportunities, as well as the movement dynamics. Some individuals with ASD have a tendency to become over-excited and may take a long time to calm down, and hence, prefer a calm, gentle approach to movement teaching, while others enjoy lively and vigorous movements. Each programme was intended to be delivered three times consecutively to facilitate accurate assessment of pupils' responses – socially, emotionally and kinaesthetically.

The programmes were delivered during all three phases, with adaptations to the model being incorporated at the end of each phase:

Phase 1:   The researcher delivered twice-weekly movement sessions to six groups of pupils at Sunfield. Each group was given the same movement experiences for a period of six weeks using the traditional SDM teaching methods.

Phase 2:   An adapted model of SDM delivery was produced based upon Phase 1 outcomes. Twelve directly comparable sessions were delivered to each group (Sunfield and two schools) by the researcher and one Sherborne consultant/trainer.

Phase 3:   Further adaptations were incorporated into the model trialled in Phase 2 to create the 'Sherborne @ Sunfield' model. The 'Sherborne @ Sunfield' SDM sessions were delivered by session leaders identified by each of the 11 schools with consultancy support from the researcher and one Sherborne consultant. Sessions were held at least twice weekly for eight weeks.

Procedure

Baseline data on each pupil's social communicative needs and levels was obtained from a synopsis provided by the class teacher, and school assessments and reports.

This information was used to facilitate the compilation of more comprehensive individual pupil profiles and the consequent decision of which SDM movement experiences to include in the initial lesson plans. Baseline data on the pupils' levels of engagement in their initial SDM sessions was collected through researcher and staff evaluation immediately following the session using a standard form devised by the researcher. Results were triangulated through documentary video evidence.

Throughout the three project phases, data was gathered using multiple methods, including interviews, a research diary, participant and non-participant observation, staff evaluation reports and documentary video evidence, which provided an opportunity for triangulation of the data (Denzin and Lincoln, 2005).

Session observations/evaluation

During Phase 1, instead of using a prescriptive observation schedule, a post-session discussion group was convened in order to allow key elements relating to pupils' sociability to emerge. It was decided that a prescriptive, fixed observation schedule would be limiting since the capacity of SDM to support the social communicative development of individuals with ASD was still unclear. However, for Phases 2 and 3, participant and non-participant observers were given a structured observation/ evaluation grid which focused on key research themes, including sociability indicators, prompting strategies, types and/or levels of engagement, as well as teaching techniques. Non-participant observers recorded data during sessions, while supporters completed the evaluation sheet immediately after each SDM session.

A research diary (Phases 1, 2 and 3)

This was an on-going record of field notes from SDM sessions, key points from informal discussions (e.g. those leading to programme modification) and informal observations.

Semi-structured interviews with supporters, session leaders and head teachers (Phase 3)

Pre- and post- intervention interviews were carried out. The questions within the semi-structured interview schedule related to the focus of the research and invited participants' opinions upon adaptations made to the SDM session delivery. Although interviews were tape-recorded, key interviewee responses were noted as the interviews proceeded. Pre-intervention interviews involved teaching staff (n=12), non-teaching staff (n=7) and one parent working with the pupils; post-intervention interviews involved a staff focus group (n=23) and four head teachers.

Questionnaires (Phase 3)

A questionnaire was distributed to all the leaders and supporters at the end of Phase 3. The format and content was similar to the interview schedule. It was piloted on a small sample of participants prior to its distribution. Eighty-two questionnaires were distributed with a return of 68.

Documentary video evidence: (Phases 1, 2 and 3).

Video evidence was used to corroborate other data.

Analysis of data

The data derived from the observation notes (Lord et al., 2000), staff evaluation sheets, interview transcripts and documentary video evidence were subjected to categorical content analysis (Robson, 2002). Coded data was organised into themes and subcategories. The categories identified emerged from implicit, as well as explicit, data (Radnor, 1994).

The explicit data covered different views of the staff on the effectiveness of the programme, while the implicit data was derived from the researcher's personal judgement of the pupils' responses and supporter/leader perceptions (Cohen et al., 2000). Hycner (1985, cited in Cohen et al., 2000) refers to this as 'delineating units of general meaning, entailing a thorough scrutiny of both verbal and non-verbal gestures to elicit a participant's meaning'. It is important to note that data collection and analysis ran simultaneously and informed one another.

Research outcomes

The researcher's initial assumption in this study was that pupils with ASD would find the form in which the SDM movement experiences were presented challenging, and therefore that other ways of providing the same movement experiences would have to be devised. However, during Phase 1, it emerged that most of the pupils were able to take part in the individual movement experiences, and did not appear to find the form of the movement experiences confrontational. After observation and informal discussion between the researcher, the consultants and supporters/leaders, it emerged that the fundamental issue to be addressed was pedagogical style. Instead of adapting the movement experiences, it was the teaching techniques that required modification.

Phase 1 outcomes

The outcomes during Phase 1 were derived from leader and supporter observation, video documentary evidence and diary notes of informal discussions and included:

- Recommendations for the adaptation of SDM session delivery
- The identification of indicators on which observation/evaluation schedules could be based, relating to levels of pupil engagement in movement experiences and levels of pupil interaction with supporters.

Adaptation of Sherborne Developmental Movement session delivery
Environmental adaptations
Higher levels of pupil engagement were noted when the environment was contained, and visual distraction (e.g. non-essential notices, tempting apparatus) was minimised.

Communication of supporters with pupils
Verbal communication
There was a majority consensus among supporters that the use of simple, clear and consistent language by both the session leader and the supporters was vital for supporting pupils' engagement. Supporters suggested that pupils were confused by complex verbal directives which appeared to increase their levels of disengagement. This observation is commensurate with the difficulty which many pupils with ASD are

known to have with receptive language processing (Wing, 2002). As one teacher stated:

> *...because of the information processing difficulties these children experience, it is vitally important that simple and short instructions be used at all times.*

Supporters were therefore encouraged, when communicating verbally with their partners, to use appropriate one- or two-word statements supported by a visual prompt (see next section). They were also asked to give their partners enough time to process the information given, as many pupils with ASD experience difficulties with auditory processing (Wing, 2002).

To facilitate consistent delivery and communication, an A3 sheet with written instructions, breaking down each movement experience into small achievable elements was designed and posted at a strategic position on the wall along with other visual cues (A4 symbols[1] and photographs) to guide supporters and pupils.

Visual prompts
Supporters suggested the introduction of visual cues such as symbols and photographs as a means of communicating session developments to pupils. Visual communication systems build upon the strength of pupils with ASD as visual learners (Mesibov and Howley, 2003; Mesibov et al., 2005). Most pupils with ASD at Sunfield and elsewhere routinely use visual communication and scheduling systems; for example, through the Picture Exchange Communication System (PECS; Bondy and Frost, 2002) and the TEACCH model of structured teaching (Mesibov and Howley, 2003; Mesibov et al., 2005). These two approaches take account of their learning patterns and needs.

To increase manageability of symbols/photographs for communication, pupils and supporters were given an extendable belt attachment which held a number of visual cues relating to movement experiences. Supporters were then easily able to cue pupils into the next movement experience, without having to retrieve symbols from elsewhere to do so.

Enhancing communication using other modalities
While the significance of visual cues in facilitating communication was recognised, classroom observations and video evidence revealed that there was an increase in positive outcomes and more sustained engagement in movement experiences whenever clear demonstration preceded a movement experience. It was equally noted that when supporters used other prompting strategies with their partners (e.g. physical, gesture, signing, modelling), there was also a higher level of active engagement from the pupil.

Structuring Sherborne Developmental Movement sessions
Beginnings, transitions and endings
Supporters reported, and video evidence corroborated, that pupils appeared confused by transitions from one movement experience to another during sessions. Discussion suggested that this was due to lack of session structure. While the four lesson plans

provided the researcher and the supporters with a framework to follow, and formed the basis of inter-session comparability, the experiences were arranged in no particular order. There was nothing to signal the beginning or ending of an on-going activity or session.

Two movement experiences – 'Rocking' and 'Sliding on a blanket' – were favoured by most pupils, even if they had been unable to engage in the rest of the session. Following a supporter's suggestion, it was decided that 'Rocking' would be used as an initial and transitional activity between movement experiences, and 'Sliding on a blanket' would be used as the last movement experience before the final gathering together of the group. Thus these experiences became 'kinaesthetic cues', signifying the end of one experience and preparation for another.

Providing familiarity and challenge

Pupils with ASD are often made anxious and stressed by unfamiliar situations due to their difficulties around sequencing and predicting events without reference to concrete cues (Mesibov and Howley, 2003; Mesibov et al., 2005; Worth, 2005). It was therefore decided that new movement experiences, aimed at promoting specific interactional skills, would be introduced very gradually, while retaining a session framework of familiar movement experiences. Each new movement experience was repeated at least three times to consolidate the experience for the pupils. The retention of familiar movement experiences helped these pupils with severe learning difficulties and ASD to achieve success in the learning process in the same SDM session as they were challenged to learn new skills.

Supporter engagement

Analysis of video evidence showed that pupil engagement increased when their supporter was engaged and animated. Partnerships were most successful when the adult was able to channel pupils' natural preferences for, for example, free-flow activities, or rough-and-tumble games into positive social communicative experiences in a playful way. Pupils' continuing engagement also relied upon their supporter's ability to judge how long to sustain a movement experience, moving on before their partners become bored.

Supporter expertise

Most of the supporters felt that they lacked expertise in using SDM as an interactive strategy as it was new to them. This appeared to have compromised their confidence in supporting their partners, as a learning support assistant confirmed:

> *I would have been more confident to support Lee if I knew in advance what was expected of me and the child. I did not know whether I was doing the right thing or not as I had no previous experience using Sherborne Developmental Movement.*

On-project training was given; however, it was decided that, following the project, Level 1 SDM training would need to be offered to supporters in association with the adapted SDM approach.

Observation/evaluation instruments
Indicators of engagement

In the course of Phase 1, five levels of pupil engagement with their supporter were identified for the observation/evaluation forms against which to record participant and non-participant observations. These are listed in Table 4.2.

Table 4.2. Degree of engagement associated with pupil interaction category

Categories of pupil interaction with supporter	Degree of pupil engagement
1. Refusal • *Pupil moves away from group* • *Does not take part in movement experience* • *No interaction with supporter*	Least engaged
2. Retreatism • *Pupil remains in proximity to the group and supporter* • *Intermittently takes part in movement experience* • *Intermittent interaction with supporter*	
3. Ritualistic engagement • *Pupil remains with supporter* • *Is a passive participant in movement experience while focusing on ritualistic activity* • *No/intermittent interaction with supporter*	
4. Passive engagement • *Pupil remains with supporter* • *Is an <u>apparently</u> passive participant in movement experience* • *No/intermittent interaction with supporter*	
5. Authentic engagement • *Pupil remains with supporter* • *Contributes to/initiates movement experience* • *Frequent/sustained interaction with supporter*	Most engaged

Indicators of interaction

Following analysis of videos and participant observation records, the researcher identified the following indicators of pupils' level of interaction with their supporters:

- Eye-contact
- Turn-taking
- Joint attention
- Imitation, and
- Initiating interaction.

These elements were included on a standard form alongside information about the associated movement experience and the level of prompt for pupils used by supporters. Due to its initial complexity, the form used during Phase 2 was simplified for use in Phase 3 (see Figure 4.1).

'Sherborne @ Sunfield' programme design

Prior to the start of Phase 2, the first model of the adapted SDM approach was devised based upon Phase 1 outcomes. This included:

- Specific verbal communication strategies – minimal and focused use of simplified language in association with visual prompts
- Specific visual communication strategies, which included:
  - □ individual size Sherborne symbols or photographs attached to an extendable belt ring for use as prompts by both pupils and supporters
  - □ A4 size Sherborne symbols and photographs for pupils with visual difficulties
- Structured teaching strategies, including:
  - □ A prescribed order of movement experiences indicated visually using a left-to-right sequence of A4 symbols/photographs to form a 'wall schedule'
- Kinaesthetic cues, including specific beginning, transitional and end movement experiences
- Strategies to improve consistency, including:
  - □ Specific guidance for supporters in use of language (A3 instruction cards)
  - □ A protocol for the introduction of new movement experience elements
  - □ Consistent support.

Standard recording and reporting strategies were also put into place including an observation/evaluation schedule devised to monitor levels of interaction and engagement to be filled in by supporters at the end of each session.

Phase 2 outcomes

Findings from the trials involving the three Phase 2 schools were used to make further improvements to the adapted teaching approaches to SDM for use with individuals with severe ASD. Again, video documentation informed the process, and supporter evaluation and discussion determined further modifications to the programme delivery. While only minimal changes were made to all the four lesson plans (see Figure 4.2) – one movement experience ('See-saw') being replaced – the evaluation sheets were redesigned following requests by supporters for easier administration.

Timing of sessions

The Movement sessions were reduced in length to between 20 and 25 minutes, as a result of pupils' improved concentration, and hence increased time spent on task.

Figure 4.1. Session evaluation sheet

Sunfield Research Institute

SDM SESSION EVALUATION SHEET

Date............ Programme no............ School/class............ Name/ID............

Movement experience	Type of prompt						Type of engagement						Level of engagement					Comments
	P	VS	V	G	S	M	TT	EC	IM	II	JA	SE	R	RT	PC	RE	AE	
Rocking																		
Sliding on hips																		
Exploring space with arms																		
Back to back push																		
Swaying by arms/legs																		
Wriggling through a tunnel																		
Sliding on blanket																		

Type of prompt:		
G = Gesture	M = Modelling	
P = Physical	S = Sign	
V = Verbal	VS = Visual cues	

Type of engagement:		
EC = Eye-contact	II = Initiate interaction	
IM = Imitation	JA = Joint attention	
TT = Turn-taking	SE = Shared experience	

Level of engagement:		
AE = Authentic engagement	PC = Passive compliance	
RE = Ritual engagement	R = Refusal	
	RT = Retreatism	

Figure 4.2. Example of a lesson plan for an adapted Sherborne Developmental Movement session

Sunfield Research

LESSON PLAN 2.1

CLASS:	NO. OF PUPILS:	NO. OF ADULTS:	DATE:	DURATION:

AIMS: 1. To develop basic skills which improve relationship play, communication, creativity and an awareness of self, others and space
2. To ensure that the quality of interaction between the caregiver and the child has positive effect on the child

LESSON DEVELOPMENT

Learning experience/Target	Learning activities	Class organisation	Class Development	Assessment opportunities	Dynamics
1. Developing body and spatial awareness and an ability to move safely avoiding others	Rocking	Pairs	1. Partners sitting one behind the other 2. Place hands on partner's shoulders 3. Rock gently forwards/backwards or sideways	1, 3, 5, 6	Bound/free Slow/fast
2. Developing creative and communication skills	Sliding on hips	Pairs	1. Sit on the floor with straight legs and palms on the floor between the legs of a partner 2. Shuffle on hips saying hello to others 3. Use arms and feet to propel the body	1, 2, 3 and 5	Slow/fast Straight/flexible
3. Developing trust and confidence in self and others	Appearing/disappearing knees	Single/pairs	1. Sitting on the floor with bent knees 2. Press and flatten knees 3. Bend and stretch knees	3, 4 and 5, 6	Strong/fine Fast/slow
4. Developing an ability to form positive relationships	Sliding on stomach/back	Pairs	1. Lie on stomach next to partner 2. Feel parts of own body in contact with the floor 3. Wriggle/slide on the stomach/back towards/from a target	1, 2, 3, 4 and 5	Free/bound Direct/flexible
5. Acquiring and improving performance in basic movement skills	Wriggling through a tunnel	Pairs	1. Adults on all fours 2. Partners wriggle through the 'tunnel'	1, 3, 5 and 6	Low/medium High Fast /slow
6. Providing access to the curriculum	Sliding on blanket	Pairs	1. One partner lies on blanket 2. Other partner pulls blanket by head or leg end	1, 3 and 4	Fast/slow Flexible/direct

RESOURCES: Blankets, cues (pictures and symbols)

COMMENTS:

Engagement

During Phase 2, there was a notable improvement in both supporter and pupil engagement. The majority of pupils were able to respond positively to most movement experiences. The improvements were attributed to:

■ Supporter endeavour and their ability to make the pupils feel safe and nurtured. This increase followed additional briefing on the shared goals and objectives of the project, where concerns were resolved.

■ An increase in pupil understanding and confidence.

Communication

Pupils' communication skills also improved. Some pupils became able readily to recognise the visual cues and vocalise the movement experience. Many pupils demonstrated an improved ability to maintain eye-contact. The data collected demonstrated that, by the end of Phase 2, the majority of pupils showed improvement in their social communicative skills – 40 out of 43 of the participants had remained fully engaged with their supporters throughout these sessions, which showed improvement from Phase 1 figures (see Figure 4.3). The remaining three pupils had found elements of the SDM sessions confrontational, and persistently retreated or completely failed to join in. Supporters from all three Phase 2 schools reported that the symbols/pictures helped them gain confidence in supporting their partners.

Sensory sensitivities

Pupils' sensitivities, which had characterised Phase 1, appeared to reduce, and individual pupils who had shown high sensitivity to touch began to accept being held and touched.

Phase 3 outcomes

At the beginning of Phase 3, the 11 schools were given packs containing the lesson

Figure 4.3 Pupils' levels of engagement over Phases 1 to 3

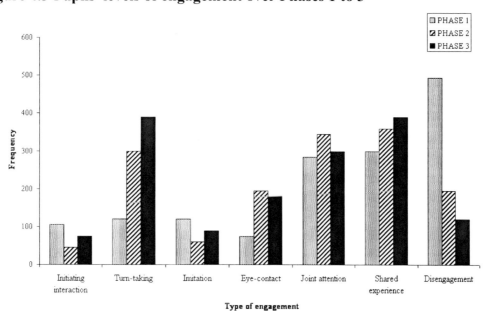

plans, evaluation schedules, symbols and extendable belt rings for individual use, wall symbols and photographs, protocols for verbal prompting and introduction of movement experiences. The leaders were, however, given autonomy to produce A4 ring-bound booklets of the symbols/photos to support pupils who had difficulty accessing the small cues.

During Phase 3, supporters and leaders took part in semi-structured interviews with the researcher prior to and following the intervention to elicit their perceptions of the adapted SDM approach. The following were derived from categorical content analysis of the data generated from interviews.

Communication

Traditionally with SDM, the cues have been auditory, vocal and kinaesthetic, but using visual prompts is a new approach. Although it cannot be claimed that the improvement observed was due only to the use of visual cues, during sessions it was noted that, following introduction of symbol prompts, pupil engagement with movement experiences increased. Thirty-five supporters (n=120)[2] had observed that the visual communication strategies led to pupils feeling more in control and more confident, and a simultaneous increase in attention span, noted by eight supporters, may suggest an association between the two. Commenting upon the use of visual cues, one supporter remarked:

> *...the visual cues have made a big difference in the delivery of the sessions. Both the staff and pupils have found them clear and self-explanatory – immensely reducing verbal input in terms of instruction.*

Three supporters/leaders perceived that the introduction of visual cues to augment verbal prompts had improved pupils' levels of engagement (see Figure 4.4). In the following quotation, a leader describes her experience with one pupil:

> *In the course of the project, Doll appeared to take more interest in others and was less detached. He became happy to interact with other pupils...checking to see that everyone was ok. He would approach his peers and show them visual cues of the next activity.*

The visual cues provided the pupils with opportunities to communicate their preferences regarding movement experiences in a much clearer way. For example, the supporters reported that some pupils would intermittently refer to the set of visual cues on key rings to ensure that their favourite movement experience was scheduled. Access to symbols associated with specific movement experiences ultimately enabled some individuals to start initiating interactions and taking the lead on certain movement experiences as a supporter confirms:

> *I felt that I formed a much more positive relationship with Sunil, and his level of concentration grew as the project progressed. He communicated with me more at the end. He also began to initiate the movements and began to do actions such as sitting behind me and rocking me.*

While there were many positive remarks (15)³ regarding the effectiveness of the visual cues, some supporters/leaders (3) expressed the opinion that particular symbols and photographs were not clear enough, and hence required further development. However, a disadvantage of photographs is that they carry specific visual and environmental cues all of which may deflect the pupil from assimilating the core message of the cue, which can be isolated within a symbol (Porter and Ashdown, 2002).

Structure of the Sherborne Developmental Movement session

Seven supporters/leaders (n=120) were positive about the increased structure within SDM sessions. One teacher observed that through her pupil's responses to structure, she had learnt a lot about 'how an ASD child needs an ordered regime to put him at ease'. Another teacher commented that 'the adapted approaches to the SDM delivery have opened a whole new world to learning styles with pupils with ASD'.

The benefit of using 'Rocking' between movement experiences was particularly remarked upon (45 supporters/leaders) as being useful in reassuring anxious participants. A teacher described this transitional strategy as 'very useful and reassuring [for the pupil]'.

The A3 and A4 cues posted on the wall were a great help to both the supporters and pupils who were not very familiar with the programme in terms of structure. For example, there were instances when people with no previous experience in using SDM were deployed to support individual pupils, but because the visual cues were clear and self-explanatory, they were able to provide effective support to their pupil partners.

Repetition

The significance of repeating known movement experiences and gradually introducing new ones into the sessions was highlighted by 18 supporters/leaders (n=120). One supporter/leader pointed out that:

> *The gradual build-up by increasing the movements whilst still retaining some of the known movements gave stability to the programme with measured challenge to the participants.*

Responses to the adapted programme

Nineteen supporters/leaders (n=120) remarked upon the effectiveness of the adapted teaching approaches to the SDM programme in supporting pupils with ASD to assimilate skills in the areas of engagement (11 supporters/leaders) and communication (8 supporters/leaders). A head teacher asserted that:

> *In relating to those children who find interpersonal relationships very difficult and who are locked in their own worlds, our perception is that the practical and interactive nature of the programme meant that those children were interacting without necessarily knowing that they were interacting. So relationships were being developed, some of the proprioceptive needs of the children were being met and obviously the programme was fulfilling some of their needs as well as empowering their communication.*

Case Study 1

Jimmy is a 13-year-old pupil in a class of four others with severe ASD. The TEACCH approach is used within Jimmy's class. This system provides him with a high level of structure and support for all of the day's activities. It ensures that Jimmy knows what he has to do, how much he has to do, when it is finished and what is next. He uses symbols to transition from activity to activity, and this has provided him with a great deal of independence. He also uses PECS to communicate his needs to staff. In addition, Jimmy is able to use Makaton signs and speech alongside symbol communication, and these skills continue to improve. He also has access to a choice board at other times; however, he does sometimes need reminding that it is available.

Obuya, Jimmy's teacher, felt that he would benefit from SDM sessions, given his difficulties in interacting with the staff and his peers. During Phase 1, Jimmy found the unstructured teaching approach confrontational and kept withdrawing from the group. He seemed to be unsure of what was expected of him, as there was nothing to show him what was coming next. He spent much of the session sitting on the periphery with his supporter, watching what his peers were doing. He would rejoin the group for short periods then retreat.

However, as soon as the structured teaching approach was introduced, he started to join in the movement experiences. Video footage indicates that by the end of the project, he was able to remain focused throughout the session. Jimmy started initiating interactions and using relevant language. During the session, he also started communicating with other staff and pupils. He now greets all staff members involved with Sherborne as he passes them in school.

Two supporters/leaders reported that some pupils made progress from being dependent on visual cues to being listeners and verbal communicators.

> *It was great to see my partner develop and have the opportunity to express herself freely. It was interesting to see the progress made from the beginning to the end of the programme and watch the communication channels open up.*

Discussion

The initial hypothesis in this study was that pupils with ASD may find Sherborne Developmental Movement experiences problematic. However, it emerged that the movement experiences themselves were not a problem, as most pupils were able to take part in the activities. It seemed that for many of them, instead, the unstructured teaching approach was the main issue. Cyndi Hill, the Sherborne consultant commented:

> *I cannot believe how well these children with Autistic Spectrum Disorders coped with the programme. I expected most of them to find the programme and activities confrontational, but, as children often do, they have proved me wrong. My view of these children's abilities has completely changed. All we need to do is change the way we teach them.*

This resonates with the findings from Kasa-Hendrickson's (2005) study. Pupils' ability to take part in the movement experiences prompted a shift of the research hypothesis from a child focus (adapting the programme content) to a teacher focus (modifying pedagogy) in order to secure pupils' engagement.

Structured Sherborne Developmental Movement delivery

While the SDM programme is traditionally delivered through an open-ended teaching approach, centred around the responses of the participants with no predetermined order of movement experiences (Hill, 2006), the more structured approach to SDM sessions proved very helpful to pupils involved. Firstly, most of the participants found the programme more acceptable because of the predictable sequencing of movement experiences. Each session always began with 'Rocking' and ended with the most popular activity, 'Sliding on the blanket'. Secondly, the use of rocking as a transitional movement experience was particularly recognised as being crucial in reassuring vulnerable participants. This suggests that rocking can be used as a kinaesthetic cue (Farnell, 2003) to prepare the pupil for the introduction of a subsequent movement experience, just as symbols are visual cues (Bondy and Frost, 2002).

Trevarthen et al. (1998) recognise structured repetition and practice as being crucial in the effective delivery of any new intervention with children with ASD. The gradual introduction of new movement experiences while retaining some familiar ones proved beneficial to the participants since regular use of the retained, known movement experiences allowed the pupils to achieve success while still struggling to learn the new ones.

Iconic values of visual cues

The significance of structured teaching approaches in the context of autism has been well articulated (Mesibov et al., 2005; Worth 2005). Evidence from this research has highlighted the significance of visual cues targeted to autistic pupils' strengths as visual learners (Worth, 2005). Visual cues indicated to pupils which movement experience was scheduled 'next' and significantly reduced the need for verbal instructions and other prompting strategies by improving the pupils' levels of understanding of the expectations. This may have been associated with the simultaneous improvement in pupils' ability, observed by supporters/leaders, to make eye-contact, sustain joint attention and share experiences.

Demonstration

While a study by Charlop-Christy and colleagues (2002) recognised the merits of video modelling against direct modelling, the evidence from video analysis during this research suggests that clear direct demonstration appeared to be motivating and engaging for children with ASD.

Pupils' sensitivities

Sensory sensitivity is a major factor for individuals with autism (Grandin, 1995; Worth, 2005). While evidence showed that some pupils craved close personal contact, some initially resisted touch, but eventually overcame the barrier by the end of the project. Perhaps these pupils accepted touch during the movement sessions because in that context it was not irrational; rather, it was focused, predictable and part of a cohesive experience incorporated into their kinaesthetic learning modality (Farnell, 2003; Jones, 2002).

Issues raised by the research and implications for practice
The adult supporters remained central to the development of pupils' engagement (Sherborne, 2001; Tilston and Layton, 2004) – both experientially with the movement and socially with their supporter. The adults' bodies were a conduit for the pupils' experiences of movement. A need for the adults to have expertise in SDM, high motivation and understanding of the needs of pupils with ASD emerged as being crucial if they were to provide effective and confident support, and ensure a high quality delivery of the adapted teaching approaches to SDM. Training is therefore a high priority. Supporters appeared to become more involved after being briefed thoroughly, with a resulting increase in pupil engagement.

Regularity of sessions and consistency of support is essential for maximum pupil engagement. Staffing during the project remained problematic, which meant the session leader needed to work with individual children throughout each session. This perhaps compromised observation. However, the impact of this was minimised by the involvement of one of the consultants as an independent observer. Progress among pupils who had had a consistent supporter appeared to be greater than those who did not. A teacher commented:

> *We thought hard about who should work with pupils. Because the purpose of the project was social engagement, we wanted pupils to work with someone they had a daily relationship with and that relationship would continue after the project so that we could see generalisations and perhaps build on it. We invited parents, and we did have one working with a child which was lovely.*

Limitations
Although attempts were made to maintain the focus of the study on engagement as a major theme, it became apparent that some of the predetermined elements were not exhaustively explored. First, it became impossible to isolate issues relating to SDM and ASD in relation to the concept of engagement. The challenge was further exacerbated by the limitation of literature on both SDM in relation to ASD and engagement as an emerging concept. There was, therefore, little recorded data with which to compare the findings.

Conclusion
The current philosophical climate and interest in supported interaction with young people with intellectual disabilities is providing a platform for the re-establishment of SDM and the development of other reciprocal communication initiatives (Pauli, 2006; Thornton and Taylor, 2005). There is also a growing realisation that these approaches can be set within the National Curriculum (Department for Education and Science (DfEE)/Qualifications and Curriculum Authority (QCA), 1999; Hill, 2006). SDM has the flexibility to accommodate the individual's learning needs and patterns within its philosophical approach, and this liberates teachers to modify the approach to meet these on a day-by-day basis.

It has emerged from this study that movement programmes delivered through a structured teaching approach may have the potential to ameliorate some of the social communicative difficulties experienced by children with autism. Moreover, it is important to make appropriate decisions about the teaching approaches based on the strengths and learning preferences of individuals with ASD, and that the staff should have adequate programme-specific training. This should include the Sherborne Association's SDM Level 1 training, together with instruction on 'Sherborne @ Sunfield', the adapted teaching approach to SDM for individuals with autism, and associated familiarisation with ASD if needed.

Within the scope of this research project, the main objective of enhancing the social engagement of pupils with ASD through SDM by implementing adapted teaching approaches was achieved. The results indicated that the pupils involved experienced improved levels of eye-contact, joint attention and shared experiences. In addition, supporter/leader evaluation reports indicated that participants' attention spans and turn-taking abilities had increased.

Many headteachers and staff from the participating schools acknowledged the effectiveness of the 'Sherborne @ Sunfield' programme and expressed their readiness to offer it to a wider pupil population in their schools. One headteacher, who was personally involved as a supporter in the sessions at his school, said that he had never been involved in such a valuable piece of collaborative work. One of the Sherborne Association UK consultants involved with the project said that she felt that the 'Sherborne @ Sunfield' model would be tremendously important for the future of SDM – not only from the point of view of children with ASD, but also in that the framework would give new leaders of traditional SDM confidence during their first sessions.

Prior to the development of an ASD-specific approach to SDM, the programme did not articulate a pathway for pupils with ASD. 'Sherborne @ Sunfield' is not a deviation from Sherborne's work but a specific application within the spirit of Sherborne's own approach to 'Developmental Movement'. As she stated:

> *Each teacher or caregiver can make use of the materials described in this book in his or her own way. Teachers develop their own variations and ideas as do the children they teach.* (Sherborne, 2001, p. 111)

Acknowledgements

I would like to thank all who have given time to this project, not least all the head teachers, staff and pupils who agreed to take part in this research. There have been many other people without whose help and support this research project would not have been possible, but, in particular, my thanks to go: the Three Guineas Trust for their invaluable financial support and to the Sherborne Association UK for endorsing the project; Barry Carpenter (Chief Executive, Sunfield) and Cyndi and George Hill (SDM Consultants/International Trainers, Sherborne Association UK) for their professional guidance and help with session delivery, data collection and analysis; Jackie Buscombe (Senior Occupational Therapist, Sunfield) and Cate Detheridge (Widgit Software; www.widgit.com) for their work on symbol design. My thanks also go to

Julie Grove (Teacher), Teresa Whitehurst (Research Officer) and other members of the project management team whose support has been invaluable, and finally to Barry Carpenter, Cyndi and George Hill, Stuart Daniel (ex-Teacher, Sunfield) and Jo Egerton (Publications Manager/Research Fellow, Sunfield) for their contributions to this report.

References

Bell, J. (1999) Doing Your Research Project (3rd edn). Buckingham: Open University Press.

Bondy, A. and Frost, L. (2002) *A Picture's Worth: PECS and other visual communication strategies in autism.* Bethesda, MD: Woodbine House.

British Educational Research Association (2004) *Revised Ethical Guidelines for Educational Research.* Nottingham: BERA.

Charlop-Christy, M.H., Carpenter, M., Loc, L., LeBlanc, L.A. and Kellet, K. (2002) 'Using the Picture Exchange Communication System (PECS)with children with autism: *assessment of PECS acquisition, speech, social-communicative behavior, and problem behavior'*, *Journal of Applied Behavior Analysis,* 35 (fall), 213–231. [Online at: http://seab.envmed.rochester.edu/]

Cohen, L., Manion, L. and Morrison, K. (2000) *Research Methods in Education (5th edn).* London: RoutledgeFalmer.

Denscombe, M. (2003) *Ground Rules for Good Research: A 10 point guide for social researchers.* Milton Keynes: Open University Press.

Denzin, N. K. and Lincoln, Y. S. (2005) *The Sage Handbook of Qualitative Research.* London: Sage.

Department for Education and Employment /Qualifications and Curriculum Authority (1999) *The National Curriculum for Physical Education in England.* London: HMSO.

Farnell, B. (2003) 'Kinaesthetic sense and dynamically embodied action', *Journal of Anthropological Study of Human Movement,* 12 (4), 133–144.

Grandin, T. (1995) *Thinking in Pictures and Other Reports from My Life with Autism.* New York, NY: Doubleday.

Hill, C. (2006) *Communicating through Movement: Sherborne Developmental Movement – towards a broadening perspective.* Clent: Sunfield Publications.

Hycner, R.H. (1985) 'Some guidelines for the phenomenological analysis of interview data', *Human Studies,* 8, 279–303.

Jones, G. (2002) *Educational Provision for Children with Autism and Asperger Syndrome: Meeting their needs.* London: David Fulton.

Kasa-Hendrickson, C. (2005) '"There's no way this kid's retarded": teachers' optimistic constructions of students' ability', *International Journal of Inclusive Education,* 9 (1), 55–69.

Lord, C., Risi, S., Lambrecht, L., Cook, E.H., Jr., Leventhal, B.L., DiLavore, P.C., Pickles, A. and Rutter, M. (2000) 'The Autism Diagnostic Observation Schedule–Generic: a standard measure of social and communication deficits associated with the spectrum of autism', *Journal of Autism and Developmental Disorders,* 30 (3), 205–223.

Mesibov, G. and Howley, M. (2003) *Accessing the Curriculum for Pupils with Autistic Spectrum Disorders.* London: David Fulton.

Mesibov, G., Shea, V. and Schopler (2005) *The TEACCH Approach to Autism Spectrum Disorders*. New York: Kluwer Academic/Plenum.

Pauli, D. (2006) 'Contact through colour', *Special Children,* June/July, 30–33.

Porter, J. and Ashdown, R. (2002) *Pupils with Complex Learning Difficulties: Promoting learning using visual materials and methods*. London: National Association of Special Educational Needs.

Radnor, H.A. (1994) *Collecting and Analysing Interview Data*. London: Open University Press.

Robson, C. (2002) *Real World Research: A resource for social scientists and practitioner-researchers* (2nd edn). Oxford: Blackwell.

Sherborne, V. (2001) *Developmental Movement for Children: Mainstream, special needs and pre-school* (2nd edn). London: Worth Publishing.

Stalker, K. (1998) 'Some ethical and methodological issues in research with people with learning disabilities', *Disability and Society*, 13 (1), 5–20.

Sunfield (2006) 'Code of ethical practice'. Clent: Sunfield.

Thornton, K. and Taylor, E. (2005) 'Play and the reduction of challenging behaviour in children with ASD and learning disabilities', *Good Autism Practice,* 6 (2), 75–80.

Tilstone, C. and Layton, L. (2004) *Child Development and Teaching Children with Special Educational Needs*. London: RoutledgeFalmer.

Trevarthen, C., Aitken, K.J., Papoudi, D. and Robarts, J. (1998) *Children with Autism: Diagnosis and interventions to meet their needs (2nd edn)*. London: Jessica Kingsley.

Wing, L. (2002) *The Autistic Spectrum: A guide for parents and professionals*. London: Constable and Robinson.

Worth, S. (2005) *Autistic Spectrum Disorders*. London: Continuum.

Endnotes

[1] Sherborne-specific symbols were developed by the researcher and the Senior Occupational Therapist at Sunfield, Jackie Buscombe. These symbols were later adapted by Widgit Software and are now available as part of the Writing With Symbols computer programme (see www.widgit.com).

This, and similar instances in this format, indicate the total number of staff responding to the question

[3] Numbers in this format indicate the number of staff who expressed the viewpoint described.

CHAPTER 5

Improving the Movement Vocabulary and Social Development of Children in the Early Years

Elizabeth Marsden, Mario Hare and Carrie Weston

Introduction
Improving movement vocabulary
Veronica Sherborne's work was rooted in movement principles and movement experience after her time working with Laban. Her observation and planning were grounded in the four categories of *Body, Space, Dynamics* and *Relationships* described in Chapter 2. She often spoke of her desire to help children, both those in mainstream education and those with special needs, expand their movement vocabulary and become 'at home in their own bodies' (Sherborne, 1990).

Movement vocabulary, in this context, is the term given to the building blocks of movement experience, such as the ability for the body to move fast, and recognise and perform its opposite of moving slowly. Another example of what is meant by movement vocabulary might be the understanding of how to move only a part of the body as opposed to the whole body. The parallel in literacy would be the acquisition of vocabulary at an early age in order eventually to form sentences and paragraphs and, finally, a whole story. Similarly, in movement education, children should learn movement vocabulary at an early age in order to build movement sentences, movement paragraphs and finally movement stories.

Today, as in Sherborne's time, children enter their compulsory schooling with a wide variety of movement experiences. However, modern environments and lifestyles may have resulted, for some children, in their having little space for moving and playing either indoors or outside and in prolonged periods of playing computer games or watching TV (Penn, 2004). Others may already have been exposed to swimming, dance classes or sports development projects (e.g. mini-kickers football skills) at playgroup or nursery school. Yet other children may have had enthusiastic families who spent time outdoors and encouraged their children to climb, swing, slide, run, jump or skip from a very early age. Nowadays, early years education documentation throughout the UK supports the idea that children, as they grow, not only learn *to* move (and thus develop early movement vocabulary), but also learn *through* moving. PE that meets the needs of these young learners is, therefore, very important.

Presently, there is a drive to increase 'quality' PE for all children, although until the National Summit on Physical Education held on 24th January 2005, there had been no consensus on what quality PE might be. The 'commonsense' viewpoint of politicians, the media and many members of the general population regarding quality PE was that it should produce elite performers and sportsmen and women (Kirk, 2004). Others insisted that good quality PE must primarily be concerned with fitness and health and lifelong participation (Pate et al., 1997; Scottish Physical Activity Task Force, 2003). For children in their early years at school, neither model alone would have been acceptable to those concerned with child development and well-being (Siraj-Blatchford and Sylva, 2002). Delegates at the National Summit on Physical Education (NSPE), however, addressed physical, psychological, social and moral developmental issues, culminating in a Position Statement published in the *British Journal of Teaching Physical Education* (NSPE, 2005).

The Position Statement prioritised the development of 'physical literacy' in which the learning of movement vocabulary in the early years plays a vital part. Movement vocabulary is an essential building block in physical literacy. The Sports Council (1991) recognised the importance of physical literacy, stating that it was as 'vital to every person as literacy in verbal expression itself'. Similarly, some PE philosophers today stress its fundamental importance:

> *As a capacity integral to the individual, and influencing much of life as we know it, the achievement and exercise of physical literacy plays a very significant part in the development of self realisation, self awareness, self confidence and positive self esteem.* (Whitehead, 2001, p. 8)

Maude (2001), investigating the concept of physical literacy, argued that it incorporates all seven of Gardner's (1993) intelligences and includes all movement achievements, experiences, knowledge, understanding and applications in both functional and expressive performance. She was convinced that physical literacy for any child will change over time, depending on the developmental stage that the child has reached. As children learn more movement vocabulary, so they are empowered in their physical literacy.

Maude, along with Sherborne and Whitehead also embraced the concept of 'embodiment' (Whitehead, 2001). The idea of 'feeling at home' in one's own body (Sherborne, 1990) is similar to that highlighted by Whitehead's (2001) description of 'embodiment', when she attempted to explain the concept of physical literacy. Both Sherborne and Whitehead promote an existentialist, monistic view in which existence is embodied as opposed to the more common Cartesian, dualist view where the body merely houses the mind and may be treated as an object to feed, to exercise and to enskill for performance. Acknowledging physical literacy in PE recognises the child as a whole, embodied being.

Kay (2006) described quality PE as that which is inclusive, builds self-esteem and physical confidence, is fun, ensures safety and a supportive environment, is holistic and prepares participants for life-long learning. Quality PE should obviously respond to children's needs which, in turn, change at different stages of development. For our youngest children in compulsory schooling, their needs of being active, developing motor skills, experimenting with gaining movement vocabulary, and therefore improving body mastery and learning to share, co-operate and play with their peers in an atmosphere of fun and appreciation are regarded as a priority at this early stage (Davies, 1995; Fisher, 2002; Gallahue and Donnelly, 2003; Wright, 2004).

A PE programme that incorporates all of these elements and is taught with skill would meet the needs of children in their early years. The National Curriculum for Physical Education 2000 (Qualifications and Curriculum Authority (QCA), 1999) emphasises skill learning and physical activity, and the concept of 'fun' is also mentioned. It is more difficult to find references to movement vocabulary or partner and group work at Key Stage 1 (ages 5–7). The 5–14 Guidelines (Scottish Office Education Department, 1992) in Scotland are based on movement principles (p. 57) which incorporate movement vocabulary. The Guidelines include strands concerned with developing fitness, skills, creativity and co-operation. Unfortunately, these high ideals are rarely found in the actual teaching of PE in primary schools (Her Majesty's Inspectorate (HMI), 2001).

Sherborne (2001) claimed that her movement education programme had a profound effect on the movement vocabulary and social development of participants. Bogdanowicz and Kasica (2003) have collected a series of research reports in Poland to show the effects of Sherborne Developmental Movement (SDM) on a wide variety of populations. Loots and Malschaert (1999) offer a psychological view of why communication was improved in a Belgian population using SDM. Filer's (2006) work in the UK in early intervention family therapy and work with excluded 5–7 year olds is based on SDM (see Chapter 6). Through gains in movement vocabulary, especially that associated with the *Relationships* principle, children's self-esteem and ability to trust adults both physically and emotionally also grew, and Filer saw family relationships restored and children being able to return to work peacefully in school.

There are many *anecdotal* reports of how children in mainstream education have improved in physical, social and emotional development after following SDM teaching, but, to date, there has not been a controlled study to examine the claims of SDM practitioners. This research project was designed to examine Sherborne's claims that her movement education programme increases children's movement vocabulary and leads to better social development. If these claims stand up to scrutiny, then SDM should add to the 'quality' PE debate for children in the early years.

Improving social and emotional development
Earlier studies have failed to show consistent relationships between PE and effects on physical, social and emotional development, although Pollatschek's work (1989) suggested a relationship between *daily* PE and physical and cognitive improvements in upper primary children (10–11-year-olds). However, a more recent study from New Zealand (Parrott, 1997) has shown improved social and affective development for babies and pre-school children through participation in physical activities designed to incorporate play actions, such as swinging, jumping and rolling, and also play

involving others. Improved self-esteem, physical confidence and feelings of well-being have been reported in participants. The physical activity programme in the New Zealand study is based on principles similar to SDM, but has only been used with babies, toddlers and pre-school children.

Expanding children's movement vocabulary was initially the basis of Sherborne's work. Young children and older children with special needs often had a limited experience of movement. But she realised early on in her use of SDM that children were learning to communicate and relate to each other in a new and powerful way. This seemed to be the result of something that was happening both between the children and between the children and their teacher. Sparkes (2001) recognised the innovation involved in SDM:

> *To understand the Sherborne approach to movement teaching is to understand movement in the context of early child development and to engage oneself in an analysis of the teaching method... It is a way of working which sets out to give confidence, to engage the participant in non-judgemental teaching, to develop an individual's self-esteem and to ensure both consolidation and progression in personal learning.* (Sparkes, 2001, p. xi)

Sherborne made claims that her style of movement education affected both the physical and psychological domains of participants. She believed that the unique way in which the SDM leader interacts with participants results in improved self-esteem and feelings of well-being for both (Sherborne, 2001). Hill (2006) highlighted the importance of the delivery: 'A carefully selected balance between movements that are developmentally appropriate, and the way those movements are presented, are fundamental to the success of the SDM session' (p. 11).

One of the main differences between SDM and other child-centred pedagogies rests in the teaching style adopted. The SDM leader strives to create an atmosphere of trust and equality between all involved in the session. It becomes a shared experience where effort, not performance, is celebrated. The process is the priority, not the product. Emotional safety and security are important, and each participant is valued for their individual contribution, rather than reaching a predetermined attainment target. It is a movement session where physical and mental challenges are presented, movement problems are tackled, opportunities are explored, creativity and fun are championed but, most noticeably, relationships are forged.

Loots and Malschaert (1999), approaching SDM from a developmental psychology analysis perspective, stated that the affective climate created and the style of interaction of the teacher trained in SDM are of critical importance. The teacher is not primarily an instructor giving teaching points and feedback to improve a specific skill, but rather someone who practises 'sensitive responsiveness'[1] and thereby gives children more trust and responsibility in their movement learning. They suggested that the interactive style of the movement teacher influences the development of a child's confidence in a profound way. This can be explained by reference to the simplified Riksen-Walraven developmental psychology model (1989) illustrated in Figure 5.1.

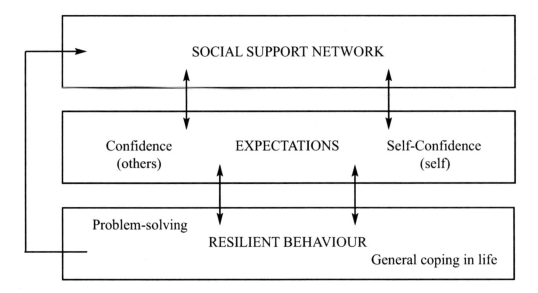

Figure 5.1. Simplified Riksen-Walgrave model

In this simplified model, it can be seen that the two expectations in the centre (confidence in others and self-confidence) are formed under the social support given in the top section of the model. Riksen-Walraven (1989) explicitly stated that the most important influence on children's social development is the receiving of sensitive responsiveness to their signals and needs by significant others including their teachers. In Sherborne's developmental movement programme, confidence and self-confidence are central concepts which are as important as body mastery and building relationships through movement. They take shape mostly through the SDM teacher adopting a sensitive and responsive, interactive teaching style which seeks to observe children's needs and respond to them in order to give the children confidence to progress.

The bottom layer of the model deals with behaviour which consists of solving developmental tasks and 'resilience'. Riksen-Walraven (1989) considered resilience to be of great importance in the development of psychological well-being in children. She defined it as a reflection of certain expectations that a person holds in regard to self and others. She also believed that resilience as a personal dimension is vital in the realisation of potential throughout life and in dealing with stress. It is fundamental to personal well-being. Loots and Malschaert (1999) identified the similarities in the construction of the SDM programme and the progression of the developmental tasks in the Riksen-Walraven model:

> *By stimulating behaviour skills that are important for appropriately solving the developmental tasks, the relationship play of SDM can have a positive influence on the development of the central expectations and resilience in the Riksen-Walraven model.* (Loots and Malschaert, 1999, p. 28)

Finally, this model showed a feedback loop from the behaviour level to the social support level. This indicates the powerful effect certain behaviours, whether positive or negative, will have on the giving or withdrawing of social support.

It can be seen from the work of Loots and Maalschaert (1999) that SDM is under-pinned by social behaviour theory as well as the more recognisable movement theories based on Laban's movement principles (Douglas, 1995) and embodiment (Whitehead, 2004). This present study was designed to test Sherborne's claims that children exposed to SDM will show greater gains in movement vocabulary and relationship-building which will show as general social development gains both inside and outside the movement session compared to children undergoing a traditional early years PE programme.

Methodology

An infant school in rural Kent was identified, as the head teacher was very supportive of this research project, and one of the Year 1 teachers was trained in SDM. The school was a new and very well-equipped school with around 250 pupils aged between four and seven years of age. There were three classes in each year, and the children came from a wide socio-economic background.

Participants

Three Year One classes (Class A, Class B and Class C) were identified for this study. The head teacher estimated that each class contained an even mix of children from similar backgrounds, was of a similar age range and was developmentally similar to the others. All children received traditional early years PE input three times per week, normally taught by their own class teacher who followed the school's yearly PE plan which was based on the National Curriculum for Key Stage 1. Fourteen children (seven boys and seven girls) from each class were randomly chosen from the register as research subjects (n=42) as this was deemed the maximum number of children who could be successfully observed under the project's limitations of time and number of observers.

Procedure

a) Movement vocabulary

Each group of 14 children was observed during a whole class movement session that contained the same general movement material (e.g. jumping, running, rolling, balancing) for each of the three classes. The teacher/leader for these sessions had chosen a series of movement tasks appropriate for Year 1 children, and she just presented the tasks to the children. She did not attempt to *teach* them except if there was a safety issue. Video recordings of each session were made by a professional photographer. Neither the participant group nor their classmates were aware that they were being observed specifically.

Observation instruments for movement vocabulary

Movement vocabulary was measured over 14 different activities using a movement observation schedule based on Laban's Principles of Movement (Laban, 1998) and Motor Development Stages (Gallahue and Donnelly, 2003). The 14 activities were chosen as developmentally appropriate for Year One children (5–6 years old) and were sufficiently varied to reveal the amount of movement vocabulary acquired by each subject. For instance, the 'ballooning' activity (where two children are given the task of creating the shape of a 'balloon' with their own bodies) would show whether the subjects could hold and change shape (*Body*); change levels and extensions fluently (*Space*); change speed and flow of movement (*Dynamics*); collaborate with and observe partner (*Relationships*). Each activity was observed, videoed and later analysed by an expert PE teacher (Research Assistant 1) using Laban's four movement principles of *Body, Space, Dynamics* and *Relationships* (in those activities using partners), and graded on a scale of 1 to 10, with 10 being the highest score.

For the total observation schedule, the *Body* element consisted of the sum of 21 measures so that a child's score could theoretically range from 21 to 210. The *Space* element consisted of 19 items, that of *Dynamics* consisted of 23 items and *Relationships* consisted of 20 items.

b) *Social development*
Research Assistant 2 was experienced in the observation of the behaviour of children in their early years. She spent a full day tracking one of the three classes, observing children's behaviour both inside and outside the classroom.

Observation instruments for social development
Although *Relationships* is the fourth element of Laban's Principles of Movement and was analysed in the previous movement analysis, Sherborne had claimed that children's relationship-building improvements, gained by participation in SDM, could be seen in contexts other than movement. The schedule developed by Sylva, Roy and Painter (1980) was used by Research Assistant 2 in both the classroom setting and during break times to test this claim.

Each child was observed over a total of 10 minutes. During this time, it was recorded whether they were working alone, in a pair, a small group or a large group. Behaviours were scored for co-operation, for turn-taking and for sharing. If the specified behaviour was observed, the child scored one point; if the specific behaviour was not observed, then the child scored minus one; and if the activity at the time meant that the behaviour was not applicable (for example, listening passively to an adult) the child scored a zero.

Delivering the PE and the SDM programmes
In January of the school year, the 14 identified subjects had been observed and baseline measures taken. For the next six months (i.e. until July), Class A participated in two traditional PE lessons (gym, dance and games) per week taught by their own teacher and then one SDM session taught by the teacher of Class C, who was specially trained in SDM. Class B participated in three traditional PE lessons (gym, dance, games) per week taught by their own class teacher. Class C participated in two traditional PE lessons (gym, dance, games) and one SDM session per week, all taught by their own teacher. The aims and learning objectives for the traditional PE lessons were the same for each class and based on the school's yearly PE plan. The two 'intervention' classes, however, did experience a weekly SDM session, and Table 5.1 shows the learning outcomes and main activities involved in this 18-week SDM programme for the intervention children.

Table 5.1. Sherborne Developmental Movement programme over 18 weeks

Week	Learning outcomes	Movement experiences
1	Identifying and naming how body parts move	Variety of movement patterns, e.g. stepping, sliding, jumping
2	Differences in movements between feet and knees	Visible + invisible knees Light + heavy feet Taking off + landing
3	Differences in movement between hands, elbows + shoulders	Where in space each part can move how: grip, stroke, push, pull
4-8	Identifying importance of centre of body in 'joining' upper + lower limbs Simple partner work	Bend, curl, stretch Curl, roll, stretch roll With partner, gentle rock, back-to-back push, turn the turtle, cradling
9-10	Identifying partner shape and space for moving	Holes + barriers Moving close/far away from partner
10-14	Trusting partner with own body weight (partial) Simple partner balances	Cradling, partner-slides along floor, rising + falling together, leaning (counter-balance/tension)
14-18	Small group co-operation + simple observation of other children's movement	Holes + barriers Problem-solving tasks Groups, group trust activities

Research subjects in Classes A and C became the intervention groups (n=28) and those in Class B acted as the control group (n=14). Two intervention groups were required because it was hypothesised that Class C may have been further influenced by their teacher who was specially trained in SDM and may have been showing a consistently different type of teaching style as shown in the Riksen-Walgrave (1989) model, thereby affecting the results by a much longer exposure to a sensitive-responsive style than the other intervention group.

After six months, the observation tests were repeated by the same research assistants using the same schedules. The same general movement session was used as in January. The session contained the same tasks, and the same approach to presentation only, as opposed to teaching the children, was adopted. The research assistants were not informed whether the children that they were observing were from a control group or an intervention group.

Results
Baseline data analysis for movement vocabulary
In January, all the four elements scored well for reliability. Cronbach's Alpha for *Body* was 0.885, for *Space* was 0.882, for *Dynamics* was 0.865 and for *Relationships* was 0.872. All were well over the accepted values for reliability.

All the distributions were unimodal and, with the exception of *Dynamics,* they were mostly symmetric. However, using the Kolmogorov-Smirnov test, none of them were significantly different from a normal distribution (Table 5.2). Hence, despite the small sample sizes involved, the use of parametric tests would be acceptable.

Table 5.2. Kolmogorov-Smirov test to determine whether the initial distributions of the four Laban elements can be assumed to have a normal distribution

	Kolmogorov-Smirnov		
	Statistic	Degrees of freedom	Significance
Body	.087	42	.200
Space	.082	42	.200
Dynamics	.115	42	.187
Relationships	.109	42	.200

It can be seen (Table 5.3) from the pre-intervention scores (January) that there were no significant differences between the three groups on any of the four elements (ANOVA; p = 0.109 for *Body*, p = 0.299 for *Space*. p = 0.309 for *Dynamics* and p = 0.231 for *Relationships*). These results were confirmed using the non-parametric Kruskal Wallis test.

Table 5.3. Mean scores on *Body*, *Space*, *Dynamics* and *Relationships* elements by group

Group		*Body*	*Space*	*Dynamics*	*Relationships*
Sherborne (outside teacher)	Mean	102.42	92.64	108.65	117.00
	N	14	14	14	14
Sherborne (class teacher)	Mean	114.70	98.94	114.27	125.43
	N	14	14	14	14
Control group	Mean	112.43	99.61	121.19	130.85
	N	14	14	14	14
Total	Mean	109.85	97.06	114.70	124.42
	N	42	42	42	42

Change over six months in movement vocabulary development

All the children were re-assessed six months later using the same four elements. The change in scores was calculated for each child and can be seen in Table 5.4.

Overall there were mean increases for every group, as would be expected from normal child motor development over six months. However, the increase for the two intervention groups were well over *four times* as large as those for the control group.

Table 5.4. Mean scores on the four Laban elements before and after treatment by group

Laban element	SDM with class teacher (Class C) (N = 14)				SDM with outside teacher (Class A) (N = 14)				Control (Class B) (N = 14)			
	Before	After	Diff	P-value	Before	After	Diff	P-value	Before	After	Diff	P-value
Body	114.7	170.49	55.79	< .000	102.42	163.41	60.99	< .000	112.43	126.05	13.62	.004
Space	98.94	154.82	55.88	< .000	92.64	149.79	57.15	< .000	99.61	115.42	15.81	< .000
Dynamics	114.27	186.55	72.28	< .000	108.65	173.01	64.36	< .000	121.19	136.49	15.30	.006
Relations	125.43	178.17	52.74	< .000	117.00	169.18	52.18	< .000	130.85	140.89	10.04	.064

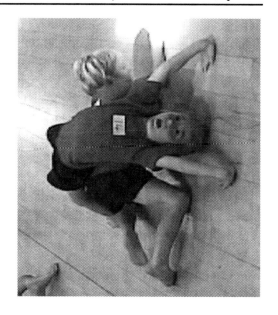

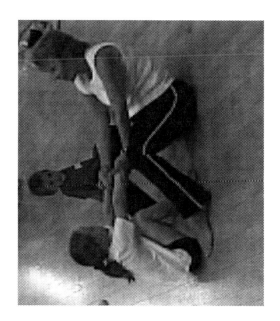

The differences between the two intervention groups and the control group were highly significant (ANOVA; p < 0.001 for all four elements: *Body, Space, Dynamics* and *Relationships*). These results were confirmed using the non-parametric Kruskal Wallis test.

There were no significant differences between the two intervention groups, Classes A and C (ANOVA; p > 0.05 for all four elements: *Body, Space, Dynamics* and *Relationships*). These results were confirmed using the non-parametric Kruskal Wallis test.

The control group, Class B, showed slight but significant improvements from their baseline measures in three elements, *Body, Space* and *Dynamics* (T-test; p<0.05), but the improvement in *Relationships* was not significant (T-test; p=0.064).

Baseline analysis for social development in a classroom setting/break time
Social development was observed in both a classroom setting and at break times. The three measures for co-operation, turn-taking and sharing scales showed good internal reliability with a Cronbach's Alpha of 0.684 for January.

The baseline mean scores were negative for all classes at pre-intervention (January) indicating that, in general, children were mostly not engaging in social relationships when the opportunities presented themselves. The distribution of the social development scores was non-normal for January (Kolmogorov-Smirnov test, T = 0.220, p < 0.01).

Change over six months
The three measures for co-operation, turn-taking and sharing scales showed good internal reliability with a Cronbach's Alpha of 0.861 for post-intervention (July). It can be seen from the results in Table 5.5 that following the six months' intervention period, there was a marked improvement in both intervention groups (Classes A and C), while the control group (Class B) had got slightly worse. As the sample sizes were small, the non-parametric Wilcoxon signed rank test was used to test for significance. The improvements in both intervention groups were significant, while the slight decrease in the control group was not significant.

Table 5.5. Social development scores before and after treatment by group

	Mean social development score		Difference	P-Value*
	Before	After		
SDM with class teacher (Class C; N = 14)	-.036	4.71	5.07	.025
SDM with outside teacher (Class A; N = 14)	-1.43	5.29	6.72	.002
Control (Class B; N = 14)	-0.71	-2.14	-1.43	.529
* Using Wilcoxon signed-rank test for non-parametric data				

Discussion

Movement vocabulary development

The statistics show the three observed groups of children in Classes A, B and C had a similar grasp of movement vocabulary by January in their first year of compulsory schooling. After a further six months of growth and development, all children would be expected to score higher. Figures 5.2–5.5 show that these changes were not of the same magnitude for each group.

The control group's scores on *Body, Space* and *Dynamics* had risen to the $p < 0.05$ significance level which would suggest that the traditional early years PE programme had affected the children's development in these areas. It is interesting to note, however, that the *Relationships* score improved only slightly. On checking the traditional PE programme covered during these six months, it was clear that the children had had little opportunity to work with partners or in a group.

Those children undergoing six months' intervention of SDM had, in contrast, had many opportunities in which to engage with each other. Some of the SDM work had involved sharing another's weight and space; some had involved testing one's own

Figure 5.2. Measures of the *Body* element by group

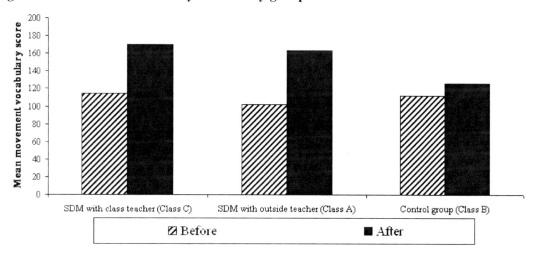

Figure 5.3. Measures of *Space* element by group

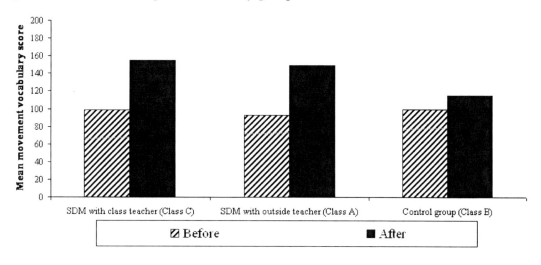

Figure 5.4. Measures of *Dynamics* element by group

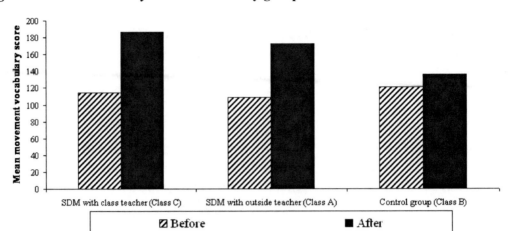

Figure 5.5. Measures of *Relationships* element by group

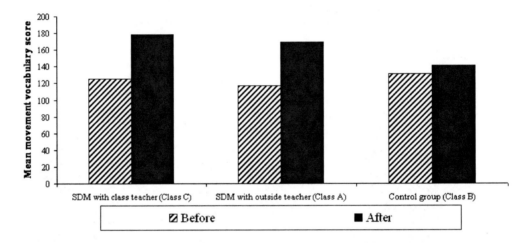

strength against another; and some had involved matching another's shape. The improvement by the intervention groups in the *Relationships* section of the movement vocabulary test was, therefore, not surprising. The *magnitude* of the improvements in movement vocabulary in all four elements by the intervention groups *was* surprising.

The scores of the intervention children had risen four times more than the control group. The differences between the intervention and control groups was highly significant (p<0.001) Given that all three groups were evenly matched in January, this change can be attributed only to the SDM programme.

The children were assessed on the four Laban movement areas of *Body, Space, Dynamics* and *Relationships*. Eleven out of the 14 activities observed during the assessed movement session had involved work with a partner, and three had involved activities alone. During the 18 weeks, the intervention groups were experiencing their once-a-week session of SDM; 14 of those sessions involved partner work, but none of the control group's equivalent traditional PE sessions involved partner work. It could easily be argued, therefore, that the intervention groups were at an unfair advantage for the assessment of *Relationships*. It could also be argued, however, that the control group, spending less time on partner work, were in fact, spending more time learning *Body, Space* and *dynamic* movement vocabulary alone. But the results for these three movement elements were also significantly lower for the control group. These results suggest that SDM allows children in their early years opportunities for learning movement vocabulary in ways that traditional infant PE programmes may not.

Both the National Curriculum for Physical Education 2000 (QCA, 1999) and 5–14 Guidelines (Scottish Office Education Department, 1992) in Scotland recommend that partner work be encouraged once children have learned movement skills alone (i.e. they recommend that children in Key Stage 2 and P4–7 work with partners and in groups rather than those in the infant stages). Sherborne, during her professional movement career, had observed young children learning new skills in relation to others. She regarded the communication, co-operation, trust, competition and adaption that children practise in good partner work to be extremely important in helping them learn about their own bodies (Sherborne, 2001). She emphasised how babies and very young children learned from mimicking others, especially the main care-giver, and how they might learn movement by being in very close contact with another who was moving. These results suggest that children aged five and six years old may still be learning their movement vocabulary in this way.

There were no differences between the scores of the two intervention groups. If there was any effect of special SDM teaching style as suggested by Loots and Malschaert (1999), it was not evident in this study, otherwise the scores of Class C, who were exposed to the sensitive-responsive teaching style of the SDM teacher throughout the day, would have been higher. It could be argued, however, that the intervention groups' scores were affected somewhat by the SDM teacher, and to control further for teacher effect, it would have been necessary to ensure that the control group in Class B also had one lesson of traditional PE taught by the SDM teacher. This was impossible to organise without severe disruption to the school timetable.

Lastly, with regard to movement vocabulary, it was important to check that the activities used in the assessment tool were not the same as those taught during the SDM sessions so that it could be determined that the intervention children were not being taught for the test. On examination of the Year One class lesson plans, both for the traditional programme, and also for the SDM programme, only two activities were found to be the same as those activities in the test. These were 'Holes and barriers' and 'Partner push'. 'Holes and barriers' was taught in the traditional gym sessions and in the SDM sessions, but 'Partner push' was taught only in the SDM session. There was only an unfair advantage for the intervention children during the assessment on 'Partner push', which had not been encountered by the control children. Given that there was only one item out of 14 on which the children could have been primed, it can safely be assumed that priming was not a factor in this study. The results of this study showed the combined package of SDM, and the SDM teaching style, had had a significant effect on the acquisition of movement vocabulary by Year One Class children compared to traditional early years PE sessions.

Social development

In January, all groups scored negatively on the social development scale. This shows a sensitivity of the instrument as it would be expected that children after only four months of school would not have learned many turn-taking, sharing or co-operation skills. Table 5.5 shows that by July, however, the scores of both intervention groups on the social development scale were significantly better than those of the control group.

This would correspond with Sherborne's premise (2001) that her movement programme helps children to form relationships, to care for another, to communicate and to compete. It also affirms the Riksen-Walraven model (1989) because the social support and the expectation levels have been extended after exposure to SDM. This shows improvement in behaviour. This behaviour was imprinted sufficiently strongly in the movement class that it showed itself within a classroom situation and during playtime. It seems likely that behaviours learned in the SDM sessions had a strong effect on the children's relationship-building generally.

Conclusion

The results of this fieldwork were of sufficient magnitude in the degree of difference in movement vocabulary acquisition and relationship-building between traditional early years PE and SDM in these very young children that more attention is warranted. The quest for good quality PE should also apply to the early years stage, as it is at this stage that so many future behaviours are effected (Sirij-Blatchford and Sylva, 2002). Despite the present emphasis on the physical activity/obesity and the grooming of future sporting heroes, it is important to remember the needs of every child (Kay, 2006). Sherborne's claims that her type of movement education programme meets the two basic needs of all children – to feel at home in their own bodies and to form relationships – has been very evident in these results.

The next step

There are inherent difficulties involved with research on real children in real school situations. Disruption of the timetable and normal running of a school needs to be avoided. This research, however, could have been more robust if the teacher trained in SDM could have also taught all of the PE and SDM sessions of all of the classes. In future research, this may be possible. Since the difference in movement vocabulary observed was of such a great magnitude, it is important that a similar piece of work is carried out with a different early years population. The observation and analysis of children's movement is very time-consuming and should, in future, be shared with more than one research assistant, if funds can be made available.

Sherborne's approach to movement holds some real treasures for early years PE, and attempts must be made to persuade policy-makers and initial teacher trainers of these benefits.

References

Bogdanowicz, M. and Kasica, A. (2003) *Ruch Rozwijajacy dla Wszystkich*. Gdansk, Poland: Harmonia.

Davies, M. (1995) *Helping Children Learn through a Movement Perspective.* London: Hodder and Stoughton Educational.

Douglas, M. (1995) 'The essence of Sherborne's work: the way forward'. In: J. Dibbo and S. Gerry (eds) *Caring and Sharing: Physical Education, Therapy and Sherborne Developmental Movement.* Plymouth: University of Plymouth Press.

Filer, J. (2006) 'SDM and its role in family therapy'. In: Hill, C. (2006) *Communicating through Movement.* Clent: Sunfield Publications.

Fisher, J. (2002) *Starting from the Child: Teaching and learning from 3 to 8.* Oxford: Open University Press.

Gallahue, D. and Donnelly, F. (2003) *Developmental Physical Education for All Children.* Champaigne, Illinois: Human Kinetics.

Gardner, H. (1993) *Multiple Intelligences.* New York: Basic Books.

Her Majesty's Inspectorate (2001) *Improving Physical Education in Primary Schools.* Edinburgh: The Stationery Office.

Hill, C. (2006) *Communicating through Movement.* Clent: Sunfield Publications.

Kay, W. (2006) 'Physical education – a quality experience for all children', *British Journal of Teaching Physical Education,* 37 (1), 6–30.

Kirk, D. (2004) 'Framing quality physical education: the elite sport model or sport education?', *Physical Education and Sports Pedagogy,* 9 (2), 185–197.

Laban, R. (1998) *The Mastery of Movement (5th edn).* London: Northcote House.

Loots, G. and Malschaert, E. (1999) 'The use in Belgium of developmental movement according to the work of Veronica Sherborne: a developmental psychology view', *European Journal of Special Needs Education,* 14 (3), 221–230.

Maude, P. (2001) *Physical Children, Active Teaching: Investigating physical literacy.* Buckingham: Open University Press.

National Summit on Physical Education (2005) 'Position statement on physical education', *British Journal of Teaching Physical Education,* 36 (1), 33.

Qualifications and Curriculum Authority (QCA) (1999) *National Curriculum for England: Physical Education, Key Stages 1–4.* London: QCA.

Parrott, K. (1997) *The Contribution of the Kiwi Baby Programme to Meaningful Health Gains.* Waikato, New Zealand.

Pate, R., Pratt, M., Blair, S., Haskell, W., Macera, C., Bouchard, C., Bulhner, D., Etting, W., Health, G., King, A., Kriska, A., Leon, A., Sauis, J. and Wilmore, J. (1995) 'Physical activity and public health', *Journal of American Medical Association,* 273 (5), 402–407.

Penn, H. (2004) *Understanding Early Childhood: Issues and controversies.* Oxford: Open University Press.

Pollatschek, J. (1989) 'The Linwood Project: quality daily physical education', *British Journal of Physical Education,* 20 (4), 197–201.

Riksen-Walraven, J.M.A. (1989) 'Meten in perspectief: een levensloopmodel als achterground bij het meten en beinvloeden van gedrag en interacties', *Tijdschrift voor Orthopedagogiek,* 28 (1), 6–33.

Scottish Office Education Department (1992) *National Guidelines 5–14: Expressive arts.* Edinburgh: Scottish Office Education Department.

Scottish Physical Activity Task Force (2003) *Let's Make Scotland More Active.* Edinburgh: The Stationary Office.

Sherborne, V. (1990) *Developmental Movement for Children: Mainstream, special needs and pre-school (1st edn).* Cambridge: Cambridge University Press.

Sherborne, V. (2001) *Developmental Movement for Children: Mainstream, special needs and pre-school (2nd edn)*. London: Worth Publishing.

Sirij-Blatchford, I. and Sylva, K. (2002) *Researching Effective Pedagogy in the Early Years*. London: Department for Education and Science.

Sparkes, J. (2001) 'Forward to the second edition'. In: V. Sherborne (2001) *Developmental Movement for Children: Mainstream, special needs and pre-school (2nd edn)*. London: Worth Publishing.

Sports Council (1991) *The Case for Sport (Publicity leaflet)*. London: Sports Council.

Sylva, K.D., Roy, C. and Painter, M. (1980) *Childwatching at Playgroup and Nursery School*. London: McIntyre.

Whitehead, M. (2001) 'The concept of physical literacy', *British Journal of Teaching Physical Education,* 32 (1), 6–8.

Wright, L. (2004) 'Preserving the value of happiness in primary physical education', *Physical Education and Sports Pedagogy,* 9 (2), 49–163.

Endnote

[1] The ability of parents to receive signals and needs from children, to interpret them adequately and to react to them in such a way that the child becomes more competent (Riksen-Walraven, 1992.

CHAPTER 6

Bonding through Developmental Movement Play

Janice Filer

Introduction

Background

Developmental Movement Play is an innovative early intervention that addresses the needs of two generations by providing a service for both the parent and child. It was developed in the 1980s by the writer as the result of a lifetime's work in the field of dance and movement. The original idea came from a union between children's wish to dance and the need to develop a programme to address the poor attachment relationship and negative parenting styles of some of the parents attending movement workshops.

From 1999 to 2002, Developmental Movement Play became foundational to a multi-disciplinary research project, established as a service for vulnerable families facing social exclusion, with children eight years of age and under who were experiencing emotional and behavioural disturbance (EBD) and/or mental health difficulties at home, at school or both. It was funded by Education, Health and Social Services. From 2002 to 2004, the project was funded by the government through the 'On Track' programme and, in 2004, it was granted funding by The Children's Fund until March 2008 under the Behaviour Support Service.

All children and their parents can be included in the practice of Developmental Movement Play regardless of their stage of development, physical ability, class or culture. Participants can engage creatively in a process to further their emotional, cognitive, physical and social integration, develop confidence, self-esteem and self-worth. Developmental Movement Play is a very personal form of dance and movement that is not easily explained in words. There are no steps to learn, and the only way to understand this style of practice fully is to do it.

This psychotherapeutic use of movement and dance is based on the principle that movement reflects an individual's patterns of thinking and feeling. Emotions and perceptions of disability are invited into the dance activities to be expressed and released as a natural part of what is happening in the sessions. It uses movement as a means of communication to engage parents in playing with their children in order to improve their relationships with each other. Participants learn to listen to themselves through moving.

Developmental Movement Play provides opportunities for the parents to grow as individuals alongside their children through shared dance and movement activities based upon the theory, philosophy and practice of Rudolf Laban (Thornton,1971). It incorporates Sherborne Developmental Movement (SDM; Sherborne, 2001) which is recognised as being highly effective not only for children with special educational needs but also for all individuals, whatever their ability (Department of Education and Science, 1991; Sherborne, 2001). Although most of Sherborne's work was carried out in special schools, this study demonstrates the benefits of this socially inclusive practice for children in mainstream education and their parents/carers.

Research question and main aims of the study

The broad aim of this study was to determine the effects of Developmental Movement Play on the attachment relationship between parents and children attending the programme. Within an ethos of social inclusion, it also aimed to:

■ Improve the relationship between parent and child by giving them the opportunity to learn to feel relaxed and enjoy one another's company through physical play

■ To address some of the issues concerning communication, relationships, emotional, behavioural and mental health difficulties for both parents and children

■ Provide parents with knowledge, skills and positive experiences to enhance their relationships with their children

■ Encourage participants to have fun playing with each other as they learned to trust and respect each other

■ Develop confidence, self-esteem and self-worth in both adult and child participants by using movement and touch as a means of communication to enable them to achieve a deeper understanding of each other's thoughts and feelings

■ Provide a means to release pent-up emotions and stress

■ Raise parents' awareness of their role in promoting self-confidence and resilience in their children and encourage them to develop strategies for promoting positive behaviour.

Methodology

Participants in the research study

The participants in this Developmental Movement Play study were 10 mainstream children between the ages of 18 months and 8 years, and their parents/carers. They were referred to the project by Health, Education and Social Care professionals because they were experiencing emotional, behavioural and/or mental health difficulties at home, school and in the community, and were at risk of social exclusion. The majority of adult participants were mothers of the children attending the project. Two of them brought along younger siblings/relations who were allocated play workers as partners so that the parents were able to concentrate on the focus child. Two of the mothers had severely poor attachment relationships with their children, and were taking part in the movement group work in the hope that their attachment relationships would improve. One of these children was at risk of being taken into care by the local authority due to the lack of emotional attachment and allegations of physical abuse by the mother. All of the mothers had a history of postnatal depression; all but one of them were experiencing on-going clinical depression and were taking anti-depressants for the duration of the group programme. During the programme, two of the parents experienced the breakdown of their relationship with a partner; one mother attempted suicide, and her children were placed into short-term care for three weeks. Another parent was struggling to come to terms with her own sexual abuse as a child, and five others were suffering from very low self-esteem due to past violent relationships. Two of these women were experiencing domestic violence throughout the duration of the group work process. Everyone was interested in participating in the group.

Environment

The working space was a place which was safe and where children and parents invented group rules to create a situation which the group itself had defined. Participants were responsible for themselves as well as for certain collective tasks, and were encouraged to be both the care-giver and recipient. Everyone had the right to sit out, but they were encouraged to join in. Everyone agreed to work within the defined frame of reference.

Procedure

Parents' comments were recorded during discussions before the start of the programme, at the end of every session when they had had the opportunity to view the video recording taken, and after they had completed the programme.

The seven phases of the project

The project took place over seven phases which are identified in the schematic diagram below (Figure 6.1). Assessments were made throughout, and parents were given the opportunity to withdraw from the programme up to the point of delivery or to withdraw from the research at any point. Once the programme had started, parents were expected to make a commitment to it.

Baseline assessment

These assessments provided information regarding the aspects of Developmental Movement Play which needed to be planned into the programme to suit the needs of both the group and individual members. The assessments also gave an insight into the relationships between adult and child participants, their general attitude, behaviour patterns, parenting styles and the mental health state of both child and adult.

Delivery of the programme

Parents accompanied their children to a series of 10 programme sessions which took place for three hours on one morning each week. Each session included: a welcome circle; the Developmental Movement Play aspect of the programme based on activities found in SDM (Sherborne, 2001), in particular the work on relationships and 'Blanket Play' (Filer, 1994); a plenary/goodbye circle; refreshments (after which the children were taken back to class or the crèche provided by the project); time for parents to watch and discuss the video recording of the movement session; and, at the end of each session, a participant satisfaction questionnaire.

End of programme assessment

At the end of the programme, parents were asked to repeat the assessments taken before the start of the programme to determine change, if any, as a result of taking part in it and to complete a final satisfaction questionnaire.

Analysis, findings and reporting

During the final stage of the project, the questionnaires and video recordings taken by a co-worker were analysed alongside any notes of mental observations and the evaluations made of each session. The findings were reported back to the parents in a final group meeting and the stakeholders in the project received a written report.

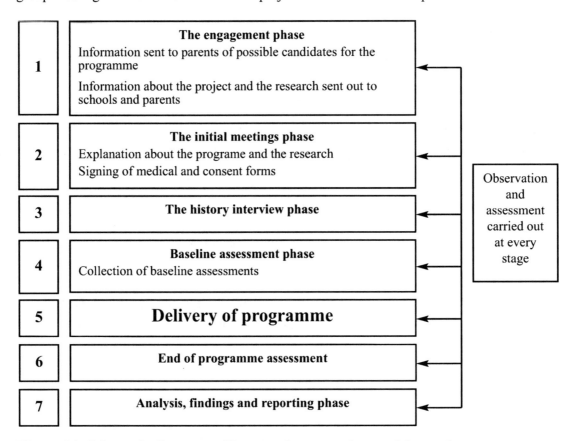

Figure 6.1. Schematic diagram to illustrate the seven phases of the project

Assessment

The main tools used to measure change in participants from start to end of the programme were:

- A checklist for evaluating adult–child play interaction (Webster-Stratton, 1985)

- The Parent Defined Problem Visual Analogue Scale (PDPVAS)/Likert Rating Scale (Ollier et al. 1999)

- Eyberg Child Behaviour Inventory (Eyberg and Ross, 1978).

Parent Satisfaction Questionnaires, devised by the researcher, were also used throughout the programme.

Results
Attendance
Although at first it was feared that attendance would be poor as many of the parents were serial non-attendees to services offered to them, the graph below (Figure 6.2) shows that this was not the case as the attendance was recorded at a level of 78%. This high level of attendance reflected the parents' commitment to the programme. Some of the absences were due to holidays (Child 3, 7 and 9) or because the parent or child had been ill (Child 4, 5 and 6). One child (Child 9), a relation of Child 3, was looked after at home on two occasions to make it easier for the parent to concentrate on the focus child. The mother of Child 6 was hospitalised due to a mental breakdown during the programme, and they both missed four sessions due to the state of her mental health and the child being taken into temporary care by the local authority.

Interestingly, as can be seen from Figures 6.2–6.6 below, the parents and children who attended the most movement sessions were not always the ones who made the most progress. Although parents initially felt uneasy about attending the programme, once they got into the practical aspect of Developmental Movement Play, they looked forward to it, and attended apart from times of genuine illness or holidays.

Figure 6.2. A graph to show the levels of attendance for the Developmental Movement Play programme

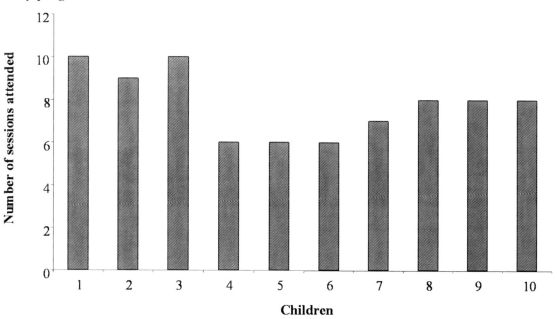

Assessment
The Eyberg Child Behaviour Inventory Scale (Eyberg and Pincus, 1999) was administered at the start and end of the programme to determine if there were any changes in the children's behaviour as a result of taking part in Developmental Movement

Play. This inventory provides a checklist of 36 child behaviours characteristic of behaviourally disruptive children. Parents rate the severity of these behaviours on a scale from 1 (never) to 7 (always) and whether these behaviours are considered a problem for the parent now (yes/no). The results of the inventory were converted into an Intensity Score (range: 36–252; clinical threshold: 131–133) and a Problem Score (range: 0–36; clinical threshold: 15).

Five children were rated above the clinical threshold indicating that their behaviour was a cause for concern at the start of the intervention. At the end of the intervention three children remained above the clinical threshold, but the intensity of their difficult behaviour was perceived to be reduced by their parents. The intensity of the difficult behaviour exhibited by the children decreased in all cases. Although two of the children were rated below the clinical threshold at the start of the programme their parents still noted a reduction in the intensity of the difficult behaviour they sometimes experienced. As can be seen in the figure below, these results indicated that every child's behaviour, except for the child with an incomplete Eyberg Behaviour Inventory, improved as a result of attending Developmental Movement Play sessions.

Figure 6.3. Graph to show the children's Eyberg Behaviour Inventory Scale Intensity (EBISI) scores at the start and end of the Developmental Movement Play intervention programme. (The dotted horizontal line represents the lower clinical threshold limit of 131 and the black line represents the upper clinical threshold limit of 133.)

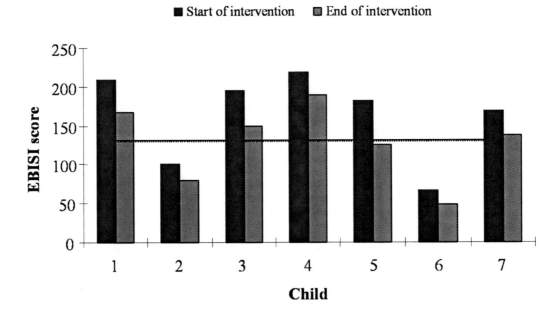

The nature of the work
The group was defined as a space for individual and shared exploration, discovery, experience and learning through dance and movement play. After agreeing guidelines to ensure safety, participants were invited to sit on the floor in a welcome circle. During the first session many children who found it difficult to sit next to their mothers who exerted full parental control to pull them harshly down, wriggled wildly and struggled to be free. Two of the mothers, who felt too self-conscious to join in, sat on the sidelines watching as their children ran uncontrollably around the space. They

used the excuse that they did not want to sit on the floor. Soon they joined the group, saying that they 'felt more embarrassed sitting out than taking part, and it looked as if the others were having fun'. During discussions after the first session, all but one of the adult participants revealed that they had felt embarrassed and self-conscious, and that they had been dreading taking part in the programme, but were forcing themselves to do so because they thought it would help their children. This improved, and by the end of the fourth session all except oneparent, Sara, was happy to join in.

During the movement sessions, the adults became increasingly aware that their bodies had limitations, rules and possibilities, but gradually they learned to listen to them and use them accordingly during the relationship play with their children. The movement took place within the defined frame of reference agreed at the very beginning. Although some principles needed to remain unchanged, everyone recognised that the nature of the movement programme inevitably led to changes. In the beginning, suggestions for movement ideas were fed to the group; for instance, participants were invited to explore different ways of sitting closely to each other without actually touching. They were asked questions, such as: 'How does it feel?'; 'Can you find different ways of sitting next to each other?'; 'How do you think your child feels?'. Sometimes the parents were asked to lead the movement; at other times, the children were asked to do so; and at times both shared the lead. Soon participants invented different ways of sitting next to each other rather than waiting to be told what to do. This process was repeated for various movement experiences (Sherborne, 2001) during the first three sessions of the programme. By Session 4, it was no longer necessary to demonstrate ideas or give suggestions to the group.

After this stage, the problems that participants were experiencing were being worked out individually or in a relation to someone else. Pairings and groupings occurred naturally during the movement workshops. Sometimes, when there were obvious difficulties between parents and their own children, participants instinctively worked with each other's children in an attempt to offer group support. Relations between participants, forms, rhythms, sequences, groupings and interactions were studied in the way that the group moved together in 'movementscapes'. Moving from one feeling to another, and examining them from the participants' individual perspectives, gave the researcher an overview of what was happening in the group. In this way an insight into the nature of our work together was developed. The participants learned to transform energies to turn feelings of depression into those of joy, and lack of attachment into constructive relationships. Touch became the means of communication between parent and child when once it had signalled only repulsion and anger. Slowly, by the second half of the programme, participants were able to use the movement in a therapeutic way.

As parent and child interacted in movement, they talked about their feelings and relationships with each other, which were then worked out within the frame of reference or in the guise of it. This might happen in relation to someone who was working with a similar type of problem, rather than what was actually happening between participants. The participants were given the opportunity to dance their feelings towards one another, expressing them in movements, or dance out certain aspects of the person towards whom the feelings were directed (Meekums and Payne, 1993).

Breathing activities were included, as many participants were experiencing problems associated with shallow breathing and anxiety. This experience created awareness of the quality of the breathing and its influence on the body and importance in learning to control feelings of anxiety.

When, as was usually the case particularly for the first half of the programme, participants came to the sessions feeling angry, they danced out their anger and left with an inner feeling of calm that lasted for the rest of the day and resulted in no school exclusions on movement day! In the group, everyone was allowed to feel angry, but they danced out their anger rather than take it out on each other. Some sessions felt flat and quiet, as many of the participants were suffering from depression, and the dark silent moods permeating the group were danced out, leaving participants feeling exhausted but lifted into lighter frame of mind. The realisation that things were not always what they seemed came when the group experienced the silences of deep depression that seemed to scream out loud.

Meaningful communication between participants was made possible as they juxtaposed, paired and fused in movement play experiences. When Sara, mentioned earlier, was finally ready to dance out her feelings in Session 6, a turning point in the group's relationship was reached. It became clear to Sara that the feeling of repulsion she had for her son had nothing to do with him. Through movement, reality was separated from fantasy (Bateson, 1985; Haley, 1955), and the whole group arrived at a new, more open conception of life.

Results of the checklist for evaluating adult–child interaction, Part A (Webster-Stratton, 1994)

79% of assessment questionnaires were completed by parents, indicating a high level of commitment to the programme. As can be seen in Table 6.1 and Figures 6.4 and 6.5 below, there were significant levels of improvement in the adult–child play interactions after completing the programme. A high number of parents had reported before the start of the group that they hardly ever played with their children because they did not really know how to or that they felt uncomfortable playing with them.

Results of the checklist for evaluating adult–child interaction, Part B (Webster-Stratton, 1994)

In Part B of the checklist for evaluating parent–child play interactions (Webster-Stratton, 1994), the parents were asked a further 14 questions about their interactions with their child. At the start, many parents expressed their discomfort about playing with their children, particularly in physical, hands-on way. Table 6.2, and Figures 6.6 and 6.7 below, demonstrate how much more positive they were about playing with their children by the end of the movement programme.

Results of the Parent Defined Problem Visual Analogue Scale (PDPVAS)

Parents were asked to rate various aspects of the parent–child relationship on a scale from 1–10, from 'Not a problem' to 'Couldn't be worse' at the start and end of the programme.

Table 6.1. Part A: Parents' responses to questions about their relationship with their child (Webster-Stratton, 1994)

Qu No	QUESTIONS	PARENT RESPONSES TO QUESTIONS					
		'Almost always'		'Sometimes'		'Never'	
		Before programme	After programme	Before programme	After programme	Before programme	After programme
1	How often do you encourage your child to solve problems?	1	4	5	4	2	0
2	How often do you encourage your child to play independently?	4	6	4	2	0	0
3	Do you encourage your child to be creative and inventive?	1	5	3	3	4	0
4	Do you encourage your child to express their feelings and ideas?	0	6	2	2	6	0
5	When playing with your child, how often do you direct and structure activities?	0	5	4	3	4	0
6	When playing with your child, do you criticise and correct mistakes	7	1	1	4	0	3

The results of the PDPVAS, adapted from the Likert Scale (Hobday and Ollier, 1998) regarding the play/relationship aspect of the programme, show that the parents of all 10 children felt that their child grew in confidence as a result of attending the Developmental Movement Play programme. Overall, parents recorded a 44% increase in their child's confidence from the start to the finish of the programme. There was an increase in the amount of time every parent spent playing with their child at home as

Figure 6.4. Part A: Results of the checklist for evaluating adult–child interaction taken at the start of the Developmental Movement Play programme (Webster-Stratton, 1994)

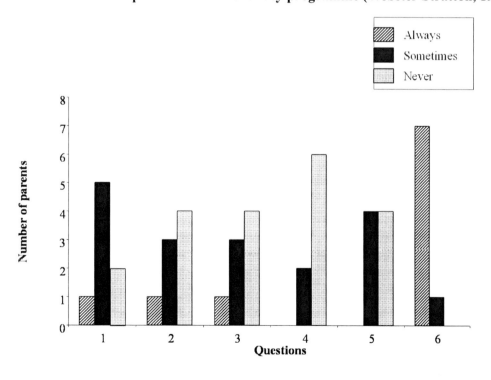

Figure 6.5. Part A: Results of the checklist for evaluating adult–child interaction taken after completion of the Developmental Movement Play programme (Webster-Stratton, 1994)

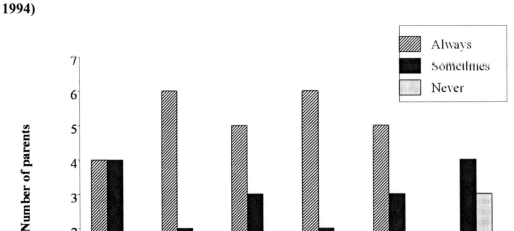

a result of attending. Overall this increase was recorded at 40%. All parents indicated that there had been an improvement in the relationship they had with their child by the end of the programme; overall, the level of improvement in parent–child relationship was rated as being 35% better by the end of the programme.

Analysis of the PDPVAS taken at the start of the programme showed that the majority (7) of the children experienced very little, if any, opportunity for any control in their relationship with their parents at the start of the programme. Two children experienced an extreme lack of control and were allowed to do exactly as they pleased, and the remaining child had a more balanced parent–child relationship with his mother. Interestingly, by the end of the programme there was only a 9% improvement in the balance of control between the parents and their children, but on reflection this could have been down to the fact that it appeared that one parent (the mother with the most evenly balanced relationship with her child) had not understood the question. She had recorded a shift of control from 100% in favour of herself at the start of the programme to her child having 100% of the control by the end of the programme.

This result does not reflect the shift towards a more even level of control between all the parents and their children noticed during the weekly observations of the group, parent feedback during interviews and the rating scales of the other seven parents. All these parents recorded that they had a more evenly balanced relationship with their child as a result of attending the programme. The five parents who felt that they always wanted to be in control by setting harsh, unrealistic boundaries and insisting their child stayed within them regardless of the difficulty or outcome, realised that their relationship with their child improved if they occasionally allowed the child some choice, the opportunity to take the lead or make decisions rather than always telling the child exactly what to do. The remaining two parents at the opposite

Table 6.2. Part B: Parents' responses to questions about their relationship with their child (Webster-Stratton, 1994)

		PARENT RESPONSES TO QUESTIONS ASKED					
		'Almost always'		'Sometimes'		'Never'	
Qu No	QUESTIONS When playing with your child how often do you...	Before programme	After programme	Before programme	After programme	Before programme	After programme
1	Direct or structure play?	6	1	2	5	0	2
2	Create the rules of play?	5	0	3	4	0	4
3	Criticise or correct your child's mistake?	8	0	0	5	0	3
4	Force your child to finish a project?	5	0	3	3	0	5
5	Allow participation only in sex-appropriate activities?	3	1	5	5	0	2
6	Feel uncomfortable if your child expresses fear or helplessness?	8	0	0	5	0	3
7	Compete with your child?	2	0	6	2	0	6
8	Become engrossed with your own play, and ignore your child's play?	3	0	4	2	1	6
9	Ask a lot of questions?	2	2	4	5	2	1
10	Impose your own ideas?	4	0	4	1	0	7
11	Give too much help?	4	0	4	0	0	8
12	Prohibit pretend play?	0	0	5	0	3	8
13	Demand perfection?	3	0	5	1	0	7
14	Place emphasis on the ultimate product of play rather than on effort?	4	0	4	2	0	6

extreme at the start of the programme of allowing their child free rein to do what they wanted, had also developed a more balanced approach to the parent–child relationship by the end of the programme by setting appropriate boundaries during the relationship play and taking some responsibility for their child's behaviour. It was hoped that a more even balance of control between parents and children would be achieved so that the children would be given the opportunity to be in control of some areas of their lives, but not all.

The main outcomes for parents and children who experienced the programme were emotional liberation, improved mental health, raised levels of confidence and self-esteem and improved parent–child relationships, with participants recording a 34% increase in the amount of enjoyment experienced from playing with each other. At the start of the programme, parents were also asked to describe three behavioural

Figure 6.6. Part B: Results of the checklist for evaluating adult–child interaction taken at the start of the Developmental Movement Play programme (Webster-Stratton, 1994)

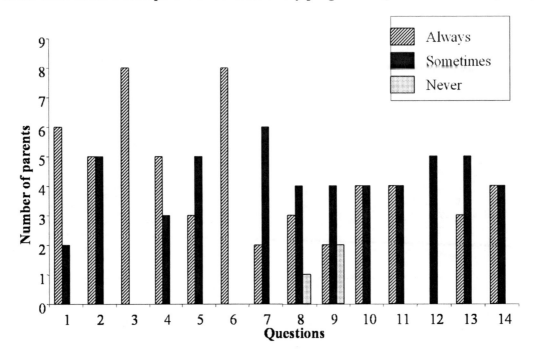

Figure 6.7. Part B: Results of the checklist for evaluating adult–child interaction taken after completion of the Developmental Movement Play programme (Webster-Stratton, 1994)

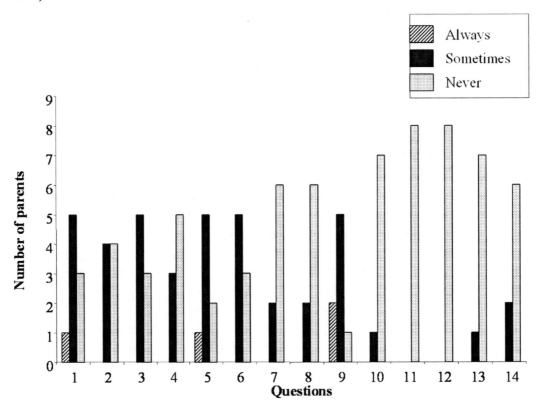

problems that their child was experiencing at home that they would like to change. They rated the severity of each of these on a PDPVS by marking along a 10 cm line (the opposite ends of which represented the two extremes of 'Not a problem' and 'Couldn't be worse') the points which represented their perception of their child's problems. This was repeated at the end of the programme. These behaviours included:

> *...having violent temper tantrums, refusing to do what they were told, swearing, shouting, hitting and spitting, always saying no, raising his fist to me when told he can not have something, aggressive behaviour, is spiteful to others, has no confidence, is always miserable and moody, always throwing things, destroying things and answers back.*

As a result of attending the programme, there was significant overall improvement in the three main problem areas in child behaviour identified by parents at the start of the programme. By the end of the programme, eight parents recorded a reduction in severity of at least two of the three behavioural problems they were experiencing with their child at home. As can be seen in Figure 6.8 below, Parent Defined Problem 1 (PDP1), seven parents revealed that there was a 72% improvement in the areas of the children's behaviour rated as being the most difficult by their parents. One parent recorded that their child's problem had slightly deteriorated. This 7% regression was possibly due to the parents trying to exert more control or becoming more aware of their child's behaviour due to the activities they experienced in the group and the opportunity they were given to explore the issues of parenting and reflect on their behaviour.

Six parents recorded a reduction in the severity of their child's second most difficult behavioural problem, one rated their child's behavioural problem as worse and one rated it as staying the same. Findings regarding Parent Defined Problem 2 (PDP2), indicated an overall 64% improvement in the behaviour of six of the children, a regression of 11% in one child's behavioural difficulty and one child's behaviour stayed the same. Six parents recorded that there was a reduction in severity of their child's third behavioural problem; one parent said that the child's problem had got

Figure 6.8. Chart to show results of the PDPVAS for Developmental Movement Play

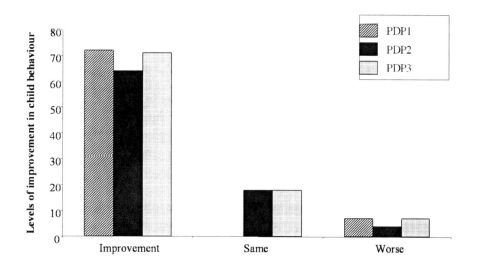

worse; and another said the third behavioural problem had stayed the same. For Parent Defined Problem 3 (PDP3), there was an overall 71% level of improvement in the behaviour of six children; one child's behaviour showed a regression of 7%; and one child's behaviour remained unchanged.

Parent Satisfaction Questionnaires

78 weekly Parent Satisfaction Questionnaires were completed. On a scale of 'unhelpful', 'neutral', 'quite helpful' and 'very helpful', the findings (Figure 6.9 below) of the weekly feedback evaluation sheets suggest that the main activities and discussions were very helpful (84%), while 14% were recorded as helpful, and 2% as neutral. No parents found the programme unhelpful.

Figure 6.9. Chart to show parent satisfaction levels with the Developmental Movement Play Programme

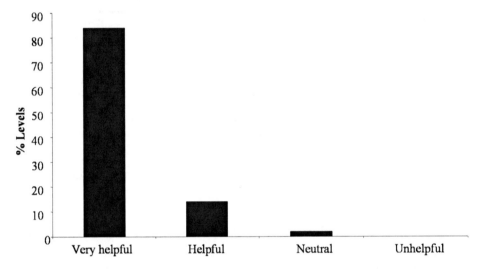

Parent comments

At the start of the programme, all but one of the parents felt uncomfortable interacting with their child. Typical comments made were: 'I don't feel comfortable in playing with my children, 'cos something always needs to be done'; 'I hardly ever play with my children. I spend all of my time shaking'; and 'I feel that play is valuable, but I need to feel comfortable in doing it.' By the end of the programme, comments made by parents were very different:

> *I did not realise just how much fun I would have playing with my child and how much he enjoyed playing with me. We especially enjoyed the blanket play and rolling together on the floor. We both felt good afterwards, and it lasted all day. I was surprised because he had a good day in school which is unusual for him.*

Another parent reported:

> *I dreaded it at first, but I got into it and really enjoyed myself. It was a shame when it had to end because I felt so much better in myself when I was doing the movement and had something to look forward to each week.*

Another parent mentioned the effect the programme had on her mental health state:

After the movement group, I felt much better about myself and my relationship with my child. We had done something good together. My mood changed and I felt more positive, and it made everything much calmer at home, and we seemed to have more good days than bad, when once all days were bad especially the mornings.

The one parent who enjoyed interacting with her child from the start reported that:

Nothing interferes with the playing side of things as I would drop anything to play with them. Almost every evening time is spent playing with them. I do feel that playtime is a valuable time.

During discussions at the end of the programme she reported:

I did not realise that physical play could be so much fun for us. Normally his dad does the rough and tumble stuff. It brought us closer together, and I join in with it a lot more now because I realise how much I was missing out on. Our relationship was good to begin with, but it's even better now.

Other comments from parents included 'It's something for us to look forward to together' and, 'Thursdays are always good in our house now. Doing the Movement Play together gives us a good start to the day.' One mum who was having particularly severe problems in her relationship with her child said that she did not realise just what a difference it had made to them until she saw it for herself on the video and that she could tell by her son's body language that he liked it:

Normally he flinches if I go near him because he thinks I am going to do something to him. He doesn't do that in the movement play. He even looks as if he is smiling, and so do I. I can't believe the change in us; everything is beginning to get better now. Don't get me wrong – he still demands attention, but when I remind him about the group he cheers up.

The children were also given the opportunity to discuss their views of the programme during the refreshment time immediately after the session each week. At first they were quite sceptical, and made comments about their parents' lack of involvement in their play: 'Everything is "in a minute", but she never comes 'cos she's always too busy.' Several children reported that their parents 'never play with us', but that they would 'always tell us what to do and shout at us'. One child reported that her mother was 'always in the kitchen or tidying up' and that she never had time to play ''cos she's always in a bad mood'. One boy said that his mum was always talking to her friends and that she was always too mad to play with him.

As the programme progressed, the comments changed, and the children began to look forward to their Thursday mornings playing with their parents: 'I love movement playing with my mum; she likes it now'; 'It's such a laugh. We always have fun together when we come, and I think it makes it better at home 'cos mum seems happier now she's coming to you'. One child reported that his mum '...doesn't shout at me so much now, especially when it's movement days.'

Although some of the children were too young or did not have the verbal communication skills to express their feelings, it was quite clear from the body language and movement seen in the video recordings of the group that there had been a significant positive shift in their levels of self-esteem, confidence and self-worth. During discussions, some children reported back that they felt their mothers loved them more now because they touched them more when they were playing:

> *My mum used to smack me all the time. She doesn't do it so much now. She used to shout all the time, but now it's calmer at home especially on Thursdays 'cos we come to group and can play together.*

One child said that he loved cuddling up to his mum in the group because his mum didn't push him away any more:

> *I like cuddling my mum in the group. She lets me wrap her up in the blanket and roll her, but at home she does not let me do anything 'cos she always sends me to my room when she's sad or mad at me.*

The parents all felt that the children looked forward to attending the group each week and that they had 'no problems in getting them up and ready for school on Thursdays' when it was the movement group. One mother said her child asked every day 'Is it the group today'? And was disappointed if the answer was no.

Case studies
These two case studies show the empowering effect that Developmental Movement Play can have on individual parents and their children.

Case Study 1
The cases of Sara and Milan illustrate the powerful effects the programme had on participants. At the start of the programme, Sara was trapped in a harsh, negative parenting style with her seven-year-old son, who was in the habit of seeking negative attention through frequent violent episodes of aggression and temper tantrums. Sara came to the group 'to help her son before it was too late and to stop him turning into a violent adult who would do something bad and end up in prison'. Sara suffered severe depression, and attending the group enabled her to continue parenting her two children adequately.

Due to the severe difficulties, depression and violence Sara had experienced during her pregnancy, by the time Milan was two years old there was a lack of attachment between them. She came to the movement group expressing a deep hatred for her son, saying that she could not bear to be near him and that she felt physically sick when he touched her or asked for a cuddle. She felt that she could no longer meet his emotional needs, and wanted him put into care. Milan liked dancing, so she joined the programme as a last attempt to try to work things out with him. Sara attended every session of the Developmental Movement Play programme, and reported at the end of the programme that it had been a lifeline to her without which she would not have been able to cope at all with her son's behaviour.

Milan, her son, was a small, watchful boy who demanded constant attention. He loved to dance, but at first his movements had a jerky, artificial unbounded quality, and he was unaware of his own safety or that of others. By Session 4, Milan had begun to understand the power of dance movement. That day, he came to the group feeling depressed because everything had gone wrong for him since he had got up in the morning. At the start of the session he said, 'I will dance myself happy today.' By the end of the session, he was clearly in a happier mood. Sadly, there was no response from his mother when it was clear that Milan was trying to encourage her to join him, as it took Sara a couple more sessions before she too understood it.

Sara, too, eventually realised something good was happening with her. In the beginning she had felt sceptical about the programme as it was different from anything she had previously experienced. Slowly, as the programme unfolded, she started to experience a feeling of warmth within the group, although at the end of the programme she continued to view the world outside the group as a cold place to be. She noticed that her movement range had increased, and that, while at first she had always needed to think hard and remember what she was supposed to be doing, by the end of the programme, she was beginning to enjoy the movement experiences without having to think so much about them. For the first time, she learned to relax and enjoy her son. Video observations showed that her movement quality had become softer, freer and her body less tense. In one video clip, she could be seen in what appeared to be an instinctive 'mother love' movement, gently guiding her son's body in towards her own in an attempt to cuddle him for the first time in many years. Milan responded to her touch and reciprocated the feeling expressed in the movement by shuffling close to her body and nestling under her arm towards her. From this position, their movements unfolded as they rocked gently side by side together enjoying the experience of the shared movements of a 'together' relationship, a deeply touching moment for everyone. They then moved to an upright position and danced around the room together holding hands until together they fell to the floor laughing in exhaustion. Their movements were centred, integrated, graceful and expressive. Their shared dance made a deep impression on the whole group as everyone felt that something special was happening. Her breathing had a deepened light quality and became integrated with her movements, which were showing the harmonious quality of being centred. She had learned to move from the centre of her body – the most difficult thing to learn in terms of movement (Sherborne, 1974).

This incident was the catalyst for change in Sara's state of mental health. Her mood changed, and she said she felt overwhelmed by her own inner warmth. She was tearful and her breathing heavy as she explained what had happened to her. She felt that she could begin to love her son and wanted to work towards repairing their damaged relationship. For the first time, she had naturally reached out to touch her son and had done so without feeling repulsed or physically sick. This defining moment was a significant turning point in Sara's life. She said:

> *I know I can love Milan now, and I am going to fight to keep him. I know it's going to be hard but I think I can do it. He's missed a lot, my boy, and most of it has been down to me.*

Through their taking part in Developmental Movement Play, the attachment relationship between mother and son had improved to such an extent that, by the end of the programme, both were able to touch each other safely and with love, and to play and show genuine pleasure in each other's close company. Showing Sara video recordings of their improving relationship helped her to realise that she could love her son. She no longer needed to take anti-depressants and felt much happier. Milan's behaviour also improved as he no longer demanded or craved attention from negative situations as his mother had more time for him.

After the programme, Milan frequently asked group facilitators to look out for his mother:

> *Mummy was crying again this morning. Can you talk to her when she comes in later? She's always better when she comes home after the movement group.*

He reported that:

> *She does not shout at me so much any more. Sometimes we talk now, and all my toys don't get taken out of my room anymore. I think she loves me again like she used to when I was a baby like Jo [his new brother]. I liked playing with my mum in your dance group – it was fun. When can I come again?*

Case Study 2

Tanya and her two children – an eight-year-old daughter and a five-year-old son, had been attending the Family Support Service for one year. At the beginning, she was sceptical about the value of the group, but was encouraged to attend by a friend who had previously taken part and credited the support of the group for helping her to achieve a high level of success in turning her life around for the better.

Tanya was experiencing difficult relationships with both her children. She was caught in the negative parent trap, and was continually smacking and 'grounding' her children in long time-out sessions. She was frightened that she 'might loose it one day and really hurt one of them'. She was being treated for depression, and felt and looked thoroughly fed up with life in general. By the end of the programme, Tanya understood the reasons for her children's aggressive, attention-seeking behaviour and worked hard to improve her attachment relationship with them. Tanya no longer smacks her children, as she has learned and uses many strategies to help deal with their and her own aggressive behaviour. Tanya is no longer depressed, has stopped taking anti-depressants, and appears to be more self-confident, reporting that:

> *When I first came, I could not talk in the group or join in with the movement. I just felt too embarrassed and self-conscious. I did not really want to come, but now I think the group is brilliant. It has changed my life. Don't get me wrong – we still have bad days, but I can handle them better now. I realise why my*

daughter is so aggressive, and I can listen to her and even touch her. I could not stand her anywhere near me before and would shout at her to go away. Since trying things out in the group, we talk, and I even ask her if she wants a cuddle now... I realise that a lot of the problems were down to me. I've changed a lot, and the group has really helped me to understand how to cope more. It's brilliant. I feel good about myself now, and I enjoyed playing with my child in the movement. I think every parent should come to a group like this because we all get problems, and it helps you deal with them without loosing it all the time.

Discussion

In the results above, general comments from participants illustrate the improvement in parenting skills, both child and adult behaviour, states of mental health and the attachment relationships between parents and children as a result of attending the Developmental Movement Play programme.

As a result of the experiences in the group, everyone learned to shift viewpoints, communicate across many levels of understanding, create transformations and new concepts, and learn to learn. Participants learned skills which would transfer into other areas of learning (Bateson, 1985). The effectiveness of this programme was due to the holistic practice of the movement methodology – a practice where the flexible orientation of the movement teacher enables her to move freely among participants, shifting position, levels and viewpoints while acting as a unifying agent, a catalyst in relation to others in order to facilitate change in relationships, behaviour and states of mental health.

Conclusion

This study suggests that the relationship between the parents and children involved, and consequently children's behaviour, improved as a result of taking part in movement experiences outlined in the Developmental Movement Play programme. The programme paid close attention to encouraging in the participants awareness of others, self, relationships, safety and emotional expression, all of which showed considerable improvement among the group and were valuable attributes that could be transferred into real life settings. Although it was not possible to ascertain if the changes reported by parents were long-term, as 10 weeks was insufficient time to ensure permanency, the parents involved believed that this programme was the vehicle for their positive engagement with their children. They all noticed changes at home, which suggested that the bonding reached further than the intervention. All the children's usual teachers reported a considerable improvement in the children's behaviours. The assessment results, too, related to positive changes in the adult–child relationship, mental health, attitude, behaviour, self-confidence and well-being of participants. The researcher believes that Developmental Movement Play should be adopted more widely to address issues related to the attachment relationship between parents and their children, particularly in relation to parenting skills.

The limitations of this study are more fully discussed elsewhere (Filer, 2006), and include participant group size, the recognition of long-term issues around sustainability

87

of improvement for the participants (e.g. training of facilitators), and participant effectiveness (e.g. the father–child and carer–'looked after' child bond), .

This study has demonstrated the potential of Developmental Movement Play for these parents and children coping with the difficult parent–child relationships often associated with emotional and behavioural difficulties. It has shown positive changes in children's behaviour, and concludes that this programme, with its high diversity of experiences, gives enormous scope for young children and their parents to develop alongside each other. The beauty of this intervention is that, once it has been learnt and barriers have been broken down in the safety of a supportive group, it can be sustained by parents and children in the home environment to continue to nurture their relationship.

References

Bateson, G. (1985) *Steps to an Ecology of Mind*. New York, NY: Ballantinc Books.

Department of Education and Science (1991) *National Curriculum Physical Education for Ages 5–6*. London: HMSO.

Eyberg, S. and Ross, A. (1978) 'Assessment of child behavior problems: the validation of a new inventory', *Journal of Clinical Child Psychology*, 7, 113–116.

Eyberg, S.M. and Pincus, D. (1999*). Eyberg Child Behavior Inventory and Sutter-Eyberg Student Behavior Inventory: Professional manual*. Odessa, FL: Psychological Assessment Resources.

Filer, J. (1994) 'Blanket play', *Nursery World,* 98 (3635), 22–23.

Filer, J. (2006) 'SDM and its role in family therapy'. In: C. Hill (2006) Communicating through Movement. Clent: Sunfield Publications.

Haley, J. (1955) 'Paradoxes in play, fantasy, and psychotherapy', *Psychiatric Research Reports (American Psychiatric Association)*, 2 (December), 52–58.

Hobday, A. and Ollier, K. (1998) *Creative Therapy: Activities with children and adolescents*. London: The British Psychological Society/Blackwell.

Meekums, B. and Payne, H. (1993) 'Emerging methodology in dance movement therapy research'. In: H. Payne (ed.) *Handbook of Inquiry in the Arts Therapies: One river, many currents*. London: Jessica Kingsley.

Sherborne, V. (1974) 'Utvikling av Kroppsbevissthet' ('Development at Kroppsbevissthet'), *Fysioterapeuten (Oslo)*, 41.

Sherborne, V. (2001*). Developmental Movement for Children: Mainstream, special needs and pre-school (2nd edn)*. London: Worth Publishing.

Thornton, S. (1971). A Movement Perspective of Rudolf Laban. London: MacDonald and Evans Ltd.

Webster-Stratton, C. (1985) *Dyadic Parent–Child Interaction Coding System – Revised (DPICS–R): Manual*. Seattle: School of Nursing, University of Washington.

Webster-Stratton, C. (1992) *The Parents and Children Videotape Series; Programmes 1–10*. Seattle, WA: Seth Enterprises.

CHAPTER 7

Quality Physical Education in the Early Years

The Influence of Sherborne Developmental Movement on Teacher Approach

Carrie Weston

To move, to run, to find things out by new movement, to feel one's life in every limb; that is the life of early childhood. (McMillan, 1930)

Focus of the research

Given the differing needs of children in the early years (aged 4–8 years), it was hypothesised that there would be a difference in the planning, teaching, aims and influential factors in Physical Education (PE) teaching between teachers trained specifically for early years and those trained in primary teaching and beyond. It was anticipated that teachers trained in Sherborne Developmental Movement (SDM) would have similar traits to those with early years training, regardless of their Initial Teacher Training (ITT) age range. This is because, as in all quality early years practice, SDM considers the needs of the individual within the group and begins with the abilities and experiences of the child (Bruce, 1991; Moyles, 1992; Nutbrown, 1994; Sherborne, 1992). The study also set out to explore differences in planning and teaching PE between teachers who were PE 'specialists' (i.e. those that had taken PE as their major subject in teacher training) and those who were SDM-trained. The hypothesis was that teachers trained in SDM would plan and teach PE to encourage individual development, enjoyment and exploration of physical learning while 'specialist' PE teachers would depend more on their subject knowledge leading to a greater emphasis on skill acquisition.

Introduction

The early years classroom

Any practitioner working with young children (aged 4–8 years) in schools will know that there exists a difference between the infant and junior years. Not only are there differences in the way that children experience learning, with the early years curriculum being more integrated, and having more opportunity for play- and exploratory-based learning, but also the school day is usually structured to reflect different needs of young children. In the early years, lunchtimes are earlier and last longer; children have an afternoon break; the classroom has a play area; and the school day often finishes earlier. Practice in the early years is not a diluted version of what is to come, but recognition of the affective and learning needs of younger children.

The Foundation Stage curriculum (Qualifications and Curriculum Authority, 2000), for children between the ages of three and five years, emphasises the need for learning to build on what children can do and to begin with what is familiar. In recognising that young children are naturally curious and eager to learn, play, talk, exploration and direct experience are valued within the curriculum. It is acknowledged that children learn best when they feel confident and secure, are surrounded by positive attitudes and have the freedom to make choices (Rodger, 1994). The Rumbold report (Department of Education and Science, 1990) identified that, in the early years, the context and process of learning is more important than prescribed content. This requires practitioners who understand how young children develop, who can observe and respond appropriately, and who can plan for individuals as well as groups.

The importance of Physical Education for young children

The world of the young child is a physical one as they use their body to explore, play, communicate and make sense of the world around them; the body is the young child's most valuable means of learning. It is, therefore, essential that children are able to capitalise on the movement abilities of their bodies.

The physical body is the most accessible means of communication and self-expression for babies and young children, providing a freedom not fully available yet through spoken or written words. PE is, arguably, the only area of the curriculum where this natural inclination to use the body can be fully explored and enhanced.

The need for 'physical literacy' (Whitehead, 2001) is paramount if we, as humans, are to interact fully and meaningfully with the world around us as embodied beings – and this is quite different from the ability to 'do' or 'perform' certain physical acts. Children move to learn, so capitalising on motile potential will not only enhance an embodied human existence, but expand learning opportunities for young children too. It is the physical *education* experiences of young children that will enable them to understand the physical and movement capacity of their bodies, thus providing for both learning and an embodied, physical, lifetime ahead.

The early years curriculum and quality in Physical Education

Any interrogation of teaching and learning in the early years will, inevitably, include reference to the theorists and early pioneers of practice such as Fröbel (1826), Pestalozzi (1894), McMillan (1930), Erikson (1950), Piaget (1953), Montessori (1967), Vygotsky (1978), Bruner (1986), and others. While this chapter has no room to analyse and synthesise these theories and practices, it is possible broadly to summarise that a quality early years curriculum is acknowledged to be child-centred, holistic, integrated, social, practical, rooted in the everyday lives of children and founded on the enjoyment and pleasure children derive from exploring and making sense of the world around them. This is, as it should be, reflected in the aims of the Foundation Curriculum (for children aged 3–5 years) which dovetails with Key Stage 1 (for children aged 5–7 years).

However, within accepted theories, there has, traditionally, also been an acceptance of Developmentally Appropriate Practice (DAP) within the early years curriculum, often derived from theorists such as Fröbel (1826), Freud (1926), Piaget (1953), Bruner

(1986) and others. DAP is based on the notion of definable stages of intellectual and physical development in children and is rooted in our educational system; it can be seen in the different stages of the National Curriculum, the testing of children and school transfer stages.

More recent critics, such as Corrie (1995), Dahlberg et al. (1999), and Yelland (2005), have questioned DAP from a postmodernist perspective. With origins in Western thinking, considering what is 'developmentally appropriate' for all individuals will potentially privilege certain ways of doing things and reduce individuality. In addition, by stating what is developmentally 'right', we create a binary opposite; that which is developmentally inappropriate or abnormal. In this way, DAP, embedded in our educational system, fails to reflect the modern, complex and diverse lifeworlds of children in our society. Furthermore 'child-centredness' in a curriculum dominated by cultural and historical practices can assume things about children and childhood (Corrie, 1995) that exclude other possibilities.

In recent years, schools, teachers, children and parents have seen teaching and learning influenced by the arrival of new initiatives, from the National Curriculum through to the Literacy hour and Numeracy strategy. More recently, we have seen a focus on children's health and fitness through both interest in what children eat and what they do. As a result, a spotlight has fallen on PE, as this represents to most people the part of the curriculum where children's activity and fitness might be addressed. However, universal assumptions about what children should be doing physically are dangerous. They ignore the diversity and complexity of childhood experiences, inscribe the physical body with social value and meaning (Evans, 2004) and make PE a form of compensatory education with an end product deeply embedded in a modern and culturally influenced view of the 'healthy child'.

When we consider what constitutes 'quality' in early years PE, it is useful to reflect on Dahlberg et al.'s (1999) critique of DAP and child-centredness: that it is dominated by a small group of experts at the exclusion of a wider range of other stakeholders. What is argued for is a *real* child-centred curriculum which embraces multiple perspectives and is contextualised, spatially and temporally, to be able to recognise all forms of diversity.

Can Sherborne Developmental Movement provide a model of quality Physical Education in the early years?

Taking what we know to be effective in early years teaching and learning from established theorists, pioneers of practice and the Qualifications and Curriculum Authority (QCA), adding to that acknowledgement of contemporary critiques of child-centredness and DAP, together with an acknowledgement of the primacy of movement experiences for young children, then it is possible to see where the current PE curriculum is largely misplaced in the early years. An emphasis on fitness and health, physical skill and competition even between the ages of 5 and 7 years (Key Stage 1/P1–3 in Scotland), coupled with the Physical Education, School Sport and Club Links (PESSCL) initiative and its inclinations towards school sports and games, are strong forces pushing PE for young children away from the very roots of quality early years pedagogy.

Table 7.1. Considerations for quality Physical Education in the early years

	Quality early years practice	Games and skill development	Sherborne Developmental Movement
Class-based practice	Integrated curriculum, related to the real lives and experiences of children. Begins with what the child is able to do, and positively develops through increasing confidence and ability. Focuses on holistic development: the social as well as academic. Opportunities for exploration and self-expression in a supportive environment.	Current curriculum emphasises games, gymnastics, dance and knowledge of health and fitness. Emphasis on skill development, rules, competition, performance and limited creativity. Preparation for later games-dominated curriculum.	Focus on the individual child within the social context to develop physical knowledge of self and self in relation to others. Physical self-expression, self-esteem and self-confidence nurtured to enable children to be comfortable within their own bodies.
Review of DAP	Curriculum appropriate to traditionally understood developmental needs of children. Danger of excluding other possibilities through accepting dominant culture and ways of being.	Activities and skills rooted in traditional and culturally embedded games and sports. Privileges children with access to and experience of such activities.	Emphasis on child's growth of knowledge and confidence in relation to their own body and the experience of movement in relation to others. Culture-free and responsive to the needs of children.
PE Curriculum	A widening remit. Concerned with promoting health and fitness in children and encouraging activity. Children must be confident in their physical and motile capacities before this can be achieved.	Focus, derived from financial input, on clubs and specific sports working in partnership with schools. Some curriculum room for dance and movement, but greatly reduced emphasis. Team membership, rule following, games strategies and skill development emphasised in 'mini' versions of many popular sports and games.	Through nurturing confidence in and understanding of one's own body, SDM provides a foundation on which children build other physical skills and develop physical knowledge more meaningfully. Emphasis is on bodily knowledge and confidence, relationship-building and the quality of movement, to build a 'physical vocabulary'.

As a model of a quality PE approach in the early years, SDM appears to have a great deal to offer. The definition of the word, 'developmental', differs from that used in DAP. The emphasis of SDM is on movement, with the 'developmental' aspect being the evolving understanding of self and others through movement, rather than a linear progression of movement achievement or capability. To facilitate this, SDM requires the teacher to have an understanding of the child's current physical, social and psychological state and knowledge of appropriate positive experiences necessary for the child to grow and develop physical and social competence with confidence. Through this different understanding of the term, 'developmental' – as personal evolution – it is possible to embrace individuality while maintaining the collective context of learning and experience.

The philosophy of SDM has been explored in an earlier chapter, but it can be summarised as initiated and supported social, physical and psychological experiences to enable children to explore, understand and extend their physical capabilities in the social and physical world around them. The emphasis is on learning through exploration, curiosity, creativity, a sense of fun and using physical and relational interaction in order to gain a wider vocabulary of physical self-knowledge and to enhance self-esteem and physical self-worth through positive experience. It is hard to see how this could be better suited to the early years pedagogy!

Yet academic or theoretical fit is not enough. While it makes intuitive sense that SDM *per se* is a valuable model for PE in the early years, Hill (2006) postulates that the teaching style, method of delivery and the planning methods of those teachers trained in SDM take on a particular hue. She highlights the following traits adopted by such teachers:

- *Child-centredness*: the lessons planned do not contain prescribed skill acquisition coaching

- *Flexibility*: teachers actively encourage exploration and set 'open' movement tasks

- *Inclusiveness*: due to enhanced observation skills, teachers can plan differentiated lessons which include all children in the class

- *Sharing*: teachers and children are equally valued by each other, and often traditional roles are reversed, and children take on 'care/trust responsibility' for the adults

- *Creativity*: children are given confidence to explore, to initiate, to problem- solve

- *Positivity*: teachers plan the session so that children can be successful in responding to the tasks and be applauded for the effort that they show

- *Sense of fun*: the ability and enjoyment of play and laughter is positively encouraged.

Sherborne (2001) was convinced that the relationship between the children and the teacher was of paramount importance in enabling children to feel safe, motivated and confident. She placed equal importance on planning and on the adoption of the appropriate teaching style:

The movement lesson should be carefully planned. An experienced teacher will be able to see if the activities planned are appropriate and will be able to adjust accordingly. A teacher who is skilled in movement observation can have a flexible approach to the plan and will develop activities which the children discover for themselves. (Sherborne, 2001, p. 83)

Methodology

A comprehensive questionnaire was developed through a study of PE curriculum guidelines and current documents, and pilot interviews were carried out with teachers about the factors that influenced them in their PE planning and teaching. A pilot study was conducted with follow-up interviews, and the questionnaire modified in response. The final, detailed questionnaire was sent to 196 schools throughout the UK, which had been selected through professional recommendation. Of these questionnaires, 138 were returned (70% return rate), and 131 were used to compile the data. Seven were unable to be included within the data because either the teacher was not involved in planning or teaching PE, or the respondent was not a qualified teacher on the school staff.

The aim of the questionnaire was to capture a detailed and comprehensive picture of the way that teachers planned and taught primary PE and to interrogate the factors that influenced their planning. Teachers responded to a range of questions in sections relating to PE planning, long- and short-term aims, PE teaching and practice, the place of PE within the curriculum and their personal reflections on PE. They were asked to select the most apt from a list of possible answers, and their primary responses are the focus for analysis in this chapter. Following the collation of data from the questionnaires, some follow-up interviews were arranged with a cross-section of teachers from the study in order to investigate areas in greater depth.

To analyse the data, the respondents were placed into different groups. For the majority of the analysis, comparison was drawn between qualified teachers with early years specialism and no SDM training (EY no SDM), qualified teachers specialising in the primary years and beyond with no SDM training (Non-EY no SDM) and qualified teachers with SDM training regardless of the age-range they were trained to teach (SDM) (see Table 7.2a).

In some cases, in order to look at whether subject knowledge of PE produces the same effect as being trained in SDM, comparison was drawn between teachers with no specialist PE training (No PE), teachers with specialist PE training other than SDM (PE) and teachers trained in SDM. In a very small number of cases, teachers were both PE specialists and SDM-trained. The numbers are indicated in Table 7.2b. Following the pilot study, it was decided that in these cases the teacher would be placed in the SDM category. This is because the individual felt that SDM training had had a far greater influence on planning and teaching than other PE training, and this is reflected in the responses of this small group of teachers.

Table 7.2a. Breakdown of respondents with/without Sherborne Developmental Movement training

SDM training	Frequency
Early Years with no SDM (EY no SDM)	42
Non-Early Years with no SDM (non-EY no SDM)	51
SDM-trained (SDM)	38
Total	131

Table 7.2b. Breakdown of respondents with/without a specialism in Physical Education

PE training	Frequency
No PE specialism	76
PE specialists	17
SDM-trained	38
Total	131

Results

Influences on planning

The question, 'What influences your planning of PE most?', produced stark differences between the respondents grouped in Table 7.2a: EY no SDM; Non-EY no SDM; and SDM.

Figure 7.1 Influences on planning

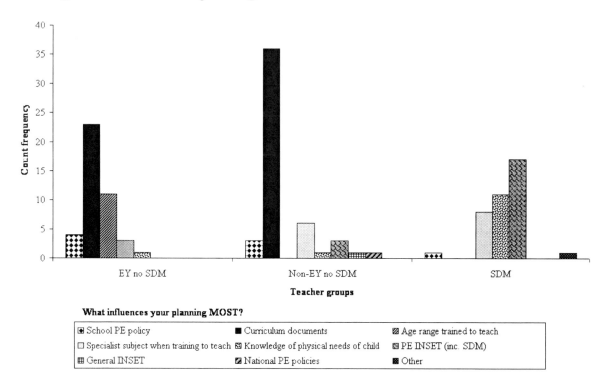

What influences your planning MOST?

⊞ School PE policy	■ Curriculum documents	▨ Age range trained to teach
☐ Specialist subject when training to teach	⊠ Knowledge of physical needs of child	▨ PE INSET (inc. SDM)
⊞ General INSET	▨ National PE policies	▨ Other

The National Curriculum (Department for Education and Employment (DfEE)/QCA, 1999) was, substantially, the strongest influence among non-EY no SDM teachers. It was also the strongest influence among EY no SDM teachers. The National Curriculum did not feature at all as the most important influence when planning PE among teachers who were SDM-trained. Rather, the SDM training itself (PE in-servicetraining) and knowledge of the physical needs of the child were the most influential factors.

All teachers have a specialist subject when training to teach, and this is usually a curriculum area or, in the case of some early years teachers, may be the specialist age range. The specialist area was a greater influence among SDM-trained teachers than the other groups. This corresponded with a stronger tendency among SDM-trained teachers to plan cross-curricular teaching and to use PE as a means of exploring other curriculum areas.

Teachers trained in the early years stated that they were influenced by their training for this particular age-range. The influence of the age-range which respondents were trained to teach was evident *only* in the planning of EY no SDM teachers, and indicated that the needs of younger children are of particular concern to early years teachers in their planning.

Figure 7.2. Long-term planning aims

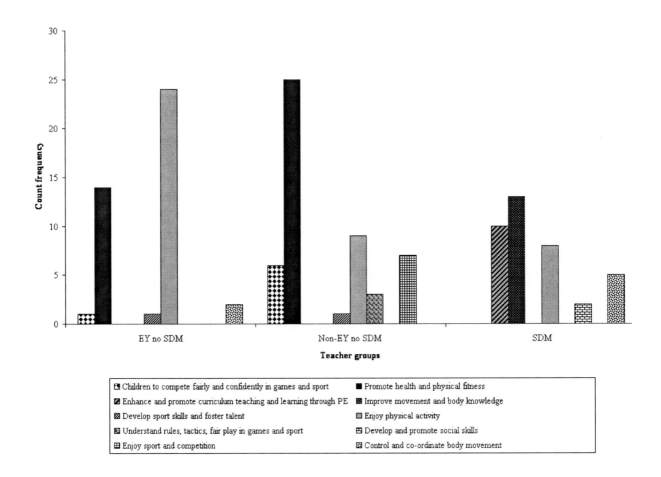

Aims of long-term planning

In terms of the main aim of long-term planning in PE, there are, again, some marked differences between the three groups of teachers.

The promotion of health and physical fitness was the leading aim on the non-EY no SDM group. It also featured strongly as the leading aim in the EY no SDM group. It did not feature at all as a leading aim in the long-term planning of teachers with SDM training. These findings were supported by the in-depth, follow-up interviews. All teachers interviewed were aware of the current climate of concern over the fitness and health of children, and understood that PE was targeted as a means of addressing this issue. However, while non-SDM-trained teachers named health and fitness as a priority in their planning, those trained in SDM expressed confidence that, as a by-product of becoming more physically confident and physically aware, children who had good experience of SDM would develop the *ability* to engage in activities promoting health and fitness.

EY no SDM teachers responded most strongly that 'Enjoyment of PE' was the most important, long-term aim in their planning. While 'Enjoyment of PE' was also a strong (although not the strongest) response from both non-EY no SDM and SDM-trained teachers, the reasons for this given in interviews varied. SDM teachers felt that enjoyment was derived from physical self-confidence, expression and exploration, so these were the long-term aims of planning, while non-EY teachers felt that PE should not be equated with 'play', and therefore the emphasis on 'fun' was underplayed.

Non-EY no SDM teachers were more likely to state their most important long-term aim was for children to develop an understanding of rules, tactics and sportsmanship, and to have a far greater emphasis on sport and competition than any other group. SDM teachers were more likely to state their most important long-term aim was for PE to enhance and support learning in other curriculum areas.

Confidence in teaching Physical Education

Using the groupings for Table 7.2a, teachers trained in SDM expressed far more confidence in the teaching of PE. EY teachers were more likely to state they were less confident teaching PE than other curriculum areas.

It might be argued that any PE training will increase confidence in teaching the subject, so this data can also be analysed using the groupings for Table 7.2b, showing the differences in teaching PE confidence between EY no PE, non-EY no PE, PE and SDM teachers. The numbers in Groups 2 and 3 are not even when the analysis is done this way, so there is no significant difference in confidence between teachers with specific PE training and SDM-trained teachers, as might be expected.

However, when this is looked at in terms of how often PE lessons meet the needs of all children in the class, then a different picture emerges showing a significant difference.

Table 7.3a. How confident are you when teaching Physical Education?

How confident are you when teaching PE?	EY no SDM	Non-EY no SDM	SDM	Total
Not very confident	2	2	0	4
Less confident than in other areas of the curriculum	21	9	0	30
Just as confident as in other areas of the curriculum	14	13	0	27
More confident than in other curriculum areas	5	12	19	36
Most confident when teaching PE	0	15	19	34
Total	42	51	38	131

Table 7.3b. ANOVA: How confident are you when teaching Physical Education?

	Sum of squares	D.f.[1]	Mean square	F	Sig.
Between groups	78.262	2	39.131	47.037	.000
Within groups	106.486	128	.832	–	–
Total	184.748	130	–	–	–

Inclusion and Physical Education

Although PE specialist teachers were highly confident in their teaching of PE, they felt less likely to meet the needs of all children in the class during their PE lessons compared with SDM teachers.

Table 7.4a is perhaps the most crucial of all. The need to be 'inclusive' is very much a part of teaching and curriculum documents today. PE is, arguably, the most difficult curriculum area for teachers when considering inclusion, as activity must be free from barriers to full participation including physical needs, behaviour, varying ability levels, cultural and gender differences and preferences. The confidence to meet the

Table 7.3c. How confident are you when teaching Physical Education?

How confident are you when teaching PE?	EY no PE (1)	PE-trained (2)	SDM-trained (3)	Non-EY no PE (4)	Total
Not very confident	2	0	0	2	4
Less confident than in other areas of the curriculum	21	0	0	9	30
Just as confident as in other areas of the curriculum	14	1	0	12	37
More confident than in other curriculum areas	5	4	19	8	36
Most confident when teaching PE	0	12	19	3	34
Total	**42**	**17**	**38**	**34**	**131**

Table 7.4a. How often do Physical Education lessons meet the needs of all the children in the class?

How often do PE lessons meet the needs of all the children in the class?	EY no PE (1)	PE-trained (2)	SDM-trained (3)	Non-EY no PE (4)	Total
Never	1	0	0	3	4
Often	1	0	0	0	1
Sometimes	17	0	2	10	29
Mostly	22	13	7	18	60
Always	1	4	29	3	37
Total	**42**	**17**	**38**	**34**	**131**

Table 7.4b. Test statistics

	How often does PE lesson meet all needs?	PE/non-PE/SDM-trained
Chi-square (a,b)	91.405	11.076
D.f.	4	3
Asymp. sig.	.000	.011

a 0 cells (.0%) have expected frequencies less than 5; the minimum expected cell frequency is 26.2.
b 0 cells (.0%) have expected frequencies less than 5; the minimum expected cell frequency is 32.8.

needs of all pupils existed most strongly within the SDM category. Twenty-nine (76%) teachers trained in SDM reported that they *always* met the needs of all children in their class during PE lessons. This compared with four (24%) PE specialists, one (2%) EY teacher with no SDM/PE and three (9%) non-EY teachers with no SDM/PE. The confidence of SDM teachers was comparable with that of PE specialists, but the confidence to meet the *needs* of *all* children was significantly higher for those trained in SDM.

Assessing children in Physical Education
If many teachers, particularly EY trained teachers, lack confidence in their PE teaching, then it is important to know what teachers feel is important for children to have achieved. Comparing the groups from Table 7.2a, as before, is useful here. Teachers with PE training (both SDM and otherwise) ranked themselves as 'confident' or 'most confident' when teaching PE. However, there was little similarity in what they were looking for when assessing children in PE.

The ability of a child to express themselves physically was the most important consideration in the SDM teacher category. This featured in the responses of a small number of respondents in the EY no SDM category and an even smaller number in the non-EY no SDM category. The ability of the child to perform skills taught was the most prominent response in the non-EY no SDM category and was virtually the joint top response in the EY no SDM category. It did not feature as a response by SDM teachers. The enjoyment of physical activity was a strongly chosen response in all categories, while the ability to use different parts of the body featured only in the SDM category.

Discussion
It is perhaps not surprising that teachers who have been trained in SDM use the associated principles and philosophies in their planning, teaching and attitudes towards PE. However, the significance of the differences recorded are substantial and reveal that teachers trained in SDM have a confidence in their PE planning and teaching that

Figure 7.3 What do you look for when assessing children in Physical Education?

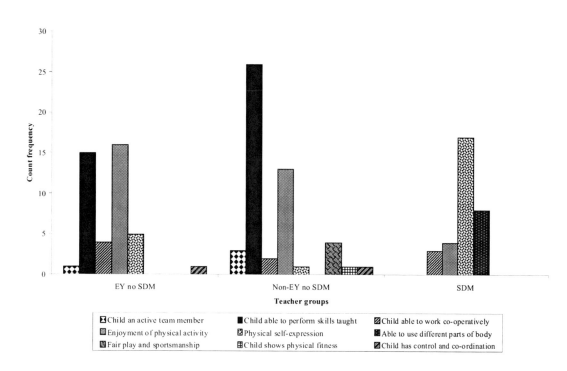

liberates them from the dilemmas that appear to be pulling other teachers away from a coherent and relevant pedagogy, particularly in the early years. These dilemmas derive from often conflicting foci, such as: concerns with child health and obesity; generating links to clubs and sports; the development and fostering of talent; the requirement to offer two hours of PE through extracurricular activity; etc. It is the *nature* of what teachers with SDM knowledge are doing in PE that is of most interest to the development of quality PE for young children.

The SDM-trained teachers were the least likely to identify curriculum guidelines as their most important consideration when planing and teaching PE. The evidence of this research indicates that SDM teachers were using their understanding of children, through both the age-range they were trained to teach and their knowledge of child development (in the sense defined above), as the most important factor in planning lessons and setting long-term aims in PE. Early years teachers were also less reliant on curriculum guidelines as the most important factor than non-early years teachers, and were most likely to be influenced by their training for this age range. Curriculum guidelines are, by their very nature, concerned with content rather than pedagogy. The fact that SDM- and early years-trained teachers are less reliant on curriculum guidelines could suggest that the nature of the teaching, rather than what is being taught, is the greater concern.

The concern with health and fitness in children was evident as the most important consideration in non-SDM teachers' planning, but was not the most important factor in those trained in SDM. Follow-up interviews with a representative sample from the group of respondents indicated that non-SDM teachers prioritised health and fitness in PE because of the current pressing public concern, elements of curriculum documents, and initiatives such as PESSCL. However, the lesser confidence in teaching PE of non-SDM teachers may indicate that this concern was not based on a strong understanding of how to address issues of health and fitness through PE. This trait was strongest in non-early years teachers. When the reliance on curriculum documents, concern with the health and fitness of children, and PESSCL strategy are considered, the dominant position of skill-specific games is not surprising. Neither is the research outcome, as it has long been recognised that games and sports dominate the PE curriculum, particularly as children get older (Kirk, 2004). However, such a PE curriculum does not resonate well with a quality early years pedagogy where the individual needs of the child within a group context and activities linked to the world of the child should have primacy.

In terms of how teachers judged achievement in PE, SDM teachers were primarily concerned with the child's ability to express themselves physically, enjoy PE and use different parts of the body, cited by individual teachers as the most important elements to assess. Among early years teachers, the ability to perform taught skills and enjoyment of PE were chosen most frequently as assessment priorities, while among non-early years teachers the most looked-for element was performance of taught skills, with enjoyment of PE being cited next frequently. Physical expression registered as the most important feature of assessment among early years teachers, but not among non-early years teachers.

Quality teaching in the early years should foster creativity. Traditionally, most competences are measured through logic and linguistic ability (Gardner, 1983), yet this is not always present to be seen in young children nor necessarily appropriate in older children. The emphasis on physical expression given in PE assessment by SDM teachers, and also evident in the responses of early years teachers, presents the opportunity for children to learn and succeed in holistic, child-centred and non-traditional ways. When children are judged against set criteria, such as in relation to skills taught, then possibilities are narrowed. Ability should not be a fixed and predetermined property in the world of early childhood, as belief about ability can have a profound effect on ability itself (Bandura, 1973). The focus for young children should be on what the child can do, not on what they fail to achieve.

Quality early years teaching should be inclusive of the needs of all individuals to allow for personal growth and development. The data reveals that many teachers who are not SDM-trained, as well as being less confident with PE teaching, felt that PE lessons largely failed to meet the needs of all children in the class. Even the PE specialists, who were even more likely to suggest that planning and teaching specific sport skills and rules was their most important aim, although they did so with confidence, acknowledged difficulties in meeting the needs of all children in PE lessons. SDM teachers, with greater confidence in their teaching and less emphasis on specific sport skills, were more likely to state they were meeting the needs of all children in PE lessons. It could be argued that, if all children are included and involved in PE lessons, then benefits to the health and fitness of children are greater than in lessons where some children are not included.

All teachers ranked 'Enjoyment of physical activity' as an important consideration, although early years teachers were the most likely to state this as the most important factor. Given what is understood about the importance of intrinsic motivation, exploration and a child-centred approach in early years pedagogy, it follows that early years teachers should place importance on the enjoyment of physical activity in their PE lessons and planning. However, when this is juxtaposed with a relative lack of confidence in teaching PE, an inclination to be strongly influenced by curriculum guidance and current public concerns, and an acknowledgement of the difficulties of meeting the needs of all children, then it cannot be assumed that 'enjoyment of physical activity' is an outcome of PE lessons.

SDM-trained teachers, with their focus on developing movement and bodily confidence in children, and their concern with the inclusion of all individuals, appear better positioned to fulfil the criteria for 'enjoyment'. Where the focus is on the child's mastery and understanding of their own body and motile capabilities through physical exploration, then as the child grows in physical confidence and relating to others, so enjoyment and pleasure in competence is more likely. A pedagogy based on exploration and interaction with peers goes hand-in-hand with quality early years provision.

In this research, teachers trained in SDM appeared to plan and teach PE differently. In particular, the concern that PE should be relevant to other parts of the curriculum was a feature seen only in the responses of SDM-trained teachers. For these teachers, this placed PE as part of a holistic curriculum rather than being compartmentalised into an isolated area. As suggested above, the world of young children is a physical one, as they move to learn and explore and understand the world around them. A view of PE that is related to learning in other areas capitalises on the young child's innate use of physical movement to explore and learn. The SDM teachers in this study were concerned in their assessment that children were able to use the different parts of their bodies as tools and vehicles for learning. The ability to use the body with confidence and in a multitude of ways must surely be a vital asset.

Limitations of the study

It is acknowledged that the study carried out has some limitations. The population sample was necessarily purposive to allow as broad a catchment of participants as possible and a valid quantity of responses from SDM-trained teachers for comparison with those from non-SDM-trained teachers. The percentage of SDM-trained teachers in this research is therefore disproportionate in terms of the national teacher population. In the absence of a randomised sample, the outcomes from this study cannot be generalised. However, trends in the research have been identified, and can form the basis for further research.

Although a pilot study was carried out, and many issues concerning the questions were revealed and clarified at this point, areas for further clarification became apparent as the data was analysed. For example, answers relating to 'child development' may have carried a different meaning for teachers not trained in SDM. It is noted that non-SDM-trained teachers did not choose this as a response.

Conclusion

The Plowden Report opens with the statement:

> *At the heart of the education process lies the child.* (Central Advisory Council for Education, 1967)

The tendency among teachers not trained in SDM to rely on curriculum documents in the planning and teaching of PE seems to place the prescribed curriculum at the centre of the education process. Further concerns with fitness, participation in activities, and obesity move the focus of learning away from the child and the world of childhood, and place it within a framework of desirable outcomes which bear little relation to the pedagogy of the early years. David (2001) suggests that learning through supported exploration and play is probably the most effective mode for young children, yet a focus on teaching specific skills is counter to this understanding of effective learning in young children.

The evidence presented through this study suggests that, among this research population, SDM supported and enhanced teaching and learning in the early years by focusing on the child's exploration of movement, space and social relationships to develop physical confidence and understanding of the world around them. The pedagogy of the early years, with the child at the heart of a process which encourages explorative, active learning, needs to liberate children to be confident and comfortable with physical movement and expression (Abbott and Rodger, 1994). A focus on skills specific to prescribed activity may actually limit the potential of children to use their bodies as an integrated, explorative vehicle for learning about and making sense of the world and social interaction.

Physical learning is an integral part of the early years classroom where children engage in activities designed to enhance understanding and develop knowledge. PE is the only area of the curriculum *specifically* concerned with the development of the physical, and it is essential that the purpose therefore is to maximise the child's experience and knowledge of physical movement within their world. An understanding of the self as a physical, motile being in a social, interactive world is to develop 'physical literacy' (Whitehead, 2001). This is not to deny children the right to learn specific physical skills in order to participate in games and sport for pleasure and health, but to provide a better, wider, more inclusive foundation from which to do so.

Liberation from the experience of body-as-an-object (Whitehead, 2004) is to enable children to feel comfortable within their own bodies and confident in what they can do. Sherborne (2001) believed that children learn through and with each other: a belief evident in the active early years classroom where children are rarely seen engaged in silent, solitary learning. It makes intuitive sense that children who are physically literate and comfortable with physical and social interaction will learn with and through each other more effectively. Therefore PE in the early years must place the child and not the curriculum at the heart of the process in order to both support and capitalise on the active, explorative, holistic learning of young children. It is suggested here, through the trend found in this study, that SDM may encapsulate these ideals.

The next step

Although teachers trained in SDM are enthusiastic practitioners of the associated principles and purpose, there appears to be little knowledge or understanding about SDM within the wider profession. Given the current thrust in PE towards activity through links with clubs, community sports and out-of-school provision, and the increasing concern with children's fitness, there is a very real danger that the curriculum may contain scant opportunity for children to become knowledgeable about and confident in the motile capabilities of their bodies before focusing on the development of specific skills related to games and sports. Unless the importance of movement in the world of young children is given greater emphasis, then the current initiatives in PE are unlikely to be inclusively successful. When a close fit between quality early years pedagogy and the principles of SDM are so evident, it is time to let others know.

References

Abbott, L. and Rodger, R. (eds) *Quality Education in the Early Years.* Buckingham: Open University Press.

Bandura, A. (1977) *Social Learning Theory.* New York, NY: General Learning Press.

Bruce, T. (1991) *Time to Play in Early Childhood Education.* Sevenoaks: Hodder and Stoughton.

Bruner, J.S. (1986) *Actual Minds, Possible Worlds.* Cambridge, MA: Harvard University Press.

Central Advisory Council for Education (1967) *Children and their Primary Schools* ('The Plowden Report'). London: HMSO.

Corrie, L. (1995) 'Vertical integration: teacher's knowledge and teacher's voice', *Australian Journal of Early Childhood,* 20 (3), 1–5.

Dahlberg, G., Moss, P. and Pence, A. (1999) *Beyond Quality in Early Childhood Education and Care.* London: RoutledgeFalmer.

David, T. (2001) 'Curriculum in the early years'. In: G. Pugh (ed.) (2001) *Contemporary Issues in the Early Years (3rd edn).* London: Paul Chapman.

Department for Education and Employment/Qualifications and Curriculum Authority (1999) *The National Curriculum Handbook for Primary Teachers in England Key Stages 1 and 2.* London: DfEE/QCA.

Department of Education and Science (1990) *Starting with Quality: Report of the committee of inquiry into the quality of the educational experience offered to three and four year olds, chaired by Angela Rumbold.* London: HMSO.

Erikson, E. (1950) *Childhood and Society.* New York, NY: W.W. Norton.

Evans, J. (2004) 'Making a difference?: education and "ability" in physical education', *European Physical Education Review,* 10 (1), 95–108.

Freud, S. (1926) *The Question of Lay Analysis.* London: Hogarth Press (1959 edn).

Fröbel, F. (1826) *On the Education of Man (Die Menschenerziehung).* Keilhau/Leipzig, Germany: Wienbrach.

Gardner, H. (1983) *Frames of Mind: The theory of multiple intelligences.* New York: Basic Books.

Hill, C. (2006) *Communicating through Movement: Sherborne Developmental Movement – towards a broadening perspective.* Clent: Sunfield Publications.

Kirk, D. (2004) 'Framing quality physical education: the elite sport model or sport education?', *Physical Education and Sport Pedagogy,* 9 (2), 185–195.

McMillan, M. (1930) *The Nursery School (revised edn)*. London: J.M Dent.

Montessori, M. (1949) *The Absorbent Mind*. New York, NY: Dell (1967 edn).

Moyles, J.R. (1992) *Organising for Learning in the Primary Classroom*. Buckingham: Open University Press.

Nutbrown, C. (1994) *Threads of Thinking*. London: Paul Chapman.

Pestalozzi, J.H. (1894) *How Gertrude Teaches her Children*. London: Swan Sonnenschein.

Piaget, J. (1953) *The Origin of Intelligence in the Child*. London: Routledge and Keegan Paul.

Qualifications and Curriculum Authority (2000) *Curriculum Guidance for the Foundation Stage* London: QCA/DfEE.

Rodger, R. (1994) 'A quality curriculum in the early years'. In: L. Abbott and R. Rodger (eds) *Quality Education in the Early Years*. Buckingham: Open University Press.

Sherborne, V (2001) *Developmental Movement for Children: Mainstream, special needs and pre-school (2nd edn)*. London: Worth Publishing.

Vygotsky, L.S. (1978) *Mind in Society*. Cambridge, MA: Harvard University Press.

Whitehead, M. (2001) 'The concept of physical literacy', *European Journal of Physical Education*, 6, 127–138.

Whitehead, M. (2004) 'Physical literacy: a debate'. Paper presented to the Pre-Olympic Congress, Thessaloniki, Greece (August).

Yelland, N. (2005) *Critical Issues in Early Childhood Education*. Berkshire: Open University Press.

Endnote

[1] The statistical abbreviations used in this chapter represent the following: Sig.– significance; D.f. – degrees of freedom; F – frequency; Asymp. sig. – asyntotic significance.

CHAPTER 8

Developing Understanding

Sherborne Developmental Movement, Gymnastics and Mainstream School Teaching

John Dibbo

This chapter identifies some positive links between Sherborne Developmental Movement (SDM) and the teaching of gymnastics in primary schools. The research project was concerned with the movement dimension of Physical Education (PE) and how children develop an understanding of movement in the collaborative and dynamic social environment of the PE lesson. Implicit within this argument is that understanding is enhanced by not only doing movement, but also by talking about movement and movement experiences. This leads to the suggestion that for PE to be educational, children need to understand what they are doing, how they are doing things and why they are doing them.

Research question

The overall question was to explore '*What happens in school PE lessons* from the point of view of the participants?' (Hammersley, 1993; my italics) by asking the children about their experiences, and observing them in action.

The aims of the study were:

- To examine the use of language by children and the teacher in PE lessons

- To identify any significant patterns in the language used by the teacher and the children

- To search for evidence of the children understanding movement through their physical actions and their use of language

- To search for links between gymnastics teaching, SDM and understanding.

Introduction

The context – gymnastics in the primary school

Gymnastics focuses on the body, and aims, in particular, to develop body management and body awareness. It is concerned with movement skill in terms of precision of movement and form. With young children, the focus on body management should allow them to discover ways of moving appropriately and becoming aware of their own capabilities and limitations. As children gain experience, demands in terms of control, finish and precision of movement can be increased (Williams, 1997). Children also bring with them to school a rich vocabulary, emanating from the vast range of experience of moving to learn and learning to move that permeated infancy and the pre-school years (Maude, 1997). At times, children work alone, in pairs and in larger groups where communication skills and the ability to work effectively with others are important.

The place of Sherborne Developmental Movement

The physical dimensions of SDM that link effectively with gymnastics are where children are encouraged to explore strength and stability, tension and relaxation and a large variety of movement experiences in individual activities and relationship play. A social constructivist approach to teaching and learning (Barnes, 1989; Bruner, 1966a,b, 1971; Hoyles, 1989; von Glasersfeld, 1989; Vygotsky, 1962; Wood, 1989) in SDM can give confidence to the individual, develop confidence in others, inspire trust, explore partnership work and provide a framework for quality (Sherborne, 2001). Learning in this way has the potential to give the children pleasure, early success and confidence. SDM does not replace existing gymnastic teaching methods, but the ideas and methods adapted from SDM contribute to the development of gymnastic competence (Maude, 2001; Maude et al., 2000; Williams, 1997). A brief illustration of some of the teaching follows.

Exploring rolling through Sherborne Developmental Movement

A number of SDM activities can contribute to the development of confidence and competence in both forward and backward rolling.

'Rowing boat' or 'See-saw' type activities (see Sherborne, 2001), with two children facing each other, holding hands, sitting and standing in turn with partner support or rocking forwards and backwards, give the children confidence in knowing the space behind them for the start of the backward roll and developing a sense of the ending of the forward roll.

'Parcels' is a simple activity where a child curls up to make a parcel or package. Partners can test each other's strength in maintaining this tight, curled shape by trying to undo the parcel. This tight, curled shape is the central part of forward and backward rolls, and practice at this activity helps children maintain their shape and tension in rolling.

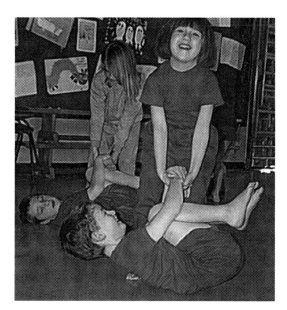

Using the 'Rock' with one partner making a hands and knees 'rock' shape, the other partner can slowly rest their weight on the 'rock', place their hands on the floor and, working together with their partner, can control a safe and gentle forward roll (Sherborne, 2001).

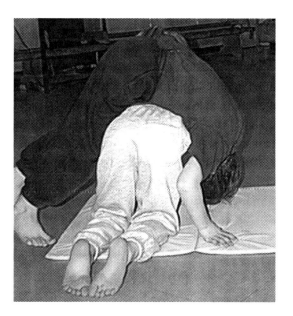

Theoretical position

PE is more than just physical, it is cognitive, affective and located within the midst of a socio-cultural canvas (Nias and Groundwater-Smith, 1992) having the potential to meet the needs of the whole child (Dibbo and Gerry, 1995a). Furthermore, to learn the learner should have access to the concepts, ideas, understandings and theories that give meaning to particular domains of knowledge, in this case PE. For this process to be successful, direct intervention by the teacher is needed with the intervention contingent (Wood, 1989) on the needs of the learner in all respects.

As knowledge is structured (Piaget, 1967), so should learning be structured. The teacher should ensure that the learning environment is appropriate to the activities and tasks intended, and that opportunities for interaction and appropriate communication are created. The teacher should establish the relevant conditions to give children access to the community of practice (Lave and Wenger, 1991) that is PE, where the learner can draw on their previous experience. The learners should be taught, but also have the opportunity to explore the learning environment. As they are taught, they should be guided by the teacher contingently, either directly or through appropriate problem-solving activities, alone or in groups. In this way, the teacher of PE structures the task and the environment for effective learning, but also ensures the children have the means to communicate. They can talk about what they are doing in language belonging to an appropriate community of discourse (Mercer, 2000) where:

> *...activities are based on foundations of past shared experience, common interests and language-based ways of thinking together.* (p. 169)

Social constructivism encompasses all the issues of constructivist thinking, but emphasises the social nature of learning based on two main premises:

- Language plays a vital role in cognitive development, problem-solving and learning
- Learning is a social activity.

Firstly, communication through language is a source of collaborative learning where discussion helps reflection and internal regulation of thought through the speaker having to modify or clarify their thinking in order to formulate the language they will use. Secondly, listening to the ideas of others is an active process that can stimulate modifications and clarifications to one's own thoughts, understandings and actions (Hoyles, 1989). Therefore, opportunities to discuss experiences help the children to develop a better understanding of what is happening, and to modify and re-try the movements. This model of working fits closely with von Glasersfeld's (1989) argument that 'to have learned means to have drawn conclusions from experience and to act accordingly' (p. 10). It also clearly reflects the ideas of Bruner (1966a, 1966b, 1971), who stressed the 'importance of action and problem solving in learning' (Wood, 1989, p. 8), and Hoyles (1989) who argues that the main aim of language is 'the communication of...an idea or process (p. 122)...and...listening becomes an active process (p. 123).

Peers can act as 'teachers' too; bridging the gap between established skills and a new skill can be achieved through paired or group learning experiences (Wood, 1989), reflecting Vygotsky's (1962) argument that 'what the child can do in co-operation today he (sic) can do alone tomorrow' (p. 104). Knowledge is operative and is the product of reflection (von Glasersfeld, 1989), where knowledge is 'what to do in order to produce an answer' (p. 12).

Superficially, in a PE lesson, this practical response can be seen largely at the physical level. However, if the children reflect on their work either alone or discuss their work with others involved in the same experience, then the response goes beyond the mere doing; through discussion and performance, each child is involved in a collaborative process of creating ever more sophisticated meanings and sense out of their experience (Barnes, 1989). Further, if discussion is facilitated by the teacher then some learning may occur, but better learning may occur if the teacher has provided the learners with the appropriate movement vocabulary and physical components to explore movement experience, and the skills (observational skills and evaluative skills) to discuss their work. The teacher here needs to teach more than the physical skills and techniques central to SDM and linking to gymnastics. Therefore, in PE, it is not just about learning the right language for different physical experiences, but it is how the children use the specific language of PE to understand their actions and develop their expertise. Arnold (1988) distinguishes two potential ends of a continuum which are 'knowing how in a *weak sense* and knowing how in a *strong sense*' (p. 23). By way of explaining *weak sense*, Arnold refers to the gymnast who is able to perform a physical skill. He uses the example of a gymnast who can perform a cartwheel, but who is, when asked how they did it, unable to explain. The *strong sense* of Arnold refers to a person who cannot necessarily complete a cartwheel, but is able to describe how it is done, demonstrating understanding.

However, perhaps one of the most significant observations from Vygotsky (1978) is how children use language as a tool for problem-solving. He writes, 'children solve practical tasks with the help of speech as well as their eyes and hands' (p. 26). Vygotsky accepts that children function according to norms of development, but that it is wrong to say that they function only at a particular level. For example, he argues that younger children can solve problems at the level of older children:

> *This difference between twelve and eight, or between nine and eight, is what we call the zone of proximal development (ZPD). It is the distance between the actual developmental level as determined by independent problem solving and the level of potential development as determined through problem solving under adult guidance or in collaboration with more capable peers.* (Vygotsky, 1978, p. 86)

Thus, teachers should know their children, know levels of normal performance, and be able to differentiate within and between tasks in PE teaching. Vygotsky argues that 'the only good learning...is that which is in advance of development' (ibid., p. 86). Hodgkin (1985) develops a definition of instruction that encompasses social constructivism in his discussion of the teacher's role in relation to the process of discovery where:

> *Instruction involves bringing the learner confidently up to his (sic) frontier so that he begins to ask interesting questions, finds some answers, creates appropriate models or pictures, and, perhaps, does some experiments.* (p. 93)

This reflects the idea of scaffolding first discussed by Wood, Bruner and Ross (1976) and developed by Applebee (1989) as instructional scaffolding. Scaffolding does not change the task, but provides the learner with the skills and tools to manage the learning experience.

Educational discourse of the initiation–response–feedback (IRF; Sinclair and Coulthard, 1975) style involves the techniques of repetition, cued elicitations and reformulations; this is one form of the discourse of teaching and learning. There is a potential link between IRF and Mercer's (1995) social modes of thinking, where the teacher-led IRF cycle provides the children with the language, models of questioning, the skills of observation in PE and the movement experience that enable children to build their own understanding through longer conversations of their own, or further periods of practice, without teacher control.

Social modes of thinking
Mercer (1995) argues that the:

> ...*important goal of education is not to get students to take part in the conventional exchanges of educational discourse ... it is to get students to develop new ways of using language to think and communicate.* (p. 80)

Through thinking and communicating, children develop understanding. This is a view supported by Edwards (1991), who writes that 'the development of understanding is a communicative accomplishment, embodied in classroom discourse' (p. 187). He sees teacher–child dialogue as comprising the development of shared understandings, shared experiences and procedures, developing a shared conceptual vocabulary that 'embodies an unnecessarily limited sense of shared knowledge' (p. 187). He argues that a different emphasis needs to be placed upon the importance of argument, disagreement, justification and criticism developing what he calls a rhetorical approach to shared knowledge. Each individual has a particular way of experiencing the world and similarly has their own way of describing their experiences. In this way, individuals account for their experiences, and try to make them intelligible and accessible to others. In SDM, children do not work in isolation, but work as one of a large group or work together in small groups and, through communication, extend the exploration of movement, where language is action and is 'situated discursive practice' (Edwards, 1993, p. 206). Mercer (1995) describes three social modes of thinking that are distinctive as they describe situations where the children are more likely to be working without the direct guidance of a teacher. He describes these social modes of thinking as analytical categories that demonstrate levels of talk among children. They are described below.

Disputational talk
Disagreement and individualised decision-making are the main characteristics, with few attempts to pool resources or to offer constructive criticism of suggestions. Disputational talk also has some characteristic discourse features such as short exchanges consisting of assertions, and challenges or counter-assertions. The relationship is competitive: information is flaunted rather than shared; differences are stressed rather than resolved; and the general orientation is defensive of one's position and sometimes aggressive.

Cumulative talk

This is where speakers build positively, but uncritically, on what the other has said. Partners use talk to construct a 'common knowledge by accumulation'. Cumulative discourse is characterised by repetitions, confirmations and elaborations. Cumulative talk seems to operate more on implicit concerns with solidarity and trust, and the ground rules seem to require constant repetition and confirmation of partner ideas and opinions.

Exploratory talk

This is where partners engage critically but constructively with each other's ideas. Statements and suggestions are offered for joint consideration, which may be challenged and counter-challenged, but challenges are justified and alternative hypotheses are offered. In exploratory talk, knowledge is made more publicly accountable and reasoning is more visible in the talk. This kind of talk has been found to be most effective for solving problems through collaborative activity (Mercer, 1995, pp. 104–105).

Methodology

In this research, a qualitative, interpretivist approach has been favoured in which evidence gathered tends to be described as 'a rich resource' of complex cultural and social contexts and is 'presented as illuminative rather than definitive' (Sparkes, 1996, p. 170). Qualitative research (Hammersley, 1993) can take many forms, but can be identified by having: i) a clear emphasis on the examination of particular educational phenomena; ii) unstructured data which reflects what the researcher saw or heard during observations or interviews; iii) evidence from a small number of cases explored in detail; and iv) explicit interpretation of the meanings and functions of human actions. Qualitative researchers argue that this approach can provide an understanding of the cultural and political processes involved in schooling because it is subjective, and relies on descriptions or accounts as observed, or otherwise recorded, by the individual researcher. Within this approach, and a feature of qualitative research, the researcher has an influence on interaction; indeed, how can interaction occur without a degree of reciprocity (Skeggs, 1992)? Language and meaning are seen as central areas of investigation, and methods of qualitative enquiry tend to use case study with different forms of observation and open-ended, unstructured research tools to get as close to those multiple subject perspectives as possible. In this mode, the researcher is a participant who influences the cultural and social contexts under investigation and who builds a theoretical perspective from the data gathered.

Clearly, such data gathered is not independent of individual views and suppositions, and presents a picture of reality which is likely to reflect those views and suppositions, and a researcher without the same views and suppositions may see the same story entirely differently. Of importance, though, is the view that we must learn all that is possible from studying only one of anything (Wolcott, 1995). Qualitative research has a particular place in that, as Sears (1992) points out:

> *The power of qualitative data, however, lies not in the number of people interviewed but in the researcher's ability to know well a few people in their cultural*

contexts. The test of qualitative enquiry is not the unearthing of a seemingly endless multitude of unique individuals but in illuminating the lives of a few well-chosen individuals. (p. 148)

Qualitative approaches can capture the real meaning of innovation and change for those *few well-chosen individuals* and this may provide a rich source of data that is illuminative rather than definitive. Pollard and Filer (1996) also discuss the need to get close to the research, which they see as vital to obtain data about the meanings of people's lives. They argue for a:

> *...deliberate attempt to establish rapport with the subjects of the research in order to emphasise and understand their perspectives, actions and interactions...and the researcher must...listen, observe, talk and ask, then describe and try to understand...search for patterns and attempt to generate a more abstracted, yet validly grounded, analysis.* (p. 303)

The writer's involvement in the research was clearly a form of interaction that may have affected what happened, and this is acknowledged though he tried to:

> *...speak sensibly about the intersubjective world of primary PE using language that everyone [the respondents and subsequent readers of the research] can understand.* (Barritt et al., 1985, p. 14)

The intersubjective world is where the teacher, the children, the researcher and the reader 'develop a dialogue with the phenomena and thus validate the phenomena as described' (van Manaan, 1988, p. 111). Clearly, the way the researcher talked to the children and conducted the interview was crucial to this process.

The subjects of this research were the children as they engaged in PE lessons, and the aim was to draw out their thoughts and feelings and to explore the language they used, so the research had to be illustrative rather than definitive. It is illustrative because it showed what was happening at that moment in time, and cannot be definitive because, as with all interpretive research, the findings are not generalisable to other contexts and times. The accounts of what happened in these PE lessons, what was said or what and how things were done, aimed to represent the phenomena identified accurately. This made the research process framework-dependent, where knowledge is transactional and the product of experience where:

> *...an individual's behaviour can...be understood by the researcher sharing their frame of reference: understanding of the individual's interpretations of the world around them come from the inside, not the outside.* (Cohen and Manion, 1994, p. 26)

The methodological choices included video data of PE lessons from which child–teacher and child–child talk was taken, audio recordings of group interviews (the researcher and small groups of children) and movement diaries written over a seven-week period. These three strategies were a form of triangulation applied in an attempt to ensure a degree of validity and reliability within and between the data gathered. Therefore, the text analysed was from these three sources, and reference to the use of language, discourse or text refers to either the spoken word or written word. However, as the children were free to choose the topic for their diaries, none selected SDM so any reference here is limited.

Discourse analysis was used to examine the data gathered and explored 'the organisation of ordinary talk and everyday explanations and the social actions performed in them' (Cohen and Manion, 1994, p. 214). The researcher and the children were familiar with and shared the same world, were part of the same cultural backdrop from which the participants in the research draw, for example, to frame their patterns of communication. The cultural backdrop comprised the different social worlds experienced by the children and the researcher which were brought to the school context. The use of discourse analysis illustrates this cultural backdrop as:

> *...the interweaving of words and phrases in different contexts that gives them their sense, and when we attempt to grasp patterns in a text we always have to carry out that exercise against a cultural backdrop...and...discourse is sometimes used to refer to patterns of meaning which organise the various symbolic systems human beings inhabit, and which are necessary for us to make sense of each other.* (Parker, 1999, pp. 2–3)

Much of the research took place through language; for example, to find out if understanding of movement (SDM) was enhanced through the use of the 'right' appropriate technical and situational language. The idea that there is a 'right' language of PE presents a dilemma, but this research draws on the constructivist view discussed by von Glasersfeld (1989, p. 16). Should the teacher of PE teach the 'right' language because someone else, a more expert adult, sees it as right? Rather, 'rightness must be seen as the fit with an order one [the child] has established for oneself [themself]' so the teacher can 'guide the student in the conceptual organisation of certain areas of experience' (von Glasersfeld, 1989, p. 16).

Parker (1999) explains this in more detail; he writes that these 'practices' include 'patterns of meaning that may be visual or spatial, that may comprise face-to-face interaction' (p. 3). In PE, this suggests four variables. Firstly, the practice of PE is visual in a private and public sense as the children perform; for example, in SDM there is a clear set of public expectations that present the children with an infinite variety of private expectations and anxieties. Secondly, SDM is spatial both in terms of the performance of movement in personal space, and the general space of the hall or room, where the child's performance takes place. Thirdly, face-to-face interaction involves the environment, the context and the other person if working in pairs or groups, as the performer meets the physical challenges of performance. Fourthly, it is with others, an audience of their classmates and the teacher, in front of whom they perform and with whom they communicate.

Limitations of the research
Firstly, it was very difficult, if not impossible at times for reasons of safety, to gather

evidence of children's talk while they were performing. Talk was recorded after a 'period of activity' when the children paused to discuss their work with the teacher. This gave a significant amount of data that matched the IRF model (Sinclair and Coulthard, 1975). Secondly, talk was recorded with the researcher present discussing movement experience, modifying Mercer's (1995) approach to ensure a focus on the PE activities was maintained; this was necessary due to constraints on the time allocated to discussion outside normal PE lessons. This potentially restricted the development of Mercer's (1995) modes of social thinking to the higher levels of his model. Thirdly, each child was asked to keep a diary about PE lessons where they recorded their experiences and thoughts; these were necessarily retrospective. These three strategies were a form of reflection by the children on past experience, whether almost immediate or delayed, and this may have restricted the development of understanding about movement through language. However, the researcher was fully involved in the research, at times adopting a teaching mode, and it must be acknowledged that his involvement in the research was clearly a form of interaction that may have affected what happened.

As a result of the collaboration with the two teachers involved in the research (schools DPS and SPS), a videotape of eleven PE lessons was filmed, interviews of all the children in small groups were conducted, and completed movement diaries were collected from all those interviewed. From the videotapes and audiotapes, 2,285 lines of talk, conversation, description or comment were transcribed. The analysis showed that both teachers commonly taught using an IRF style during PE lessons. The children responded either through action, talk or a combination of action and talk. During the interviews, the children responded through talk that matched Mercer's (1995) model of social modes of thinking either through disputational, cumulative or exploratory talk.

Results
1. Initiation–response–feedback
A number of key findings arose from the analysis of evidence linked to IRF. Both teachers initiated conversation or action with the use of appropriate technical language and questions focused on the key aspects of the skill or activity being taught. The responses by the children in the IRF cycle were either spoken, a demonstration of performance or an activity or skill or a combination of talking about an activity at the same time as the performance. The feedback in the IRF cycle from the teacher was shown to correct misconceptions or mistakes by the children and to focus on improving or maintaining the quality of the children's performance. This whole process of IRF, managed by the teacher, demonstrated the children working on understanding or showing a satisfactory level of understanding through discussion or performance (Dibbo, 2003).

Indeed, in these PE lessons, the teachers managed talk using the IRF cycle to monitor the children's understanding, directing children to the important and critical aspects of what they were attempting to learn using the appropriate technical language, but not to the extent that this language was inaccessible. The teachers were doing what Mercer (1995) argues strongly about:

...if we encourage and enable children to use language in certain ways – to ask certain questions, to clearly describe events, to account for outcomes and consolidate what they have learnt in words – we are helping them understand and gain access to educated discourse. (pp. 106–107)

There is more than this; there is the 'accumulated knowledge (experience), the specialised vocabulary and other conventions of any particular discourse community' (Mercer, 1995, p. 107). In this case, that is PE and movement being made accessible to the children.

What emerges from the analysis of the fragments of IRF talk is a picture of interaction through talk and activity. The children have completed an activity (preparation for rolling using SDM ideas), and then, as they sit and talk about it, they are thinking back and reflecting on what they have done. The teacher ensured that the children had reached a satisfactory level of understanding by monitoring the talk, clearing up mistakes or misconceptions that arose, and ensuring the correct language was being used. If necessary, the children did the same practice again or, if it was a satisfactory performance and demonstrated understanding, they moved on to the next task; i.e. the children could demonstrate understanding through talk or action. This model of working gave the children the language, skills and strategies of observation and discussion to enable them to work alone either during practice or in conversation about practice with their peers making accessible the higher order social modes of thinking (Mercer, 1995).

2. Disputational, cumulative and exploratory talk

From analysis of the data, the fragments showing disputational talk did not demonstrate children working on understanding, or showing satisfactory understanding. Clearly, some understanding is demonstrated as the children know how to answer the questions asked in the interview, but there is little or no collaboration between the children. This closely fits with Mercer's (1995) description of disputational talk where disagreement and individualised decision-making are the main characteristics, with few attempts to pool resources or to offer constructive criticism of suggestions.

There were more examples of cumulative talk, where the children gave the right technical information and together worked on sequencing the information as they talked about the skill of how to roll. There were repetitions, confirmations and elaborations with a sense of implicit concerns with solidarity and trust, the ground rules seeming to require constant repetition and confirmation of partner ideas and opinions. This whole process demonstrated the children working on understanding as they gave the right information, but not necessarily using the right language. They built positively, but uncritically on what the others said and through their conversation built a common knowledge by accumulation.

Four fragments (54 lines of conversation from the transcripts) of exploratory talk showed children working on understanding, or achieving satisfactory understanding, as they reflected back on their experiences of a rounders lesson. There was clear evidence of the children making statements and suggestions for joint consideration in these fragments. At times, there were challenges and counter-challenges: challenges were not often justified, but alternative ideas were offered. This, as Mercer (1995, pp. 104–105) describes, is exploratory talk, where knowledge is made more publicly accountable, reasoning is more visible in the talk and where partners engage critically but constructively with each other's ideas, clearly reflecting a model of constructivism in action.

Significantly, it was clear in the transcripts from the videotapes and the audiotapes that the children relished the chance to talk and demonstrate their expertise through the use of technical language, enjoying being 'fluent in the tongue of their chosen subject' (Barnes and Sheeran, 1992, p. 90). Barnes and Sheeran describe this as gaining access to and understanding of the realms of knowledge that underpin the school curriculum and the learners 'mastering (sic) the appropriate language-game' (ibid., p. 91). The eagerness to use language in this way provides 'a kind of window on the mind' (Edwards, 1993, p. 206), and can be taken as evidence of underlying and stable cognitive representations of how a child thinks, showing a child working on understanding or demonstrating satisfactory understanding.

Discussion

It is likely that the researcher's involvement with two schools and two groups of children over the period of one year may have had an influence on the research. This is acknowledged in this discussion and through the methods chosen. There was the clear intention to describe what was seen as it occurred, and when possible to make links to other research that examined children's understanding through language, communication and movement.

It was evident that in the interviews the children did not always use the technical language introduced by the teacher, but used their own language to show their understanding. Some groups of children sustained talk at the cumulative or exploratory level demonstrating they had understood what they had been taught. However, from the video evidence gathered over the period of the research, and the transcripts of discussion and conversation, all the children involved in the research demonstrated understanding of their experiences in PE lessons through their performances, and also at different 'levels' through different types of talking during interviews: Mercer's (1995) 'social modes of thinking'. This also links with Arnold's (1988) views (i.e. 'knowing how in a *weak sense* and knowing how in a *strong sense*'; p. 23) and those of Vygotsky (1978) on how children use language as a tool for problem-solving ('children solve practical tasks with the help of speech as well as their eyes and hands'; p. 26) discussed earlier.

The implications from the research, while case-specific and not generalisable, suggest that teachers should introduce the right technical language to the children with a focus on the skills and movements being taught, even though this language was not always used by the children during reflection and writing. This research did not look at children's demonstration of understanding specifically enough to identify children whose understanding was demonstrated in a 'weak sense or a strong sense (Arnold, 1988). However, teachers should try to ensure the children achieve satisfactory understanding at each stage, ensuring mistakes or misconceptions are resolved before the children move on in the lesson; either through performance or talk (Dibbo, 2003; Mercer, 1995, 2000). They need to manage the children's learning to ensure success and progress and to provide opportunities for the children to talk to each other about what they are doing during skill practice or movement activities (Department for Education and Employment (DfEE), 2000). In addition, it would be advantageous if the children had opportunities to discuss their work in PE, as they do in other primary subjects, and to record their thoughts in written form, and were taught how to talk to each other (Dibbo, 2003).

Conclusion

Understanding, talking and Sherborne Developmental Movement/gymnastics

Success in gymnastics is all about developing confidence in learners as performers. The more complex skills of gymnastics need to be built on a basic foundation of simple gymnastic activity. Progression in gymnastics can then be seen through developing competence at these basic levels, and then by exploring more complex skills – for example, by combining roll and handstand into handstand/forward roll; or by taking basic skills into a more complex environment – floor to apparatus.

Progression is challenging and may sometimes threaten children. These challenges need managing sensitively so young children can meet them with confidence. They can be managed in a number of ways:

1. Through effective and sensitive teaching

2. Through careful structuring of tasks in the lesson and over a series of lessons

3. By providing opportunities for children to explore their ideas at their own pace and level of competence.

In all these situations the children need trust and confidence in: their ability to do, think, decide and perform; their teacher; and in their peers, who may be seen as partners, coaches or competitors.

The findings clearly showed children developing an understanding of movement through actions and through talk during and after SDM lessons. SDM into gymnastics is a way of working that can help to bridge the developmental pathways to learning in gymnastics. Individual activities and relationship play are ideal approaches to developing trust and confidence in children and, when focused through SDM into gymnastic-type work, can enable children to develop effectively and safely as gymnasts in aspects of gymnastics such as rolling, understanding stability and partner work, as well as having potential to develop basic confidence in vaulting and developing travelling in a variety of ways.

The next step

Firstly, as this research developed, the focus became largely fixed on children's developing understanding of performance through talk and action, and while trust and confidence seemed to be part of the process no hard evidence was gathered to support this view. The measurement of trust and confidence may well be problematic, but worthwhile when looking at other research into PE. Shorman's (1999) findings clearly show that children view the space in which PE takes place as challenging, and Smith (1992) looks in part at the significance of past experience for those involved in PE. While I believe SDM develops mutual trust and confidence in the self and others, this is clearly an area for future research.

Secondly, it would be useful to examine individual children's understanding in relation to Arnold's (1988) notion of 'weak and strong sense' to see if those children who responded using the correct movement vocabulary were indeed those who operated within the 'strong sense' framework; similarly, to identify if those children who demonstrated understanding through performance were those operating within the 'weak sense' framework. This would develop a critique of the notion that doing and talking link closely to show understanding in PE.

References

Applebee, A. (1989) 'The enterprise we are part of: learning to teach'. In: P. Murphy and B. Moon (eds) *Developments in Learning and Assessment.* London: Hodder and Stoughton/Open University Press.

Arnold, P.J. (1988) *Education, Movement and the Curriculum.* Lewes: Falmer Press.

Barnes, D. (1989) 'Knowledge as Action'. In: P. Murphy and B. Moon (eds) *Developments in Learning and Assessment.* London: Hodder and Stoughton/Open University Press.

Barnes, D. and Sheeran, Y. (1991) *School Writing: Discovering the ground rules.* Milton Keynes: Open University Press.

Barritt, L., Beekman, T., Beeker, H. and Mulderij, K. (1983) 'The world through children's eyes: hide and seek and peekaboo', *Phenomenology and Pedagogy,* 1 (2), 140–161.

Bruner, J. (1966a) *The Process of Education.* Cambridge, MA: Harvard University Press.

Bruner, J. (1966b) *Toward a Theory of Instruction.* Cambridge, MA: Harvard University Press.

Bruner, J. (1971) *The Relevance of Education*. New York, NY: Norton and Co.

Cohen, L. and Manion, L. (1994) *Research Methods in Education*. London: Routledge.

Department for Education and Employment (2000) *The National Curriculum Handbook for Primary Teachers in England: Key Stages 1 and 2* (May 2000). Norwich: The Stationery Office.

Dibbo, J. and Gerry, S. (1995a) 'Physical education meeting the needs of the whole child', *British Journal of Physical Education,* 26 (1).

Dibbo, J. (2003) *Language and Movement: A learning experience (unpublished Ed.D. thesis)*. Milton Keynes: Open University.

Edwards, D. (1991) 'Discourse analysis and the development of understanding in the classroom'. In: O. Boyd-Barrett and E. Scanlon (eds) *Computers and Learning*. Wokingham: Addison-Wesley Publishing Co.

Edwards, D. (1993) 'Concepts, memory and the organisation of pedagogic discourse: a case study', *International Journal of Educational Research*, 19 (3), 205–224.

Hammersley, M. (ed.) (1993) *Educational Research: Current issues (Volume 1)*. London: Paul Chapman.

Hodgkin, R.A. (1985) *Playing and Exploring*. London: Methuen.

Hoyles, C. (1989) 'What is the point of group discussion in mathematics?'. In: P. Murphy and B. Moon (eds) *Developments in Learning and Assessment*. London: Hodder and Stoughton/Open University Press.

Lave, J and Wenger, E (1991) *Situated Learning*. Cambridge: Cambridge University Press.

Maude, P. (1997) *Gymnastics*. London: Hodder and Stoughton.

Maude, P. (2001) *Physical Children, Active Teaching*. Buckingham: Open University Press.

Maude, P., Hopper, B. and Grey, J. (2000) *Teaching Physical Education in the Primary School*. London: Routledge/Falmer.

Mercer, N. (1995) *The Guided Construction of Knowledge: Talk among teachers and learners*. Clevedon: Multilingual Matters Ltd.

Mercer, N. (2000) *Words and Minds*. London: Routledge.

Nias, J. and Groundwater-Smith, S. (eds) (1992) *The Enquiring Teacher: Supporting and sustaining teacher research*. Lewes: Falmer Press.

Parker, I. (1999) 'Introduction: varieties of discourse and analysis'. In: I. Parker and the Bolton Discourse Network (eds) *Critical Textwork: An introduction to varieties of discourse and analysis*. Buckingham: Open University Press.

Piaget, J. (1967) *Six Psychological Studies*. London: London University Press.

Pollard, A. with Filer, A. (1996) *The Social World of Children's Learning*. London: Cassell.

Sears, J. (1992) 'Researching the other/searching for self: qualitative research on [homo] sexuality', *Theory into Practice,* 31 (2), 147–156.

Sherborne, V. (2001) *Developmental Movement for Children: Mainstream, special needs and pre-school (2nd edn)*. London: Worth Publishing.

Shorman, S.C. (1999) *Stories from the Lifeworld of Physical Education (unpublished Ph.D. thesis)*. Plymouth: University of Plymouth.

Sinclair, J.M. and Coulthard, R.M. (1975) *Towards an Analysis of Discourse: The English used by teachers and pupils*. Oxford: Oxford University Press.

Skeggs, B. (1992) 'Confessions of a feminist researcher', *Sociology Review,* 2 (1), 4–12.

Smith, S.J. (1992) 'Studying the lifeworld of physical education: a phenomenological orientation'. In: A. Sparkes (ed.) *Research in Physical Education and Sport: Exploring alternative visions.* London: Falmer Press.

Sparkes, A. (1996) 'Interrupted body projects and the self in teaching: exploring an absent presence', *Journal of International Studies in Sociology of Education,* 6 (2), 167–189.

van Manaan, J. (1988) *Tales from the Field.* Chicago: University of Chicago Press.

von Glasersfeld, E. (1989) 'Learning as a constructivist activity'. In: P. Murphy and B. Moon (eds) *Developments in Learning and Assessment.* London: Hodder and Stoughton/Open University Press.

Vygotsky, L.S. (1962) *Thought and Language.* New York, NY: John Wiley.

Vygotsky, L.S. (1978) *Mind in Society: The development of higher psychological processes.* Cambridge, MA: Harvard University Press.

Williams, A. (1997) *National Curriculum Gymnastics.* London: Hodder and Stoughton.

Wolcott, H. (1995) *The Art of Fieldwork.* London: Sage.

Wood, D.J. (1989) *How Children Think and Learn.* Oxford: Blackwell.

Wood, D. Bruner, J. and Ross, G. (1976) 'The role of tutoring in problem-solving', *Journal of Child Psychology and Psychiatry,* 17 (2), 89–100.

PART 3

Sherborne Developmental Movement in Europe

Introduction to Sherborne
Developmental Movement Overseas

Elizabeth Marsden

During her lifetime, Sherborne travelled to many European countries as well as to North America and Australia, mostly to show others how to use movement to reach severely disabled adults and children. Occasionally, she gave presentations at conferences but, as her heart was always in practical work, this is what she enjoyed most of all. Movement work with disabled children and adults was in its infancy in most countries, but as she showed how positive her particular way of working had become in the UK, teachers and therapists in Norway, Sweden, Poland, Belgium, Canada and Japan were very keen to welcome Sherborne into their situations. Today, her work has spread to Finland, Estonia, Ireland, Germany, Brazil, Italy and Spain through the teaching of the international course leaders of the Sherborne Association.

Sherborne was so confident in the value of her work by the 1980s that she would often make a universal statement, such as: 'all children love tunnels'; 'children will learn to pay attention and to concentrate [by working with Sherborne Developmental Movement (SDM)]'; or 'in this way, children learn to form relationships' (Good Companions Film, 1986). These observations were accepted for 20 years, but the present-day culture in almost every country in the world, requires research to support such observations. SDM practitioners work differently in different countries, and this is something that Sherborne expected and encouraged. The following pieces of research from Poland, Finland and Sweden, however, have been carried out using accepted research methodologies, and it is with great pleasure that we include them in this book. Special tributes of thanks must go to the translators who have done an exceptional job.

CHAPTER 9

Sherborne Developmental Movement in Poland

A Series of Studies under the Supervision of Professor Marta Bogdanowicz

Marta Bogdanowicz
(Translator: Malgorzata Mroziak, Poland)

Introduction

The work of Veronica Sherborne is well-known throughout Poland, because of the intense and wide-ranging actions undertaken by Polish international course leaders of the Sherborne Association who have practised and have trained others. In Poland, the research on the effectiveness of Sherborne Developmental Movement (SDM) has been conducted since 1990 by Marta Bogdanowicz, who has developed a Scale of Observation of Behaviour for Children so that researchers can use this instrument in a wide variety of settings.

This paper presents a background to the development of the Scale of Observation, and three small studies using the Scale are presented in this paper. The targeted populations were a group of children with autistic spectrum disorder (ASD), a group of children with hearing problems, and a group of kindergarten children who had had polio. Results indicate that Sherborne Developmental Movement (SDM) may have improved the motor, behavioural and cognitive functioning of participants.

The Scale of Observation of Behaviour

The Scale was first devised in 1990 by Marta Bogdanowicz and tested by Lubianiec (1992). It was specifically designed to help teachers and therapists who were using SDM with groups of children with developmental delay. It was further modified in 2000, and is now widely used in Poland. The Scale consists of four subscales which relate to cognitive, emotional, social and motor development. It is a flexible instrument, and other scales can be added depending on the needs of the teachers and therapists. The assessment within each subscale consists of five chosen aspects of psychomotor behaviour. It is not a psychological testing instrument meeting all the methodological demands necessary of such an instrument; rather, it is a tool to assist practitioners observe and record behaviour. It assesses four areas of psychomotor development: cognitive, emotional, social and motor development (see Table 9.1).

Scoring the Scale

Each aspect is assessed on a 5-point scale with the option of 'staging marks' (i.e. 0.5 points). The designation for each point is as follows:

Table 9.1. The areas of psychomotor development assessed by the Scale of Observation of Behaviour

Cognitive development	Emotional development	Social development	Motor development
a) Ability to concentrate	a) Mood	a) Attitude towards the session	a) Level of physical activity
b) Ability to communicate	b) Expressing emotion	b) Attitude towards the task	b) Motor fitness
c) Awareness of own body and space	c) Ability to relax	c) Attitude towards a partner	c) Independence during motor tasks
d) Ability to perform new tasks	d) Reaction to physical contact	d) Attitude to other children	d) Ability to adapt to the task
e) Ability to show creative ideas	e) Reaction to challenges/failure	e) Attitude towards group activities	e) Ability to adapt physically to a partner.

1 point: very low development level

2 points: low developmental level

3 points: a satisfactory (average) developmental level

4 points: good developmental level

5 points: very high developmental level.

Implementing the Scale

Bogdanowicz (2003) recommends that each assessor spends a good period of time working with the Scale and practising observations with an experienced observer. She suggests that in any piece of research involving the Scale, a child should be observed simultaneously by three observers over two movement sessions *before* SDM is begun. Observers should then discuss and compare scores before deciding on one score for each part of the Scale. Other qualitative notes and/or video material can be used to give a fuller picture of each child's development. SDM would then normally be carried out for 12 months before the same observers would repeat the procedure at the end of the test period.

There are two versions of the Scale of Observation of Behaviour: one for assessment of children (above) and the second for assessment of the children's partners (parents or teachers) because SDM helps to develop not only children but their partners as well.

More details of the Scale can be obtained from Professor Marta Bogdanowicz, Psychology Department, University of Gdańsk, Gdańsk, Poland (email: marta.bogdanowicz@wp.pl).

The following pieces of research have been carried out using the Scale described above and are presented here in a 'snapshot' version. For full research information, see Bogdanowicz and Kasica (2003) or contact the author.

Research Study 1:
The effectiveness of Sherborne Developmental Movement for children on the autistic spectrum
Jacek Bleszynski

Research questions

1. Does attending SDM classes affect the development of children with ASD?

2. Is the age of the child a factor in determining the effectiveness of therapeutic work in SDM?

Introduction

It is suggested that the therapeutic effects of SDM are multidirectional, and that they support human development in many ways. It is considered to be especially helpful for children suffering developmental delay as it can nurture, support and rehabilitate.

In the early days of therapeutic work with children with ASD, SDM was treated as an experiment where the main goal was to reduce the social limitations experienced by the children. In Warsaw, the first trials took place in the 1980s. In 1994, the National Autism Association included SDM therapy as an alternative method for developmental support – first in a division in Slupsk (Bleszynski, 2001) and, since 2000, in Torun as well. The aim of the selection of this movement programme was to support children with ASD emotionally, socially and cognitively.

An advantage of SDM is that it requires little or no equipment, and can be carried out in small or large spaces. Another advantage is the opportunity for parents and siblings to participate and become the child's special partner. Thus movement activities, play and the sheer joy of having fun together help to bond the child with ASD more closely within their family unit.

Methodology

SDM classes took place in two different geographical areas – Slupsk (Research 1) and Torun (Research 2) – and were taught by different teachers. Classes took place once a week on a fixed day for 45 minutes. The participants all had a diagnosis of ASD. In total, there were 36 participants aged between 3 and 16 years. There were 4 girls and 32 boys in the study. Among those children diagnosed with ASD in Poland, there is a ratio of one girl to four boys; therefore this research group exhibited a lower incidence of girls than the national norm.

The Scale of Observation of Behaviour (Bogdanowicz, 1990) was applied at the start of the SDM programme as outlined above. Additional qualitative data were also collected in the form of responses to questionnaires from parents, teachers and any others who were involved in the education and care of the participants. After six months of SDM, the assessment measures were repeated and the results are reported below.

Results

In all cases, progress in development of examined functions was noticed following the six-month SDM programme. Table 9.2 below shows the total scores of both groups (Research 1 and Research 2) and the differences in raw data.

Table 9.2. Total pre- and post- scores on the Scale of Observation of Behaviour

Subscales	Cognitive development	Emotional development	Social development	Motor development	Overall result
Pre-SDM	2.14	2.17	2.17	2.33	2.21
Post-SDM	3.40	3.31	3.64	3.49	3.46
Difference	1.26	1.14	1.39	1.16	1.25

The most notable effects observed were in the subscales 'Social development' and 'Cognitive development' although all scores showed improvement over the six-month period of intervention with SDM.

It was interesting to compare the results of children's responses to SDM by age. In this case, the children were sorted into two groups – those under eight years and those over eight years of age. Table 9.3 shows the differences in pre- and post-SDM results for the younger group of children, and Table 9.4 for those over eight years of age. It can be seen from Table 9.3 that the results between pre- and post-SDM intervention show an increased functioning in each subscale, especially those of the cognitive and social development scales.

It can clearly be seen that the older group (Table 9.4) show much less difference pre- and post-SDM, and children with ASD in this research were still functioning on a very low level in the emotional sphere which is characteristic of children with this diagnosis.

Table 9.3. Pre- and post-SDM intervention scores for children below eight years old

Subscales	Cognitive development	Emotional development	Social development	Motor development	Overall result
Pre-SDM	2.06	2.23	2.16	2.34	2.19
Post-SDM	3.62	3.28	3.51	3.48	3.47
Difference	1.56	1.05	1.35	1.14	1.28

Table 9.4. Pre- and post- SDM intervention scores for children over eight years old

Subscales	Cognitive development	Emotional development	Social development	Motor development	Overall result
Pre-SDM	2.80	2.00	2.80	2.31	2.48
Post-SDM	3.10	2.20	3.60	3.30	3.05
Difference	0.30	0.20	0.80	0.99	0.57

Discussion and conclusion

The Scale of Observation of Behaviour for Children was obviously sufficiently sensitive to record differences in the children pre- and post-SDM intervention. The qualitative records also suggest that SDM may be very effective in socialising children with ASD. It is difficult to know why the younger age group (below eight years) showed greater changes than the older group, but this project did not take into account where on the autistic spectrum the children were, and the older group may have collectively been in a different place on the spectrum than the younger group. What is clear is that, even after six months, all children showed better scores on all the scales. Normally, it is recommended that the SDM programme be continued for at least 12 months before taking the post-intervention scores. This project may have shown even greater gains had this been possible.

Research Study 2:
Sherborne Developmental Movement and children with hearing difficulties
Urszula Chudoba and Marianna Krawiec

Research question
Does SDM help children with hearing problems and their families to form closer bonding relationships?

Methodology
The researchers were therapists from the outpatient clinic for children and young people with hearing problems in Radom. Their previous research had led them to believe that SDM would have a positive influence on these children's relationships with their families and would also support the rehabilitation process (Krawiec and Chudoba, 1994). Children in the clinic with serious hearing defects were asked to participate in weekly, hour-long SDM classes for 10 months. Their partners, in all cases but one, were their mothers. In the other case, the partner was an older hearing sister.

The therapists hypothesised that:

1. Participation in SDM classes would allow children to start good new relationships with therapists and improve contacts with parents

2. Participation in SDM classes would have beneficial influences on their social development, improve motor skills and relax them

3. As relaxed children breathe properly, that this would provide the starting point for voice production; thus SDM would have a positive influence on voice development and expression.

Measurements were taken pre- and post-SDM intervention period using the Scale of Observation of Behaviour for Children (Bogdanowicz, 1990), and an additional scale, 'Voice expression', was added. Qualitative notes were also made on the children pre- and post-SDM intervention period.

Results
Post-SDM measures showed improvement in all five subscales.

Discussion and conclusion
After the therapists had led the SDM sessions regularly for 10 months, and had worked alongside the children closely during this time, they felt they could offer the following observations – that regular sessions of SDM over a 10-month period for this group of children:

1. Supported the rehabilitation process of children with hearing problems, being especially beneficial for young children in the first phase of rehabilitation

2. Aided children to begin to form appropriate social relationships

3. Gave parents ideas for, and a means of, making contact with children in non-verbal ways when verbal communication was impossible

4. Gave children a sense of success in their first contact with a speech therapist, building their confidence

5. Improved one child's relationship with their hearing sibling

6. Created an opportunity for parents and therapists to get to know the child

7. Built and restored relationships within the family

8. And, based upon the authors' professional observations as speech therapists, allowed children to relax and breathe properly, which is the starting point for voice production; thus SDM had a positive influence for voice development and expression.

Research Study 3:
Using Sherborne Developmental Movement in a kindergarten setting with children who have suffered polio
Anna Kolasa

Research question
Does SDM have an effect physically and emotionally on children with polio?

Introduction
An experiment was conducted in Public Kindergarten No. 77 in Gdańsk, which specialises in care for children with polio. Special attention was paid to specific developmental dysfunctions suffered by those children. Often there are problems in motor development and with the ability to be physically active, as well as with emotional well-being. Children with polio often display fear, mood swings, lack of confidence and lack of self-esteem. Sometimes children with polio display problems in communication.

Methodology
Seven children, aged four to six years, were selected to take part in a series of SDM sessions, as they were having problems with entering into new relationships. For seven months, they participated in SDM sessions once a week for 30 to 45 minutes.

Figure 9.1. Graph showing changes in Scale scores between pre- and post-SDM intervention

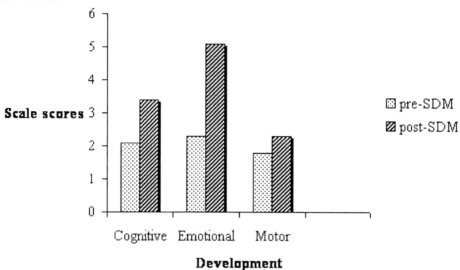

Their partners in the movement activities were high school and university students. The Scale of Observation of Behaviour for Children was used to assess three areas of development (cognitive, emotional and motor) pre- and post-intervention with regular SDM sessions. The researcher also kept a detailed diary on each child.

Results
The biggest differences after 10 months of SDM intervention are clearly shown on the 'Emotional development' subscale. However, there was some change on the 'Cognitive development' subscale also. The 'Motor development' subscale showed a slight improvement but, as the children were physically impaired by polio, this result was expected. These results are presented in Figure 9.1.

Discussion and conclusion
Comparison of pre- and post-intervention scores on the Scale of Observation of Behaviour for Children indicated that, following 10 months of SDM sessions, children became more daring and risk-taking, physically and emotionally. They also learned to trust others with their body weight, and learned that others could be reliable and helpful, and would not let them fall. Scores for self-esteem rose for each participant. It was not surprising that the scores on the 'Motor development' subscale improved only slightly over 10 months as each participant had severe physical impairments due to polio.

The diaries kept by the researcher gave some useful qualitative information on each participant and corroborated the Scale indications. She noted that each child slowly became more willing to start new relationships over the 10-month period. Children showed more positive emotional contacts, became less inhibited, showed less physical fear, began to trust others and to become more relaxed in the enviroment (Szady, 1993).

References

Bleszynski, J, (2001) 'Badania nad wykorzystaniem Metody Ruchu Rozwijajacego w pracy z dzieckiem autystycznym', *Wychowanie na co Dzien,* 12 (99), 10–12.

Bogdanowicz, M. (1990) 'Skala Obserwacji Zachowania dla Dzieci'. In: M. Bogdanowicz, B. Kisiel and M. Przasnyska (eds) (1992) *Metoda Weroniki Sherborne w Terapii i Wspomaganiu Rozwoju Dziecka.* Warszawa, Poland: WSiP.

Bogdanowicz, M. (2003) *Skale Obserwacji Zachowania (SOZ) Dzieci i Rodzicow Uczestniczacych w Zajecich Ruchu Rozwijajacego Weroniki Sherborne.* Gdańsk, Poland: Wydawnictwo Harmonia.

Bogdanowicz, M. and Kasica, A. (2003) *Ruch Rozwijajacy dla Wszystkich.* Gdańsk, Poland: Wydawnictwo Harmonia.

Krawiec, M. and Chudoba, U. (1994) 'Z doswiadczen wspomagania terapii dzieci z wada sluchu Weroniki Sherborne', *Scholasticus* 7/8, 71–78.

Lubianiec, E. (1992) 'Terapia ruchowa Weroniki Sherborne w pracy domu malego dziecka', *Problemy Opiekunczo-Wychowacze*, 10, 437–439.

Szady, K. (1993) '"Sprawni inaczej" sa wsrod nas, otworzmy przed nimi zycie', *Szkola Specjalna,* 1, 45–49.

CHAPTER 10

Sherborne Developmental Movement in Finland

Making Learning Possible for Everyone

Kirsti Lassila and Maarit Uusitalo
(Translators: Kaisu Laasonen and Tove Ruuskanen)

This chapter summarises the outcomes of a study to find out the impact of Sherborne Developmental Movement (SDM) on learning for children in 1st to 3rd grade (aged 7–9 years) who were in special education in Lapland in northern Finland. The purpose of this study was to find out whether or not SDM makes it easier for children with learning disabilities to learn, and to discover how SDM can be useful as a support to normal teaching.

Introduction
In Finland, SDM is regarded as a movement method which supports children's general development and attempts to improve children's knowledge of their own body and their relationship to their environment. SDM also helps children to develop their interaction in an emotionally secure atmosphere. An essential feature is to utilise the tactile sensations and experiences in various ways to develop body awareness. It is important to challenge the children constantly by changing movement activities depending on their responses and need. Continual observation and evaluation of the children's learning is important in order to progress appropriately.

The number of children with learning disorders is growing in Finland. Certain basic motor skills are essential for children's general development. The function of the nervous system is based on the integration of sensory information and motor experiences. Poor motor co-ordination, dysphasia and disorders in body awareness and attention are often combined with learning disorders.

In the study, Kephart's developmental theory (1971) was used as a reference frame. According to Kephart, problems or insufficiencies in development in the first three stages of life prevent cognitive skill development. The child learns differently in the different stages of the development process. Motor co-ordination, perception, self-esteem and personality develop, according to experience, in interaction with the environment. A child might refuse to perform a task, because the task is too difficult for their stage of development.

Using Sherborne Developmental Movement
According to Kephart's (1971) theory, the child needs to experience all the different

stages of movement development. In sensory integration, the actions change from simple to more complicated ones. There is nothing special about SDM movement experiences themselves. They are very typical for children, and they can be built up to functional entities where different movements and use of different sensory modalities can be systematically varied. This is how the child gets the experience appropriate to all the different stages of development. No equipment is used in SDM because the purpose is that the child gets to know their own body through working alone and with a partner.

A realistic body schema is important for development. Spatial awareness includes the comprehension of a human body in relationship to the environment and vice versa. SDM gives the child an opportunity to experience their own body in different situations. Based on experiences alone, in pairs or in groups, it is possible to awaken awareness of different positions, directions and other processes necessary for cognitive learning. The situations are always interactive. The content of an SDM-session is based on Laban's (1975) movement analysis and encourages the child to achieve progress from single tasks to controlled combinations.

SDM helps children to control their actions so that their brains will learn to separate and integrate sensory information. Sometimes we can eliminate visual information, and instead we focus on hearing – the situation changes based on perceptions. The kinesthetic sense can be widely used in relaxation, body control exercises and perception of strength. The aim is to support the child's development so that they will learn to seek for the experiences they need.

A basic precondition for learning is a feeling of emotional and physical relaxation. In SDM, there is no right or wrong way to achieve. It is important that children have a successful experience and implement the tasks in their own way. A supporter (adult assisting the child) helps only when the child needs it. They are ready to step aside when not needed, but also ready to offer immediate assistance.

Children with learning disabilities have fewer good experiences than other children. SDM is an emotionally safe way of learning and participating. SDM makes it possible for the child to be successful according to their own needs and stage of development.

Short relaxation breaks between exercises diminish the extra sensory information to brain and liberates the memory and intelligence to work. It is easier for the child to concentrate on just one of the sensory modalities at a time and act according to that modality. The child will have a chance to control their actions and to learn to relax. They can focus just on what they are doing at the moment. The programme supports children in transferring the learning experiences in the group to every day life.

Methodology
Action research was chosen as the methodology. Flexibility in responsiveness was important with the children in this study. The hypothesis was that, with the help of SDM, it was possible to support children with learning disabilities. The hypothesis

was based on several pieces of research. According to a number of researchers (e.g. Ahonen, 1990; Alahuhta, 1990) learning disabilities are combined with children's difficulties in perceiving their own body, motor co-ordination, and, quite often, interaction. SDM offers various and wide exercise experiences in interactive situations based on trust and confidence.

Research participants

The research was carried out in a middle-size municipality in Lapland in Northern Finland. A group of seven children in Grades 1–3 became the research subjects. The common factor for the children was that all of them were in special education. Their parents were involved in the study from the first meeting, when they consented to be committed to it. It was important that they were able to commit themselves to driving the children to the sessions after school. This trip could be up to 70 km per session. The group gathered together twice a week in October and once a week in November. The length of a session was 45 minutes. The co-operation with parents was intensive throughout the process. The children's teachers were also research partners, and telephone discussions and meetings with them were carried out on a regular basis.

The names of all the children have been changed in order to protect identity.

Juho was a lively, eight-year-old boy who was interested in mathematics. He had very good handwriting, but he couldn't read. He had problems in concentrating. The school and his parents had tried many ways of solving this problem.

Eemeli was a happy third-grader, who had problems in auditory perception. He left out the first consonant from words. While playing, he could not stop moving so he often ran at the other children. He often ended up in different conflict situations.

Mikko was, according to his teachers, super-active. Communicating with him was easy, but he had problems with concentrating and reading.

Emilia was one of the two girls in the group, and she was creatively talented. According to her teacher, she had a reading disability, and her fine motor performances were slow.

Milla had problems in reading, writing and understanding.

Joonas was a first grader who had dysphasia. He was communicating bravely, and he liked to exercise. He had a reading disability, and problems sitting still and listening.

Taneli had learning disabilities, and there had been plans for a personal study programme due to his problems. He liked team sports, and he was a great skater.

Before starting the study, children's body awareness was observed. In the first session, a motor co-ordination test was carried out, and it was repeated in the last session. Some of the sessions were recorded, and after each there was a discussion about the events during the session. The next session was based on that information. A study diary was also kept, and photographs were taken.

Essential themes in all sessions were body awareness, working together as a pair or in groups, concentrating, and memorising the tasks – the children chose the task they preferred in the session. The last session was the same as the third one in order to follow the progression and compare the sessions. During the last session, the parents were present. Through watching a recorded session, the parents learned about SDM. The children's teacher reported on the possible changes in cognitive actions (e.g. concentration skills, attention, durability, curiosity), motor activity, fine and gross motor skills, interaction and co-operation skills. Both teachers and parents gave very positive feedback of the training period.

Results

During the study, the children's body awareness was analysed as they worked in pairs or groups on concentration. The researchers' backgrounds (nursing/physiotherapy) and former experiences over the course of 15 years' professional practice with children were very helpful when analysing the results.

In this study, the purpose was not to make generalisations, but rather a study of methods and practices which could be used with success. Both of the researchers used the feedback differently. It would be almost impossible to get the same results in another study because the programme in this study was created just for this group of children.

Juho learned to read at the end of October. It was interesting to notice that crossing the mid-line (e.g. when touching the left elbow to the right knee) became automatic at the same time. In the beginning, Juho needed an adult to support him manually in the task, and later on he needed to see the movement to make this happen. The processes were practised during three sessions, and the teacher took into account the group actions in the planning stage. Observing the action has crucial importance. Juho's mother said that she got some good ideas on how to support him with his homework. She learned to help him to concentrate.

Eemeli suffered from problems in auditory perception and, during the sessions, he was able to find a place where the information he heard always came from places he could see. He situated himself in the corners of the room. His teacher said that she had never considered the idea that his colliding with other children was due to problems in auditory perception. Conflict situations have ceased since he took part in the SDM programme. His teacher commented, 'Eemeli dares to ask and look into your eyes.'

Mikko performed much better in the second motor co-ordination test than in the first one. He was able to concentrate better, and he was shown to have a better self-esteem.

Emilia was creatively talented and was able to make cards from different materials, but she still needed help in cognitive learning. Emilia's crawling was exceptional. The second test of motor co-ordination went dramatically better than the first test.

Milla's hyperactivity may have covered other problems. At the end of the sessions, her situation was good, even though the teacher would have preferred to choose another child instead of Milla for the group.

Joonas profited from learning to concentrate better. He became more aware of his own strength, and able to control it. It is important to be able to control sensory information and also to be able to use different sensory modalities in the learning process. Joonas learned to read during the first grade despite his dysphasia even though he didn't get special education and or special support.

Taneli needed support in basic motor co-ordination movement experiences (e.g. with balancing on one knee, rolling to the right/left, copying another person's shape) even though he was a great skater and played ice hockey.

Many children have few opportunities for experiencing movement. SDM gives children an individual starting point because there is no pressure, only the feeling of success.

Discussion

According to Dewey (1991), learning is basically a problem-solving process in which a person is an active, curious performer. A person constantly evaluates his own actions and their results. Based on these results, he rebuilds his earlier structure of knowledge. It is vital for learning to find out how one's own construction works. The children actively took part in the SDM session according to their own capabilities. The instructor helped the children to use their own strengths. The children in the group supported each other in common exercises where different interaction relationships occurred – shared, supportive or resisting ('against'). These relationships supported both social and emotional development which, together with motor co-ordination and cognitive development, positively affected the children's self-esteem. Experiencing actions related to the children's own developmental stages gave them a successful experience which motivated them to participate and have new successful experiences. Favourable factors were a positive climate, voluntary participation, self-guided action and the possibility of using multimodal information. The children had opportunities to come up with ideas all by themselves.

In the group sessions, the same problems could be detected that occurred in the classroom. Some of the children were spectators, watching what the others were doing. Another child was withdrawn; a third one came up with other things to do. A fourth was looking for a fifth child to wrestle with. A sixth child was following the instructions and found a seventh one who behaved in the same way to be their partner. In the last session, the boys' differences were not so obvious anymore, and the girls preferred to work with each other. The group was functioning together. It was an exercise group. There was no talk of special education or differences between children. The children's parents said that the children were happy to come to the group sessions even though it was after school and far away. The teachers were very interested in SDM and chose it as a theme for a teacher training day.

We felt the sessions were sometimes challenging. The recording of the sessions gave the instructor the opportunity to evaluate her own actions and instruct from a new point of view. The short relaxation breaks were important for the supervising of the group. It was important for the supporting adults to be aware of the principles of the method, and to give the children enough time to gain their own experiences. When problems occurred, it was important to maintain an emotionally safe environment.

Eggert (1994) sees motor co-ordination as a holistic skill in which movement, action and communication unite in a social situation. Because the child's development is a holistic process, motor co-ordination should also be evaluated in a situation of disorder as well as of calm.

Conclusion

Our research was very interesting and also challenging. All seven children in the group had learning disabilities, but none had problems physically. They were able to move typically, but they had problems in body awareness and motor co-ordination. SDM was a positive experience for the children and the parents, and the teachers saw many benefits as a result of their children taking part in SDM sessions, such as in learning to read.

SDM can be integrated with mainstream education. It can be used as a collaborative tool for children, parents and different professional groups. As Juho's mother said:

> *You cannot teach anyone to read by force or by urging. There has to be another way.*

The next step

As this study took place several years ago, the researchers have been able to reflect on what has happened since. Kirsti has used SDM as a tool in her work as a physiotherapist and while educating. SDM has given her an interest in looking beyond visible phenomena, and it has created interesting discussions concerning different professional views.

The success of SDM has also given the teacher courage to support and encourage parents, and it has also made her stronger professionally. Sometimes a child has become so strong through taking part in SDM sessions that they have learned to walk again, even though their situation has been neurologically challenging. It is important to give the children time to learn and develop. It is also important for the adults to have time to reflect on their own practice and attitudes

The relevance of observation has been emphasised. The problems children have in daily life can be seen during the sessions. Training in gross motor skills helps the child to manage in everyday situations. SDM enables work on the important basic skills to take place, even though the demands of environment might change. All developmental gains for children were based on coming to know their own bodies and being able to interact with other people.

SDM is a valuable method for practising basic motor skills, supporting interaction skills and also as a tool for multi-professional collaboration in individual and group situations. The action is rewarding in itself. Even though exercise takes a lot of effort, it is also fun. Seeing the children learn and develop makes everyone happy to work with SDM again and again.

References

Ahonen, T. (1990) *Lasten Motoriset Koordinaatiohäiriöt: Kehitysneuropsykologinen seurantatutkimus*. Jyväskylä, Finland: University of Jyväskylä.

Alahuhta, E. (1990) *Leikin ja Puhun, Liikun ja Luen: Puhe-lukivaikeudet ja perusvalmiuksien harjoittaminen*. Helsinki, Finland: Otava

Dewey, D. (1991) 'Praxis and sequencing skills in children with sensorimotor dysfunction', *Developmental Neuropsychology*, 7, 197–206.

Eggert, D. (1994) 'Senso- ja psykomotoriset perustoiminnot: yhteydet oppimisvaikeuksiin ja niiden pedagogiseen voittamiseen'. In: K. Matilainen and K. ja Ruoho (ed.) *Näkökulmia Oppimisvaikeuksien Arviointiin, Ennaltaehkäisyyn ja Kuntoutukseen*. Joensuu, Finland: Joensuun Yliopiston täydennyskoulutuskeskuksen julkaisuja.

Kephart, N.C. (1971) *The Slow Learner in the Classroom (2nd edn)*. Columbus, OH: Charles. E. Merrill Publishing.

Laban, R. (1975) *Educational Dance*. Plymouth: McDonald & Evans Ltd.

Sherborne, V. (1994) *Lasten Kokonaiskehitystä Tukeva Liikunta: Yleisopetus, erityisopetus ja esiopetus*. Helsinki, Finland: Hakapaino Oy.

CHAPTER 11

Sherborne Developmental Movement in Sweden 1

Adapted Relationship Play and Children on the Autistic Spectrum

Berit Astrand
(Translator: Anne Sparrow)

The research

In this volume, most research described has involved direct investigation of aspects of Sherborne Developmental Movement (SDM). However, the research referred to in this chapter uses the Kristina project, a Swedish, pre-school, curriculum approach in which SDM (Sherborne, 2001) is embedded. As the outcomes of the research relate to differences between parent and teacher perceptions of the communication and social development of children with autistic spectrum disorder (ASD) rather than directly to relationship play, the research is not described in detail in this chapter,[1] although the context of the study and the literature are described.

The research group involved was a purposively selected group of eight children with ASD, boys and girls, aged between two years five months and nine years, who were involved with the research over a two-year period, subject to parental and professional permission, and ethical considerations.

The Kristina project

The Kristina project (Astrand, 1997) explored the use of Sherborne's 'relationship play' with children with ASD. The project led to a refined communication model known as 'adapted relationship play', or the 'Kristina model', which was used in this research project. All children go to pre-school in Sweden, and relationship play is included in the curriculum in schools based upon the Kristina model.

The Kristina model is based upon Laban's theory of movement, which promoted harmony within human life. According to Laban, the flow of movement fills all human functions and actions. It releases people from detrimental, inner tensions. It is a means of communication between people – all forms of expression, including speaking, writing and singing, are carried out through movement (Laban and Lawrence, 1974)

Laban (1980) considered movement to be of fundamental importance for human development. He maintained that young children need to experience the whole spectrum of movement qualities for themselves and that, as they grow, they need to be able to adapt their movements to their environment. According to Laban, the abilities to relate to the ego and the environment as well as to another person are foundational to personal well-being, and he believed that movement assisted in this. (A summary of Laban's principles can be found in Chapter 2.)

All interactions start with the body movement (Laban, 1980; Schopler et al., 1993; Sherborne, 2001; Söderberg, 1979). Body movement and voice are the primary instruments everyone has from birth. However, people with autism have difficulties in the areas of body awareness and communication (Duvner, 1994; Gillberg, 1992; Peeters, 1998).

Adapted relationship play in the Kristina model

In the Kristina model, the movement programme is developed individually and implements a particular structure designed to suit the individual child. An adult and a child work in partnership together from the beginning; they get to know each other and bond. They learn to recognise each other's vocal and non-vocal communications and to respond appropriately, so that a deeper relationship is built (Hårsman, 1990; Mahler et al., 1990). Once a day for five days each week, every child and adult partner follow their individual programme plan. The sessions take place at the same time and in the same place each day.

The developmental stage of the child is always a consideration in the design of the programme. At the start, the adult takes responsibility for the movement, and initiates and leads, while the child can be a passive participant. The adult has to be very observant of any responses from the child, and should respond immediately. Thereafter, the child takes the initiative, or the lead in movements can be shared between child and adult. Appropriate verbal labelling accompanies the movements in order to reinforce the link between word and physical action.

During the session, sometimes one partner will imitate the other, and a certain type of 'playing' takes place. This encourages communication, trust, body awareness, self-confidence and security. The different movements provide the opportunity to experience different qualities and levels of energy (time, weight, space, flow), and the children's on-going progress is assessed.

Through this movement programme, it is hoped that the children will gradually improve against specific criteria relating to the facility of movement, enjoyment, increase in confidence, sense of security and improvement in verbal and non-verbal communication skills.

An important outcome of working in such close partnership with the children is that the adults become very aware of when the child is functioning well and when the child has difficulties; they begin to be able to see into their child's world. It is important, therefore, that the adult is a stable, sensitive and self-aware person with good observation skills. The children respond to adults with a good sense of humour, sensitivity and maturity. The children need to know that their adult partner is genuinely interested in, and cares for, them.

The outline of a basic programme below (see Table 11.1) gives an idea of how SDM experiences, described in Sherborne's book (2001), can be incorporated within an adapted relationship play session. A movement session begins and ends with the same type of movement experience to indicate when a session is beginning and when it is ending (see below). Any changes made to the session always occur between these experiences.

Procedure

The research data was gathered through questionnaires issued to the parents and teachers. The questions focused on sociability and communication, and were divided into the categories of:

- Communication and sociability

- Imitation

- Response

- Intention and information

- Social development

- Deviant behaviour.

The rationale behind the questionnaire was derived from literature.

Communication and sociability

Parents and teachers were asked to record their observations relating to gesture, eye-contact and verbalisation (Bgork-Akesson,1992; Duckworth, 1976; Johansson, 1988; Meuron, 1976; Schopler and Mesibov, 1985; Söderberg, 1979; Schwebel and Raph, 1976; Wickens, 1976).

Table 11.1. A possible sequence of elements within an adapted relationship play session

1. Slide across the floor	9. Gathering and scattering
2. Roll	10. Spinning
3. Foot and hand against partners'	11. Rocking
4. Wheelbarrow	12. Shoulder partner roll
5. Aeroplane balance	13. Tunnel
6. Ride on partner	14. Back-to-back 'against' push
7. Houses	15. Back-to-back leaning
8. Standing see-saw	16. Sliding down backs to lie with heads on each other's shoulder for rest and relaxation.

Imitation

Schopler et al. (1993) stated that imitation is essential for the development of language and the ability to learn new words. Imitation can be both verbal and non-verbal. To be able to imitate, people must work together. Learning to do this can facilitate all future learning, and gives the child and adult an early opportunity to enjoy working and achieving together. This, in turn, can create the child's motivation to develop new skills.

Preparing to imitate through careful observation encourages heightened concentration on the part of the child. Imitation can be practised very early on in development. To achieve goals set within the field of imitation, the child must be able to look at or listen to another person. They must be able to understand the concept of working as a pair, and manage to organise their sounds, movements and behaviour in general, to be able to copy what they observe. If the child experiences difficulties in any of these basic skills, they will have problems coping with imitation.

Copying the use of resources, copying physical movement and copying sound are important steps on the way to developing the ability to imitate. Many children find it easier to copy movement than sound. Schopler et al. (1993) point out that it is important not to mistake modified behaviour for real imitation. Modified behaviour does not meet up with the assessment criteria set for imitation. It is often easy for a child to learn a certain activity like clapping hands or to copy a specific sound, as in 'goodbye', without understanding the actual essence of imitation. Real imitation means that the child can switch from different activities or sounds according to what it sees another person do. This can be tested by first teaching the child two or three actions or sounds separately. Then the child is asked to copy when sounds and actions are interchanged. If this is successful, it can be assumed that the child has a basic understanding of imitation.

Response

Early interaction, notably that between mother and child, is dominated by the mother's touch, eye-contact, taking turns, controlled movements and the fact that the mother has a very special way of speaking to the child. Early on, mother and child develop a special relationship based on mutual adaptation (Björk-Åkesson, 1992).

There used to be many people, scientists among them, who believed that infants and small children were practically incapable of communicating before they had learned to talk (op. cit.). There was, and still is, a tendency to view children with speech impairments in this way, even when they get older. Today, many scientists agree that the interaction built up between infant and parent provides the base for situations of interaction with other people later in life. Being in contact with other people, and taking part in the social side of life, is essential for the development of the child's competence. Interaction and communication in the smallest children is very much about sharing a rhythm with someone and being able to pay attention, i.e. paying attention to the same thing at the same time as someone else, and taking one's own turn in the interaction (op. cit.).

Intent and information

According to Björk-Åkesson (1992), it is necessary to teach some children, who have communication that is difficult to interpret, clear signals. When the child makes the signal, even without intent, it is interpreted as though it is significant and acted upon. In this way, the wider goal is that the child will eventually learn to use the signal intentionally.

Social development

Social competence is about the social rules that guide interaction. It means knowing about the roles of interplay, taking turns and developing strategies, such as those needed to initiate, maintain and end a conversation. It is also about being able to adapt manner, content and level to suit the other person (Björk-Åkesson, 1992). Social competence also means maintaining acceptable behaviour, being able to respond to the reactions of the other person, and knowing enough about oneself so it is possible to act suitably in a social situation.

Deviant behaviour

A possible explanation for this is that, as the children grow older, the parents expect that certain behavioural patterns will cease to exist. Abnormalities are sometimes not perceived as abnormalities before the child has reached a certain age. Behavioural patterns which are considered completely normal in young children, are seen as abnormal if observed in older children (Bratt, 1972; Alin Åkerman, 1995).

Future research

It is intended that future research project will focus upon the differences in skills of communication, interaction and social behaviour between children with ASD who practice adapted relationship play, and those who do not.

Acknowledgements

I would like to thank my supervisor, Britta Alin-Åkerman, professor, psychologist and psychotherapist, for invaluable support both during this survey and in the Kristinaprojekt. Through her, I have learned that one can combine serious research with the enthusiasm and spontaneous will to know more about one's own reality.

I would like to express my warmest 'thank you' to the children. They have taught me so much, and I shall always remember them with warmth and joy. And thanks to all the parents and colleagues who have taken part in this study, and other work, very ambitiously and conscientiously. I could not have done it without you!

References

Alin Åkerman, B. (1995) *De Första sju Åren: En helhetssyn på barns utveckling.* Stockholm, Sweden: Natur och Kultur.

Åstrand, B. (1997) *Ett Steg i Sänder.* Umeå, Sweden: SIH Läromedel.

Björk-Åkesson, E. (1992) *Samspel Mellan Små Barn med Rörelsehinder och Talhandikapp och Deras Föräldrar: En longitudinell studie (Göteborg Studies in Educational Sciences 90)*. Göteborg, Sweden: Acta Universitatis Gothoburgensis.

Bratt, N. (1972) *Den Tidiga Jagutvecklingen: Några av Piagets utvecklingsteorier belysta med vardagliga exempel.* Stockholm, Sweden: Bonniers.

Duckworth, E. (1976) 'Språk och tanke'. In: M. Schwebel and J. Raph (eds) *Piaget i Skolan*. Malmö, Sweden: Beyronds AB.

Duvner, T. (1994) *Barnneuropsykiatri, MBD/DAMP, Autistiska Störningar, Dyslexi*. Stockholm, Sweden: Almqvist & Wiksell Medicin/Liber Utbildning.

Gillberg, C. (1992) *Autism och Autismliknande Tillstånd hos Barn: Ungdomar och vuxna*. Stockholm, Sweden: Natur och Kultur.

Hårsman, I. (1990) *Om Små Barns Separationsreaktioner: Teoretiska utgångspunkter för en studie av spädbarns anpassning till daghem*. Stockholm, Sweden: HLS/BUV.

Johansson, I. (1988) *Språkutveckling hos Handikappade Barn*. Lund: Studentlitteratur.

Laban, R. (1980) *The Mastery of Movement*. Plymouth: Northcote House.

Laban, R. and Lawrence, F.C. (1974) *Effort*. Plymouth: Northcote House.

Mahler, S., Pine, F. and Bergman, A. (1990) *Barnets Psykiska Födelse: Symbios och individuation*. Stockholm, Sweden: Natur och Kultur.

Meuron, M. (1976) 'Klinisk interaktionism och småbarnsundervisningens process'. In: M. Schwebel and J. Raph (eds) *Piaget i Skolan*. Malmö, Sweden: Beyronds AB.

Peeters, T. (1998) *Autism: From theoretical understanding to educational intervention*. London: Whurr.

Schopler, E. and Mesibov, G.B. (eds) (1985) *Communication Problems in Autism*. New York, NY: Plenum.

Schopler, E., Reichler, R.J. and Lansing, M. (1993) *Lära Barn med Autism: Strategier för föräldrar och professionella*. Stockholm: Natur och Kultur.

Schwebel, M. and Raph, J. (eds) (1976) *Piaget i Skolan*. Malmö: Beyronds AB.

Sherborne, V. (2001) *Developmental Movement for Children: Mainstream, special needs and pre-school (2nd edn)*. London: Worth Publishing.

Söderberg, R. (1979) *Barnets Tidiga Språkutveckling*. Lund: Liber Läromedel.

Wickens, D. (1976) 'Piagets teori som modell för öppna undervisningssystem'. In: M. Schwebel and J. Raph (eds) *Piaget i Skolan*. Malmö: Beyronds AB.

Endnote

[1] The original paper is available online (http://www.lhs.se/upload/IOL/Publikationer/D-uppsatser/Astrand%20nr%2047.pdf) or from the author.

CHAPTER 12

Sherborne Developmental Movement in Sweden 2

When the Body Becomes Music

Birgitta Althoff
(Translator: Marie Janson)

Introduction

In August 2000, Birgitta Althoff, physiotherapist, and Karin Andersson, unit manager at ProAros, together with two occupational therapists, Lena Nilsson and Pia Theander, started a research project using Sherborne Development Movement (SDM) at the Viksängs and Stallhagens day-centres in Vasteras. The aim of this research was to find out if it was possible to stimulate movements in people with multiple disabilities through SDM, and to give them new opportunities to move, communicate and develop relationships with others.

At Viksängs day centre, staff and residents had already had experience of SDM, as Althoff (1994, 2005) had introduced the method in her capacity as consultant in adult rehabilitation. The positive results seen in people with multiple disabilities had impressed both staff and families. It had been noticed that those with multiple disabilities who were the hardest to communicate with also responded well to SDM. They appeared to relax more and initiated more movement following their inclusion in the programme, and it was also noticed that relationships strengthened between staff and those experiencing SDM.

To experience movement is very important for those who are wheelchair-bound. Forsberg and Hirschfeldt (1992) showed in their research into continuous sensory stimulation that movement is necessary for functions to develop and be retained. Without movement, both body and spirit wither – the maxim, 'use it or lose it', is a true one. They observed that anxiety and restlessness increased when people could not move. This restlessness was often expressed in

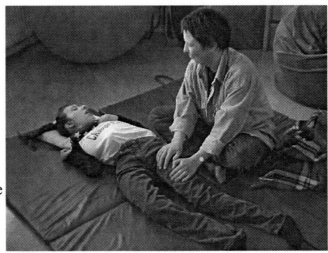

Figure 12.1. Anna, lying on the mat, enjoys feeling the flow of movement from her partner

stereotypical rocking motions, muscle tension and anxious cries. Others withdrew into themselves. These deeply human reactions are seen in people with multiple disabilities.

Bakk and Grunewald (2004) have highlighted the situation for children and adults with intellectual disability, from psychological as well as medical, social and legal perspectives. They observed that individuals with developmental delays are easily caught up in chaos and anxiety when they cannot interpret what is happening. Many have a reduced sense of time, which means that they do not know when to expect things to happen during the day or how long they will last. Since they have no speech, there are many opportunities for misunderstandings, which can make them fearful; their fear can be interpreted as aggression. Bakk and Grunewald suggested that staff can prepare the people they work with for what will happen during the day and help create a sense of time using symbols, photographs or pictures. However, they did not discuss movement stimulation.

Granlund (1993; Grandlund and Olsson, 1988) made it clear in her doctoral dissertation how, by using systematic observations, it is possible to develop communication with people with severe intellectual disabilities. She emphasised the need for different sensory modes to be stimulated; however, the need for movement was not described in any detail. Although George Hill (Hill, 1991) has described one way to work with adults with intellectual disabilities, the movement experiences in SDM are mostly suited to those who are not limited in their movements or wheelchair-bound.

Methodology
The starting point for Sherborne's ideas (2001) was that the fundamental need of the individual is that of security and trust in another person, which forms the foundation for developing relationships with others.

Participants
At the two day centres, six people with multiple disabilities were given the opportunity to try SDM for six months. These individuals had no or very limited means of communicating. They had vision and hearing, but no speech. All, except one, were wheelchair-bound. They had severely limited mobility and intellectual disabilities. One participant was autistic. None used picture support proactively as a means of communication, although three people used symbols to prepare for activities.

The delivery of SDM was tailored to each individual with multiple disabilities. A physiotherapist assessed any misalignments that could have been painful in the context of SDM sessions; for example, severe flexion of arms and legs, spinal curvature, etc. As part of the analysis, the therapist tried to find comfortable and ergonomically correct starting positions for participants as well as staff. Staff were trained in SDM, and it was emphasised that self-expression was the basis for the movement programme, not the individual's physical misalignment. To tune into the other person, to mirror and to develop sensitivity are fundamental concepts when it comes to dealing with people with multiple disabilities who have communication problems.

Those who could not move actively were prepared for the next move to be performed in collaboration with their partner. It was important to meet the individual at their own level and to go along with their movement, confirming and respecting their body language. The facilitator provided different, pleasant stimuli to encourage movement and a response from the individual. In the beginning, the individual was supported through so called 'containing'.

Collaboration develops in SDM when the participant feels secure in their body. The facilitator and the participant can sit opposite each other, next to or one behind the other. Awareness of each individual's personal space grows, as does the secure relationship with the underlying surface. The participant initially goes along with the facilitator's movements, and then begins to initiate their own movements. The partners then begin to take turns in initiating moves. This develops further by taking turns in receiving and initiating, testing one's strength against each other, and then making moves together. The facilitator has to explore which tempo best suits the participant – slower or faster. Once the participant is confident, then the 'melody of the movement' can begin to be varied.

Bobath (1980) has described how spasticity and other forms of muscle tension can relax with specific sensory input. We have developed Sherborne's method for use with people with multiple disabilities by supporting small rocking movements in their arms and legs. This movement stimulates a wave of movement through the whole body. This can give a pleasant feeling of wholeness and strengthen the subjective perception of oneself as an individual.

Tempo, force, amplitude and fluidity of the movement can be developed according to individual needs. It is good to capture the contrasts and humour in the moves to enhance the effect. The other person's moves are mirrored and confirmed to build confidence. Damasio (2003) writes that confidence develops in the body through sensory input.

Recording instruments used
Data was collected through continuous, semi-structured diary notes, analysis of videotapes based on the Marte Meo method (Hedenbro and Wirtberg, 2000), and follow-up meetings involving the occupational therapists.

Implementation
August 2000

- Nine people employed at the two day-centres were trained to become facilitators at SDM Level 1 according to the International Sherborne Association criteria (http://www.sherborne-association.org.uk/). The aim was that the staff would feel comfortable themselves in their bodies and with the way of working.

- A baseline was developed, and objectives were formulated for each participant in the project based upon what they were capable of, how they expressed their needs, and their current motional behaviour and ability to move.

- An information event for the participants' families and legal guardians was arranged to give them the opportunity to ask questions and discuss concerns. Without their approval, this project could not have been carried out.

September 2000

- Staff started to use SDM, once to twice per week at each day-centre. The writer was available as a consultant when needed.

November/December 2000

- Follow-up meetings were held with staff at both centres.

April 2001

- Further follow-up meetings with staff were held.

- Video material was viewed and observations made by staff were collated.

- Practical exercises in body self-awareness were carried out.

August/September 2001

- Videotapes were analysed and edited, and reports collated. Feedback was given to those involved in the project.

Results

The narratives below are based upon extracts from diaries, observations and reflections from the movement sessions, and analysis of the video films. All names have been changed to protect confidentiality.

Viktor

Start of intervention: August 2000

At the beginning of the first session, Viktor sat completely immobile and hunched over. He was a small and prematurely aged man with a wrinkled face and screwed-up eyes. He always brought a cuddly toy animal with him as a comforter during the day, holding it in a tight grip.

He had very little mobility. He could sit by himself on the floor, but sat with obvious tension and was perceived as uncomfortable on that surface. He did not move spontaneously, and could not stand up.

Viktor had no speech, and did not express his needs. He probably had very little understanding of time elapsed. He shunned bodily contact. Staff had almost given up on reaching him as a person.

Summary of outcomes: June 2001

Following the intervention, Viktor was perceived as more active than he had been at the beginning of the project. From being 'invisible', he had become 'somebody'. He often smiled and laughed, initiating contact and movement by stamping his feet on the footpads of his wheelchair. He had a livelier demeanour, and frowned, smiled and looked expectantly at people, seeking eye-contact. He responded to questions with a smile, and showed through body language what he wanted and did not want. Relatives noticed a marked difference, observing that he was a lot happier and was making contact with them.

Viktor also had a straighter and prouder posture when sitting in the wheelchair. He had better circulation in arms and legs, which also felt warmer to touch. In movement sessions, he now dared to let go of his cuddly toys in anticipation of the experience. He now enjoyed the physical contact with people, and did not want to end the sessions. He had developed a sense of time, and demonstrated expectations.

Inga
Start of intervention: August 2000
Inga sat in a wheelchair. She often smiled at people – a stereotypical and anxious smile. She had a small, thin, birdlike body with stiff, hook-like arms and legs. She looked fragile, as if her limbs could snap. Her arms, legs and back were misaligned, and she could not sit or stand, although she could move her left arm slightly. She waved stereotypically with one arm. Her sense of time was in the present. She became anxious when left alone, and her requests for attention could be perceived as demanding. She communicated through pictures and photos.

She was not comfortable on the floor, and appeared frightened of making movements.

Summary of outcomes: June 2001
By the end of the intervention, Inga had become more focused. Her SDM leader perceived that Inga did not only demand, but she also reciprocated. She gave clear signals – through nods, meaning 'Yes', and using the right arm to indicate 'No'. She appeared less anxious and frightened of movements, and could cope with waiting alone without crying and screaming.

She could now move without being 'contained', and did not pull her body together tightly in defence as before. Prior to the intervention, she had always screamed during physical therapy; now she seemed to enjoy the movements, and look forward to sessions. The tension in her legs seemed to disappear during sessions.

Karin
Start of intervention: August 2000
Karin was a young, wheelchair-bound woman with spastic legs. Her knees were locked in a misaligned position, and she had poor blood circulation in her arms and legs. She was able to wheel herself around the room, although she had to be strapped in across the hips so that she felt secure and did not fall out of the wheelchair when she waved her arms. She could stretch, seek contact, and show her needs. On the floor, she was able to roll her body, and sit by herself.

Although she could not speak, Karin could understand spoken words. She communicated using clear but stereotypic body language.

Karin had a strong and stubborn personality. She sometimes experienced deep anxiety, and then rocked her upper body back and forth violently, while emitting screams, extending her arms towards the ceiling in desperation and staring wildly. The staff were very upset by this. A heavy duvet sometimes calmed her down.

Karin needed emphatic and strong physical contact; for example, a strong hug. She found it difficult to accept unexpected sounds such as talking, sneezing and coughs. The sounds startled her and increased her anxiety. She needed to sit by herself while eating, so she was not disturbed, and was uncomfortable with new staff and in groups.

Summary of outcomes: June 2001
 Following the SDM intervention, Karin seemed to be more secure. She had developed a range of moves that she could perform, and understood the humour during the movements. During sessions, she was able to enjoy the movements, then relax her body and wait without becoming restless. She had developed a better sense of time.

Karin had developed a relationship with [C.], but also with others. By the end of the intervention, she was becoming a member of the group and was accepted by the others.

On good days, Karin expressed happiness, and anticipated SDM. She also coped better with minor disturbances. If she was prepared in advance for a cough or sneeze, she was now able to accept the noise. On other days, she did not want to do SDM, and clearly showed when she wanted to be left alone. Her very deep dread and fear on certain days was still a problem.

Sten
Start of intervention: August 2000
At the beginning of the SDM intervention, Sten would sit immobile, seemingly half asleep in the wheelchair. Most of the time, he seemed tired.

Sten's movement was extremely limited. He was able only to move his eyes and head, and did not initiate any other voluntary movements. His whole body was tense, with the chest kept pulled in, like a cage that was too small for his lungs. He held his arms pressed close against his chest, but made no contact with the rest of the body. His hands and feet were cold, indicating poor circulation. Staff found it difficult to move his stiff arms. When eating, he was unable to hold the spoon himself, and staff helping him to eat found it difficult.

Sten's sense of time was only in the present. He needed concrete objects and their sounds to understand what was happening; for example, a ball enabled him to realise that it was time for physical exercise, or the sound of the hoist prepared him for lifting.

Sten liked bodily contact and action, and the staff felt that they would like to do more for Sten. However, he was easily left in a corner. The regular stimulation which he received was focused on personal care; for example, to help him to change his position or to give tactile massage. The best contact Sten made with staff was through training in the therapy pool, when he could relax and balance his head for short periods.

Summary of outcomes: June 2001
Following the SDM intervention, Sten appeared more awake, and reacted more visibly to his environment. He often looked pleased. His sense of time developed, and when anticipating an exercise, his eyes were questioning and expectant. He seemed to take in everything that was happening to his body, his eyes following the movements as if he were rediscovering it.

Now, he had better circulation, and his head, arms and legs were warmer to touch. He appeared to have regained contact with his body. In a relaxed state, his whole body was more open than before. His arms were more flexible at the shoulders and elbows, and he could lower his arms to his stomach, which made it easier for staff to help him to eat.

Now that Sten seemed to be thriving, his parents felt more secure and relaxed about him, and felt able to go on holiday abroad. They noticed that Sten was more alert, that his body was more open, and that his arms were more relaxed.

Tina
Start of intervention: August 2000
Tina appeared to be a prematurely aged woman with a tense, scrunched face. She had limited facial movement, and produced a lot of saliva. She made only fleeting eye-contact with others, and wandered back and forth making stereotypical circular move-ments with her left arm. She expressed strong anxiety, sometimes crouching down on all fours and rocking herself.

During early sessions, she usually sat on the floor, turned away from the rest of the group. She did not dare to stretch out on the floor, and was anxious about moving and frightened of new moves.

Summary of outcomes: September 2001
Over the course of the intervention, Tina became calmer and her level of concentra-tion improved. She was also perceived to be more engaged and to be participating better.

Her range of movements had increased. She had become more secure with her body on the floor, and dared to rest there, even without physical contact with her facilitator. She was able to rest her body in a more relaxed and symmetrical position, and was less stuck in stereotypic movements.

Tina showed responses through her body, and made more eye-contact. She started to smile, and to make more varied facial expressions.

Anna
Starting of intervention: August 2000
Anna was a young girl who could make contact with other people using her eyes and

through a wide range of vocalisations, although she had no speech. She had integrity, humour, and communicative body language and facial expressions, which she used to indicate clearly what she did and did not want. She was also able to communicate using photos of situations and objects.

Her range of movements was greater than that of her peers. She could kick using her left leg, move her hands slightly towards her body, and turn her head and balance it. Her whole body was spastic, locked in a permanent position with bent legs and crooked back. When highly tense, her ribcage rubbed against the hip bone, and this caused her pain.

She stiffened her whole body while being moved, and it was difficult to get her into the wheelchair or move her on to the shower trolley due to strong muscle tensions in her arms and legs. She was dependent on experienced staff, and was insecure with strangers. Afraid of moving, she did not want her arms to be touched.

On the floor, she was insecure. She had strong muscular tension, and very little spontaneous movement. She could not sit by herself.

Summary of outcomes: September 2001
Anna started to laugh when we began again in September! She seemed to have positive physical memories. Her co-operation, expectation and pleasure in movements were inspiring. She was able to lie down more symmetrically, and could lie on her side without producing as much saliva as before. She had better motor control of her mouth and was more relaxed in her body. She was no longer frightened and tense when being transferred to her wheelchair or the toilet. She had become more secure on the floor, and was less frightened of moving. As her body was more relaxed, daily care experiences were more pleasant for her and easier for the staff.

Anna also showed more security in her daily life. She no longer burst into hysterical rage when a new member of staff arrived, although she kept her integrity and still wanted to get to know people before they worked closely with her on intimate tasks, such as feeding.

Discussion and conclusion
The main participants in this study had severely limited movements and multiple disabilities and, lacking speech, and they had only a limited means of self-expression. Since taking part in the SDM programme, Viktor, Inga, Karin, Sten, Tina and Anna now had the potential to develop pleasure in movements, body language, facial expressions and gestures. They were able to relax their arms and legs into more extended symmetrical positions. Their posture while sitting improved significantly in two cases. Their range of movements increased, and they made fewer stereotypic movements.

There was an especially marked difference in those who were almost totally immobile. Two participants, who were perceived as completely immobile, initiated movements for the first time during the project. In two individuals, it was noticed that there was improved blood circulation in arms and legs, as well as reduced saliva production.

The ability of the participants to communicate with others improved, and they were perceived by staff as more settled. They showed more trust in others, and eye-contact improved in those who had had a problem with this. They responded to the movements using different sounds, smiles and laughter.

Through this project, the participants also received more attention from staff members. Not only the people supporting movement sessions, but also other members of staff, noticed a positive change in other areas of daily living, such as meal times, toilet visits, lifting, etc., and parents as well as staff, in four instances, reported increased attention, increased calm and a sense of security in the home.

The nine staff who were trained in SDM were able to give the participants the safety and respect which is the foundation for co-operation. The project enabled a dialogue between the facilitators and the physiotherapist. The observations made by staff, as well as diaries and videotaping, added new knowledge about each person's disability.

The next step
Following the implementation of the SDM programme, the attitude among the wider staff group at Viksängs and Stallhagens day centres also developed, culminating in an acceptance and positive expectation of SDM. Thus, there is now a favourable climate for staff to develop their work with SDM. The approach is gentle on both staff and participants, and it creates a calm atmosphere. The staff get immediate feedback through their collaboration with people with multiple disabilities.

To maintain the engagement and knowledge around SDM, it is important that the staff maintain the dialogue with SDM practitioners and the physiotherapist. Staff members need the opportunity to try out SDM sensitively and be creative in collaboration with the participants. However, people with multiple disabilities change, develop, become ill or age prematurely which means that the ways of stimulating movement will have to be modified in on-going consultation with the physiotherapist.

Continuing research is needed to investigate further the connection between intervention using SDM and the positive changes observed. The need of people with multiple disabilities for interaction and movement stimulation needs more attention. It may be that a lack of control of the body and a lack of ability to communicate produce a sense of insecurity, which was observed as fear of movement, stereotypical behaviour and tense muscles.

References
Althoff, B. (2005) *Sherbornemetoden*. Stockholm, Sweden: Fysioterapi.
Althoff, B. and Ståhle, M. (1994) *Självtillit, Rörelseglädje och Kreativitet: Sherbornemetodens grundstenar*. Stockholm, Sweden: Sjukgymnasten.
Bakk, A. and Grűnevald, K. (2004) *Omsorgsboken*. Stockholm, Sweden: Liber förlag.
Bobath, K.A. (1980) *A Neurophysiological Basis for the Treatment of Cerebral Palsy.*

London: Heinemann.

Damasio, A.R. (2003) *Descartes Misstag: Känsla, förnuft och den mänskliga hjärnan.* Stockholm, Sweden: Natur och kultur.

Forsberg, H. and Hirschfeldt, H. (eds) (1992) *Movement Disorders in Children (Medicine and Sport Science 36).* Basel, Switzerland: Karger.

Granlund, M. (1993) *Communicative Competence in Persons with Profound Mental Retardation.* Uppsala, Sweden: Acta Uppsaliensis.

Granlund, M. and Olsson, C. (1988) *Kommunicera Mera: Teoridel.* Stockholm, Sweden: Stiftelsen ALA.

Hedenbro, M. and Wirtberg, I. (2000) *Samspelets Kraft: Marte Meo – möjlighet till utveckling.* Stockholm, Sweden: Liber AB.

Hill, G. (1991) *Sherborne Movement with Adults* (Training materials). Sherborne Association (UK) [online at: http://www.sherborne-association.org.uk/].

Sherborne, V. (2001*) Developmental Movement for Children: Mainstream, special needs and preschool (2nd edn).* London: Worth Publishing.

PART 4

Sherborne Developmental Movement in the Future

CHAPTER 13

Moving Forward

Barry Carpenter

The contributions to this book have made very clear the need to continue to research the benefits of Sherborne Developmental Movement (SDM). Research has always played a dominant and contributory role to developments in the field of disability (Rose and Grosvenor, 2001). What is unique, at the start of this 21st century, about this phase of research in the field is its potential to be practitioner-led. As Michael Guralnick (2004) has stated:

> *We now know so much about childhood disability that we must move to second generation research. This must be practitioner led and evidence based.*

Many other authors have joined him in encouraging practitioner-led research (Bell, 1994; Roberts-Holmes, 2005; Whitehurst, 2006), including the General Teaching Council for England (GTCE), which has advocated that professionally informed practice should be based on sound evidence systematically analysed by practitioners (GTCE, 2004, 2006).

Schools are gradually beginning to hear this message through journals and policy guidance (cf. *British Journal of Learning Support*, February 2006), and it is anticipated that they will see themselves increasingly as research-based organisations. The Department for Education and Skills (DfES) has a website specifically focusing upon research-informed practice (http://www.standards.dfes.gov.uk/research/resources), and the National Teacher Research Panel (http://www.standards.dfes.gov.uk/ntrp/) is among those organisations encouraging discourse among teachers around school-based research.

Sunfield School, as part of its response, established a Research Institute in January 2005. Its purpose is to promote evidence-based practice and to develop practitioner-led research. The school's aspiration is that in so doing we will find some of the complex answers needed to some of the very intricate questions posed by the children currently entering our special education system. Many of these children have a profile of disability that we have not seen before, and as such present new and diverse challenges in classroom situations. Indeed, the learning patterns of these children can be quite different to those that we have previously experienced; for example, children with foetal alcohol syndrome (Carr-Brown and Halle, 2005; Goswami, 2004; Kopera-Frye et al., 1996; Streissguth, 2005).

Sunfield School's main focus is on children with autistic spectrum disorder (ASD). The school serves the needs of children at the profound end of the autistic spectrum. The prevalence of ASD is an on-going debate (Department for Education and Skills, 2006; Gillberg, 2006; Lister, 2006; Medical Research Council, 2006; National Autistic Society, 2006; Shattock and Whiteley, 2006), and recent figures reported by Baird et al. (2006) suggest that the incidence of ASD has now risen to 1 in 86 children. There is now a pan-European initiative, the 'European Autism Information System', co-ordinated in the UK by Professor Martin Knapp at King's College, London, to establish and monitor the prevalence of ASD across Europe.[1]

I have been a Sherborne practitioner throughout my teaching career, and have seen the value of SDM with a whole range of children with special education needs and, indeed, as a medium for shared learning experiences between typically developing children in mainstream settings and their peers with learning disabilities (Carpenter, 1994). For the child with profound ASD who presents a profile of severe and complex learning needs, new pedagogies need to be evolved to embrace those needs. This is one area where I feel that SDM has been reborn in this 21st century and is poised to make a significant and meaningful response.

In taking a holistic view of the learning needs of children with profound ASD, it became obvious to me that there were elements of their learning style that were not being effectively used. Much professional practice now acknowledges the visual learning strengths of children with ASD (Jordan and Powell, 1995), and sensory approaches to learning have continued to be a significant feature in recent years within the curriculum for children with severe and complex learning needs (Bogdashina, 2001; Longhorn, 1991). Teachers regularly utilise the learning styles of the child according to visual, auditory, tactile, olfactory and gustatory modalities, but the kinaesthetic mode of learning is often missed. I therefore hypothesised that SDM could make a contribution to the learning of this group of children, which resulted in the 'Sherborne @ Sunfield' project carried out by Jotham Konaka (see Chapters 3 and 4).

As the many research projects in this book suggest, kinaesthetic learning is powerful and tangible for the child, and I believe strongly that we do not value it enough. Veronica Sherborne, in her training, would constantly remind people that children with special educational needs did not have a good concept of their bodies, particularly of the solar plexus region at the very centre of the body. This would often be reflected in children's drawings, where they would draw a person with head, arms and legs, but often with the arms and legs coming out of a very large head. This was because, as a non-weight bearing area in everyday life, their solar plexus had not been reinforced in their brain image of their body.

In SDM lessons, where children are working collaboratively and co-operatively with others, their body can be gently guided through movement patterns thus giving them a whole body experience during which the brain can assimilate complex information about the body through movement. SDM very much operates within the visual-spatial domain. Children can focus on their visual and spatial experience of movement; they can see as well as feel the way their bodies move in relation to space. Their figure–ground experience can make sense of how their body relates to the environment, and the child can ground their being literally by touching the floor. This motor reinforcement is concrete, and appeals to the learning pattern of the child with ASD, as well as those who have Down syndrome and Foetal Alcohol Syndrome among many others.

The impact of research

Some recent research in the field of neuroscience now further underpins the value of SDM. It has been known for some decades (Ramachandran and Oberman, 2006) that neurons in the pre-motor cortex of the brain fire when the brain is involved in a goal-directed activity (e.g. reaching for a food). However, when investigating a newly discovered class of nerve cells in the brain called mirror neurons, Rizolatti and colleagues (2006) discovered that when one person watched another carry out an action or experience an emotion, a similar pattern of neurons also fired in their brain. They showed that mirror neurons were not only involved in establishing another's intentions, but also in enabling individuals to copy another person's actions and inducing empathy with another person's emotional state. Their research has important resonances with SDM in areas of body concept, motor learning, imitation, connection and empathy.

Body concept

Rizzolatti and colleagues (2006) speak of 'the activity of mirror neurons [underpinning] the understanding of motor acts'. Therefore, through regular movement sessions, we may be able to improve the child's understanding of the function and purpose of various aspects of their body. High functioning writers who have ASD tell us that their own self-image and perception of their body and its interrelationship with the environment is not always well developed (Williams, 1998; Jackson, 2002). SDM could improve the physical functioning of the child and their ability to operate physically with confidence in their school, home, and community settings.

Motor learning

Rizzolatti and colleagues (2006) stated that actions performed by one person can activate motor pathways in another's brain responsible for performing the same action. In teaching SDM, the actions are often modelled by the person leading the session. Where children need a particular level of intervention due to their needs, then they are often directly supported by an older peer or a member of staff.

Imitation

Imitation has been identified as a foundation step to learning for many years. Indeed, in a recent study using data from the 1970 British Cohort Study, Feinstein and Duckworth (2006) reported that the single measure most predictive of later achievement was children's ability to copy accurately. They recommended any activity that encouraged visual-motor development in children. If we link imitation to what has been discussed earlier in this chapter, and blend it in with what is now known about brain functioning, then the following statement from Rizzolatti and colleagues (2006) has great significance:

> *Imitation requires reproduction of actions performed by another person. If mirror neurons underlie the uniquely human facility for imitation, the mirror system may serve as a bridge that allows us to teach and learn new skills.* (p. 61)

As practitioners, we need to realise that although we may have a range of effective teaching strategies, they may not be matched to the learning style of every child we teach. Neuroscience indicates that while we need to value imitation as a foundation stone for building a child's learning skills, understanding how imitation is initiated in the brain can now open up a range of opportunities for the teaching and learning of new skills, particularly to children with ASD who, like many children with significant learning disabilities, are not incidental learners.

Social development
Communication
Rizzolatti and colleagues (2006) hypothesised:

> *Mirror neurons may also underlie the ability to imitate another's action and thereby learn, making the mirror mechanism a bridge between individual brains for communication and connection.* (p. 56)

This statement not only supports the motor development contribution that SDM can make to a child's learning acquisitions, but it also indicates that SDM may be able to strengthen connectivity and communication, an outcome observed by many of the researchers writing in this volume. This is pertinent to the development of the child with ASD. Communication is a major area of the 'triad of impairment' associated with ASD (Wing, 2002), and the lack of social engagement in children with ASD is very pronounced. Therefore anything that can strengthen communication interactions and the connection of the child with ASD to another human being is to be encouraged.

Empathy
Children with ASD cannot readily read the facial expressions of others leading to impaired 'Theory of Mind' (Baron-Cohen, 2000). Consequently, their ability to engage emotionally or show empathy is also disrupted. The research of Rizzolatti and colleagues suggests that the process of reading faces relies on mirror neurons, which Ramachandran and Oberman (2006) have found are not activated reciprocally in individuals with ASD as they are with the typically developing population:

> *Studies of people with autism show a lack of mirror neuron activity in several regions of the brain. Researchers speculate that treatments designed to restore this activity could alleviate some of autism's symptoms.* (p. 64)

They suggest that the stimulation of mirror neurons through motor and movement-based activity can be helpful to the development of empathy in the child with ASD, for whom the ability to show empathy is cited as an area of difficulty (Trevarthen et al., 1996). Therefore, focusing on learning strategies such as SDM that impacts on mirror neurons early in a child's development, may have a subsequent positive effect by aiding the process of more sophisticated skill acquisition in the areas of social interaction, which are underpinned by empathy and social engagement.

Within SDM, therefore, it is possible not only to stimulate the physical/motor development of the child, but perhaps also the emotional/social development of the child. Many SDM movement experiences are based around interactive patterns and relationship play (Sherborne 2001); thus children can be encouraged in a range of social communication behaviours such as eye-contact, turn-taking and sharing.

There is much more yet to come from the field of neuroscience, but if we begin to hear some of these early messages then we can contextualise SDM in this 21st century, and see that it has yet another major contribution to make.

Sherborne Developmental Movement and well-being
I have mentioned the physical, social, emotional and cognitive benefits that SDM can have for the child with ASD and indeed for those with the full range of special educational needs. These areas of development map well into the current targets set for all children through the Every Child Matters framework (DfES, 2003, 2004). In particular, children can enjoy and achieve through SDM; their safety in those sessions is a priority, and they are taught how to use their bodies in safe and purposeful ways. Moreover, SDM can make a major contribution to children being healthy. The sense of physical well-being in children following SDM sessions is very obvious, and there are very clear motor gains for the child. Those engaged in sport often experience a sense of physical and emotional well-being derived from endorphin release during exercise. Observations of brain activity in children with ASD following physical activity demonstrates that they also experience this (Jordan, 2001). This sense of well-being is a powerful reinforce for self-image, self-esteem and self-worth.

What I do not think has been significantly acknowledged in SDM is its contribution to the emotional well-being of the child (see Chapter 6). There are many concerns around the mental health of children generally (DfES, 2003, 2004; Meltzer et al., 2000). In fact 1 in 10 children will experience some mental health problem during their childhood (Foundation for People with Learning Difficulties, 2002); however, for children with special educational needs, the Office for National Statistics (Melzer et al., 2000) predicts that 3 in 5 children with special educational needs will experience some mental health problem. Research from the Foundation for People with Learning Disabilities (2002), through a national enquiry, indicated that 4 in 10 people with learning disabilities in the 13–25 age group would develop some mental health need, and this included those with ASD. Some writers specifically concerned with ASD have indicated that this could be even higher (Ghaziuddin, 2005).

We must not wait for these problems to arise in our children, as the consequences of psychiatric intervention and medication can be very life disorientating. Rather, we must make sure that we have built preventative strategies into our curriculum. We need to offer education that keeps our children emotionally strong – a high level of emotional resilience is essential to their eventual quality of life in adulthood.

Again, I believe SDM has a significant contribution to make here. The very essence of the work developed by Sherborne looked at mother–child dyads and the interactive patterns that emerged from these dyads. The relationship play components of SDM contribute significantly to social and emotional development in children with special educational needs (see Chapter 6).

Conclusion

In this section, I have tried to indicate that new information, particularly from the field of neuroscience (cf. Shonkoff and Phillips, 2000), has helped us to re-evaluate the contribution that SDM can make to the learning of children with a range of special educational needs; in particular, for those with ASD, for whom we are still evolving appropriate pedagogies. We do not have all the answers, and hence the need for practitioner-led, evidence-based research. The research in this book has contributed towards extending our knowledge of the impact that SDM has on individuals both in mainstream schooling and those with special educational needs.

When Veronica Sherborne first developed her movement programme in the 1960s and 1970s, it was based on sound professional judgement probably supported by a fair degree of intuition, for she was an exceptional practitioner, totally in tune with her pupils. In the time in which she was working, there was not the emphasis on providing evidence for the efficacy of interventions that there is today. Now, however, there is a greater academic demand for evidence, and SDM has been open to criticism because of its lack of empirical base. Yet the programme has survived for four decades. I believe this is because practitioners see it work for children; they have continued to use it, not because they are operating in some blind belief, but rather because it has been proved effective through the quality of responses from children.

However, this is not to dismiss the need for a clear rational for the use of SDM in the modern day curriculum (Hill, 2006). SDM is a dynamic not a static programme, and the late Veronica Sherborne would be the first to say that. She was a responsive practitioner, and I believe current effective delivery can only occur through our responsivity as practitioners. Differentiation is key to our practice (Carpenter, Ashdown and Bovair, 2001); as such it has to be professionally informed routed in the true learning experience of the child with special educational needs. However, for the programme to be valued and to develop in ways that are meaningful and relevant to children, we need to ensure that it is supported in grounded evidence, which is rigorously tested and analysed.

This book, combined with the recent publication of Cyndi Hill (2006), and the recently developed 'Sherborne @ Sunfield' programme (Konaka, 2007), will leave a firm foundation upon which practice and research can build. The motivation for all of us should be what SDM can do for all kinds of children anywhere in the world and especially, the child with special educational needs. For me, it is what I have witnessed over 30 years of practice – the capacity of SDM to touch the child at their point of learning need.

References

Baird, G., Simonoff, E., Pickles, A., Chandler, S., Loucas, T., Meldrum, D. and Charman, T. (2006) 'Prevalence of disorders of the autism spectrum in a population cohort of children in South Thames: the Special Needs and Autism Project (SNAP)', *The Lancet*, 368 (9531), 210–215.

Baron-Cohen, S. (2000) 'Theory of mind and autism: a fifteen year review'. In: S. Baron-Cohen, H. Tager-Flusberg and D. Cohen (eds) *Understanding Other Minds: Perspectives from developmental cognitive neuroscience*. New York: Oxford University Press.

Bell, G. (ed.) (1994) *Action Research, Special Needs and School Development*. London: David Fulton.

Bogdashina, O. (2001) *A Reconstruction of the Sensory World of Autism*. Sheffield: Sheffield Hallam University Press.

Carpenter, B. (1994) 'Shared learning: the developing practice of integration for children with severe learning difficulties', *European Journal of Special Needs Education*, 9 (2), 182–189.

Carpenter, B., Ashdown, R. and Bovair, K. (2002) *Enabling Access: Effective teaching and learning for pupils with learning difficulties (2nd edn)*. London: David Fulton.

Carr-Brown, J. and Halle, M. (2005) 'Twitches that indicate alcohol may hurt babies', *The Sunday Times* (20 November). (http://www.acbr.com/fas/alcoholFetusUltrasound.htm)

Department for Education and Skills (2003) *Every Child Matters (Green Paper)*. Nottingham: DfES.

Department for Education and Skills (2004) *Every Child Matters: Change for children*. Nottingham: DfES.

Department for Education and Skills (2006) *First Annual Report: Autism Research Co-ordination Group*. Annesley: DfES Publications.

Feinstein, L. and Duckworth, K. (2006) *Development in the Early Years: Its importance for school performance and adult outcomes*. London: Centre for Research on the Wider Benefits of Learning. [Online at: www.learningbenefits.net]

Foundation for People with Learning Disabilities (2002) *Count Us In: Report of the Committee of Inquiry into the Mental Health of Young People with Learning Disabilities*. London: Mental Health Foundation.

General Teaching Council for England (2004) *GTC Research Digest 2000–2004*. London: GTCE.

General Teaching Council for England (2006) 'Using research in your school and in your teaching: research engaged professional practice'. [Online at: http://www.gtce.org.uk/tplf]

Ghaziuddin, M. (2005) *Mental Health Aspects of Autism and Asperger Syndrome*. London: Jessica Kingsley.

Gillberg, C. (2006) 'The prevalence of ASD and ADHD' (Powerpoint presentation). [Online at: http://www.mindroom.org/socialbrain2/assets/gillberg_s_17.ppt]

Goswami, U. (2004) 'Neuroscience, education and special education', *British Journal of Special Education*, 31 (4), 175–183.

Guralnick, M. (2004) 'Early Intervention for children with intellectual disabilities: current knowledge and future prospects.' Keynote address to the 12th IASSID World Congress, Montpellier, France (15 June 2004).

Hill, C. (2006) *Communicating through Movement: Sherborne Developmental Movement – towards a broadening perspective*. Clent: Sunfield Publications.

Jackson, L. (2002) *Freaks, Geeks and Asperger Syndrome: A user guide to adolescence.* London: Jessica Kingsley.

Jordan, R. (2001) *Autism with Severe Learning Disabilities.* London: Souvenir Press.

Jordan, R. and Powell, S. (1995) *Understanding and Teaching Children with Autism.* London: Wiley.

Kopera-Frye, K., Dehaene, S. and Streissguth, A.P. (1996) 'Impairments of number processing induced by prenatal alcohol exposure', *Neuropsychologia*, 34, 1187–1196.

Lister, S. (2006) 'Autism rate in children has doubled, say doctors', *The Times,* 14 July. [Online at: http://www.timesonline.co.uk/article/0,,8122-2269437,00.html]

Longhorn, F. (1991) 'A sensory curriculum'. In: R. Ashdown, Carpenter, B. and Bovair, K. (eds) *The Curriculum Challenge.* London: Falmer Press.

Medical Research Council (2006) 'What is Autism?'. London: MRC. [Online at: http://www.mrc.ac.uk/utilities/search/MRC002027]

Meltzer, H., Gatward, R., Goodman, R. and Ford, T. (Office of National Statistics) (2000) *Mental Health of Children and Adolescents in Great Britain.* London: The Stationery Office.

National Autistic Society (2006) 'How many people have autistic spectrum disorders?'. London: NAS. [Online at: http://www.nas.org.uk/nas/jsp/polopoly.jsp?d=299&a=3527]

Ramachandran, V.S. and Lindsay, M.O. (2006) 'Broken mirrors: a theory of autism', *Scientific American,* November, 63–69.

Rizzolatti, G., Fogassi, L. and Gallese, V. (2006) 'Mirrors in the mind', *Scientific American,* November, 63–69.

Roberts-Holmes, G. (2005) *Doing your Early Years Research Project.* London: Paul Chapman/Sage.

Rose, R. and Grosvenor, I. (eds) (2001) *Doing Research in Special Education.* London: David Fulton.

Shattock, P. and Whiteley, P. (2006) 'The changing prevalence of autism?' Sunderland: Autism Research Unit, University of Sunderland. [Online at: http://osiris.sunderland.ac.uk/autism/incidence.htm]

Sherborne, V. (2001) *Developmental Movement for Children: Mainstream, special needs and pre-school (2nd edn).* London: Worth Publishing.

Shonkoff, J.P. and Phillips, D.A. (eds) *From Neurons to Neighbourhoods.* Washington, DC: National Academy Press.

Streissguth, A. (2005) 'Brain studies show distinctions in persons with FASD', *CHDD Outlook,* 16 (3), 3–6.

Trevarthen, C., Aitken, K., Papoudi, D. and Robarts, J. (1996) *Children with Autism: Diagnosis and interventions to meet their needs.* London: Jessica Kingsley.

Whitehurst, T. (2006) 'Research tools for evidence-based practice'. In: B. Carpenter and J. Egerton (eds) *New Horizons in Special Education: Evidence-based practice in action.* Clent: Sunfield Publications.

Williams, D. (1998) *Nobody Nowhere.* London: Jessica Kingsley.

Wing, L. (2002) *The Autistic Spectrum: A guide for parents and professionals (updated edn).* London: Robinson.

Endnote

[1] Information online at: http://www.iop.kcl.ac.uk/

CHAPTER 14

Research and Sherborne

A Summary

Elizabeth Marsden

Research that involves people is complex. Education research has struggled with its identity and reputation for many years. Yates (2004) writes:

> *...we are not dealing with something as simple as finding a cure for cancer... But in education we also have a field whose end point parameters and questions are much more diverse, whose settings and agendas change. Researchers are engaged in debates about what is possible and about what is desirable and about whose interests should be served. (p. 34)*

There is a need to acknowledge the historical, social, gendered, political and cultural situated activities of education research, and the fact that what matters changes over time, in different places and depends on who is asking the question.

Veronica Sherborne lived and worked in an era when there was little demand for 'evidence-based practice', and it is easy to overlook her own quest for knowledge, understanding and problem-solving strategies. Certainly she did not undertake research as demonstrated by the authors in this book, but she did show the first and most important quality of a researcher – an open and enquiring mind. She herself said that she learned by 'trial and error' when faced with her biggest challenge in the early 1960s, when she was asked to teach movement for the first time on a course for people with learning disabilities.

> *I said, 'Well I don't know anything about them...I'll go to a local school and see if I can teach them...There was one girl with no language at all, and I beat a rhythm on my drum and she beat it back...and we began a 'conversation'...and I thought, 'This is fascinating'... My lesson was utter chaos – I got nowhere except for this relationship with this girl, who then followed me about...so I went home and thought, 'Well, I will take it on.'* (Sherborne, in Kirby, 1984, p. 47)

That was the start of a remarkable career based on problem-solving in movement and special education, and the gradual development of what is now termed Sherborne Developmental Movement (SDM). Sherborne's whole attitude to developing movement was research-like. She took the classic position described by Phillips and Pugh (1987):

> *...the classic position of a researcher is not that of knowing the right answers but of one struggling to find out what the right questions might be!* (p. 48)

Common difficulties

In the present education climate, however, a different strategy to problem-solving is required: one which follows certain criteria pertaining to methodology and rigour. Sherborne's 40 years of trial and error have produced a particular way of working with movement that has been *seen* to produce exciting outcomes, not only in movement understanding, but also in breaking communication barriers erected by disability. In turn, this has resulted in observed improvements in both children's and their adult partner's self-esteem, confidence, motivation and happiness. However, because of its very nature of flexibility and responsiveness to individuals, SDM is an extremely difficult area in which to conduct research. It could be likened to attempts to describe the shape of a moving amoeba!

The authors presenting their work in this book are all practitioners who have seen these results for themselves, and have now sought to apply accepted education research practices to test their observations. This in itself can be problematic. When a practitioner, who is either a teacher or therapist, works with a specific population, they want to help that population improve in some way. However, when the practitioner takes on the role of researcher, bias needs to be avoided and a more objective way of working must take place. The researcher needs to be clear which role they are acting out, and this can be difficult to maintain.

A variety of methodologies have been used in the research presented in this book. They include case studies, surveys, interviews and experimental studies. Attempts have been made to acknowledge the different settings alluded to by Yates (2004) above and, as this book has also warmly welcomed research carried out in Finland, Sweden and Poland, it is important to acknowledge the different values, methods and languages used in different geographical areas. The translators have been invaluable, and the editors are completely indebted to their commitment and efficiency. As in any translation from a mother tongue into English, there are sometimes language nuances that make direct and accurate translation impossible, and so these too need to be acknowledged.

SDM is about *movement,* and movement is notoriously difficult to observe and assess as it is so transient. Sherborne (1990) wrote 'The ability to observe and analyse human movement is the most important skill needed for movement teaching' (page 61), and we could add 'for movement research' also. In those research projects which analysed movement, the analysis has either been carried out by several observers and their scores correlated (Bogdanowicz; Chapter 9) or by very experienced movement teachers using video recording (Chapters 5, 6, 8 and 12). Movement observation continues to be one of the most difficult, contentious and time-consuming aspects of SDM research and yet, one of the most important.

Common threads

Acknowledging the difficulties of carrying out good education research *per se* and SDM research in particular, it can be seen that the authors in this book have done as much as is possible to carry out honest, thoughtful and rigorous research. Many thousands of words of literature have been reviewed by the authors seeking for theoretical understanding of human movement, psychology, sociology, spirituality and types of human development. Each study (except that described by Weston in Chapter 7) has used practical movement experiences, though not every study analysed the improvement in movement. This is a pity, and maybe can be remedied in the future. Sherborne (1990) herself maintained that there are *two* needs that all children have – to feel at home in their own bodies, as well as to learn to form relationships. She was always aware of the power in movement itself to affect the well-being of the person. In a controlled study, Marsden, Hair and Weston (Chapter 5) demonstrated a staggering improvement in movement vocabulary acquired by very young children after only 18 SDM sessions. Filer (Chapter 6) stated that the psychotherapeutic use of movement is based on the principle that movement reflects an individual's pattern of thinking and feeling, and so it would seem logical that improvements in movement should be sought and recorded rather than only improvements in communication and relationship building.

Every study has examined the effects of SDM on relationship-building, although different tools have been used to measure this. The importance of SDM as an intervention for improving relationships has been shown in a remarkable way in each study. It has been the breakthrough tool for some children having ASD who have been locked into a world separated from their parents and teachers. Even mainstream infants have shown much more willingness to share, take turns and co-operate with others after a relatively short time of SDM.

Weston, in Chapter 7, specifically showed the differences in attitudes, values, expectations and planning of teachers trained in SDM, and other studies have implied this. Hill (2006) drew attention to the changes in teaching style adopted by those who had been trained in SDM, and it is easy to see from the literature reviews presented in each study that the authors suspected that it was likely to be a combination of SDM teaching style and the SDM programme that would affect both children and adults in such a powerful way. Konaka (Chapters 3 and 4), Filer (Chapter 6), Astrand (Chapter 11) and Althoff (Chapter 12) particularly show how in their projects it was vital to build an environment of emotional, as well as physical, safety and care for their very vulnerable participants by adopting a teaching style based on equality, humility, acceptance, encouragement, enthusiasm and care. Dibbo and Marsden et al. have shown in their studies how such a teaching style adopted with mainstream primary children, although officially less vulnerable, has resulted in children visually responding with confidence, creativity, sociability and happiness.

Implications for the future

Barry Carpenter has demonstrated, in the previous chapter, that SDM has proved its value for a wide population of children with special needs over four decades of practice. He links new discoveries in brain research to the established practices of the SDM programme. In Sunfield's own project, 'Sherborne @ Sunfield', Konaka, under the supervision of Carpenter, and Cyndi and George Hill of the Sherborne Association UK, has shown the adaptability of SDM for the education of children with ASD. Bogdanowicz and colleagues in Poland, Althoff, Alin-Akerman and Astrand in Sweden, Laasonen, Lassila and Uusitalo in Finland have all shown the flexibility of SDM across disability labels, culture and geographical boundaries. The place of SDM within special education both in the UK and across Europe is assured.

Many understand SDM as being a special education movement programme only. They relate the name Veronica Sherborne with children with disability of some kind. But all of Sherborne's work was based on the work of Rudolph Laban and, for many years, she worked in mainstream education. Can there be a place for SDM in the world of the National Curriculum or the Scottish 5–14 Guidelines or the European mainstream curricula? Filer (Chapter 6), Dibbo (Chapter 8) and Marsden, Hair and Weston (Chapter 5) have demonstrated the value of this type of inclusive movement programme and style of teaching to ordinary, mainstream children as well as those with more challenging behaviour (Filer). In her literature review, Weston sends a warning shot across the bows of mainstream physical education in the UK. She explains that in the present political climate of grooming sporting heroes, especially with the approaching London Olympics in 2012, the Physical Education (PE) curriculum is becoming synonymous with sport, and therefore is elitist and not inclusive, leaving the majority of our children trailing in the wake of the few gifted and talented. On the other hand, the drive to tackle childhood obesity causes the political knee-jerk reaction to get all children involved in aerobic exercise. There is no room left for educating children to be at home in their own bodies or to build relationships. There is no room left for children to feel physically accepted, enthused and encouraged to have fun with gravity, a partner or in creating movement sequences. Research in today's world showing the physical, social and emotional benefits of SDM with ordinary children is every bit as important as that with children with special needs.

And finally…

Each researcher, and now author, presenting work in this book remains a practitioner first and foremost. Sherborne remained a practitioner, but she never lost the excitement of finding new ways to improve the lives of those in her care. Had she lived and worked in the present time, I believe she would applaud all our efforts to improve and become researchers in order to enhance our practice for those to whom we are responsible. In 1979, Janet Sparkes described Sherborne thus:

> *One is conscious of relating to someone who has trust in their own experience, someone who has built up a respect for their own personal thoughts and ideas and yet someone who continues to search for new truths and new ways…in returning again and again to her own experience, she clearly illustrates that she is both searching and discovering a closer approximation to truths, a closer approximation to ways in which movement experience can help… She sees her experience not as authoritative, but as the basis of authority which is continually being checked and corrected against the more immediate experience of her on-going work. (p. 2)*

In similar tones, Barry Carpenter, has appealed to all practitioners to become practise-based researchers. We trust that *Moving with Research* will be a first step.

References

Hill, C. (2006) *Communicating through Movement: Sherborne Developmental Movement – towards a broadening perspective*. Clent: Sunfield Publications.

Kirby, M. (1984) *Sherborne and Movement* (Unpublished thesis). Bristol: Bristol Polytechnic.

Phillips, E. and Pugh, D.S. (1994) *How to get a Ph.D.* (2nd edition). Buckingham: Open University Press.

Sparkes, J. (1979) *A Critical Examination of the Work and Movement Programme of Veronica Sherborne (Unpublished dissertation)*. Leeds: University of Leeds.

Yates, L. (2004) *What Does Good Education Research Look Like?* Buckingham: Open University Press.

Printed in the United Kingdom
by Lightning Source UK Ltd.
134153UK00001B/37-92/A